THE PHILIPPINES AFTER MARCOS

THE PHILIPPINES
AFTER MARCOS

Edited by R.J. May & Francisco Nemenzo

CROOM HELM
London & Sydney

© 1985 R.J. May and Francisco Nemenzo
Croom Helm Ltd, Provident House, Burrell Row,
Beckenham, Kent BR3 1AT
Croom Helm Australia Pty Ltd, First Floor,
139 King Street, Sydney, NSW 2001, Australia

British Library Cataloguing in Publication Data

The Philippines after Marcos.
  1. Philippines — Politics and government —
  1946-
  I. May, R.J. II. Nemenzo, Francisco
  320.9599   JQ1402
  ISBN 0-7099-3561-7

Printed and bound in Great Britain
by Billing & Sons Limited, Worcester.

CONTENTS

PREFACE

F. Nemenzo and R.J. May

Well before the assassination of Senator Benigno Aquino on 21 August 1983 it was clear to observers of Philippine politics that the regime of President Ferdinand Marcos was under considerable stress. Uncertainties about the president's health, combined with an economic crisis and an apparent strengthening of political opposition, created a situation in which those close to the regime became preoccupied with succession scenarios and those in opposition to it began to look hopefully to the prospects for a fundamental change in the political structure.

With these developments in mind, early in 1983 we invited a group of Filipinist scholars from Australia, the Philippines and North America, together with Philippine opposition spokesman Senator Jose Diokno, to meet in Canberra to reflect upon the likely future of Philippine society and politics when - as must eventually happen - Ferdinand Marcos has left the stage.

The assassination of Senator Aquino, and the subsequent outburst of political dissidence, expressed through popular demonstrations and the burgeoning of an alternative press, gave an immediacy and focus to the exercise.

The conference took place in Canberra in November 1983, and attracted a wide audience. The papers in this volume represent the contributions of principal participants in that conference. Three chapters - those of Senator Diokno, Filipino historian Ileto, and Canadian political scientist Wurfel - provide an overview of recent developments. Another three examine the political forces that are likely to play a critical role in the post-Marcos readjustment: the underground and the legal opposition (Nemenzo), the church (Shoesmith) and the military (Miranda). Another (May) looks at the situation of important but perhaps more peripheral elements: Muslim and tribal Filipinos. Hill and Jayasuriya provide an assessment of the economic situation. Chapters by Pinches, Fegan and McCoy look respectively at the 'urban poor' and the situation of rural dwellers in Central Luzon and Negros. Finally, Filipino journalist Doronila discusses the media and Lim addresses the subject of foreign policy. Although all of the papers have been edited and revised since originally presented, we have not attempted to establish any greater cohesion than was implicit in our initial invitation to participants; differences in assessment and prediction are left to the judgement of the reader, and of time.

There was, nevertheless, a remarkable degree of

convergence between the various contributors on certain fundamental issues. For one, there was general agreement that whatever the reasons for Marcos's departure - death, resignation or forcible removal - the changes instituted during a dozen years of authoritarian rule are so far-reaching that a return to the status quo ante is difficult to imagine. Secondly, it was agreed that a revolutionary change is not likely within the next decade, though its advent could be hastened, and society increasingly polarized, by prolonged authoritarian rule and the denial of a measure of participation in the exercise of power to the moderate opposition forces. Thirdly, it was felt that the Catholic Church, though a significant factor in Philippine affairs, is divided over political issues and therefore unlikely to act as a monolithic force. Fourthly, there was general agreement that the US government and the international banking community will exercise a critical influence in the immediate post-Marcos period, and that they are unlikely to welcome the establishment of a military regime (though whoever succeeds will have to reckon with a politicized military). Finally, there was consensus that a successor government will inherit substantial problems from the Marcos years: a huge foreign debt, a Muslim secessionist movement, a strengthened communist rebel army, politicization of the tribal Filipinos, a large urban population which cannot be supported at the present level of industrial development, and rural poverty sharpened by the introduction of capital-intensive modes of production - all of which will circumscribe the options available to it.

When the papers in this volume were first presented one of the uncertain elements affecting speculation on future scenarios was the election for the Batasang Pambansa (National Assembly) scheduled for 1984. The elections were held on 14 May on a rising tide of political activity. In January 1984 a Filipino People's Congress (KOMPIL), attended by a broad spectrum of moderate and radical political organizations, threatened a boycott of the elections unless the president acceded to a set of demands embodied in a 'call for Meaningful Elections'. Pressure came also from external sources: in October 1983 the US House of Representatives passed a resolution calling for 'genuine, fair and free elections' in the Philippines, and the international banking community, too, made it known that Marcos could not expect further financial support without having at least a semblance of popular mandate conferred on the regime. In spite of these pressures, Marcos chose to grant only token concessions to KOMPIL demands, precipitating a split between those who stood by the boycott of the elections, which they saw as a futile exercise whose outcome was bound to be manipulated to legitimate the regime, and those more conservative or opportunistic groups which chose to contest the vote.

The result was that in May 1984 three broad groupings were ranged against the Marcos-led KBL. On the one hand were the anti-Marcos opposition coalitions of the UNIDO, under the leadership of Senator Salvador Laurel, and PDP-Laban, led by

Cagayan de Oro City Mayor Aquilino Pimentel. Next to them, but standing closer to the KBL, were two groups - the Nacionalista Party (NP) faction led by Senator Jose Roy and the Social Democratic Party (SDP) faction of former Public Information Minister Francisco Tatad - referred to by some commentators as Marcos's 'loyal opposition'. Third was a broad grouping of organizations comprising the boycott movement. The nucleus of this movement was a Coalition of Organizations for the Restoration of Democracy (CORD), which included some twenty or so organizations, prominent among which were the Movement for National Sovereignty and Democracy (KAAKBAY) of Senator Diokno, the Nationalist Alliance for Justice, Freedom and Democracy (NAJFD) of Senator Tanada, the Alliance of Metropolitan Associations (AMA) led by Butz Aquino, brother of the slain senator, and a number of workers', students' and women's movements. The Liberal Party (LP) faction of Senator Salonga and the SDP faction of Assemblyman Canoy also supported the boycott, as did the vast bulk of the underground opposition. In the weeks preceding the election there was a further fragmentation when the Mindanao Alliance, under the leadership of Governor Adaza, the Bicol Saro and the Pusyon Bisaya announced their withdrawal from UNIDO following disputes over the leadership of the coalition. Although some sympathetic observers have argued that the fragmentation of the opposition is more apparent than real, basic differences of strategy and personality, and even on some issues of policy, divide the various groups. Moreover, examination of candidates standing under the banners of UNIDO and PDP-Laban revealed a number who had joined the opposition after unsuccessfully seeking KBL endorsement, and who could thus be expected to align themselves with the government if elected.

The elections eventually took place under the watchful eyes of an independent volunteer-staffed National Citizens Movement for Free Elections (NAMFREL) and an interested international press. Such scrutiny (together with that of the official Commission on Elections) probably did produce a more honest electoral exercise than the Philippines has seen for some years, but it was not sufficient to preclude numerous allegations of electoral irregularities, intimidation of voters, and a reported 200 election-related killings.

In a pre-election telecast early in May, President Marcos told his audience that if the opposition could win 30 of the 183 contested seats he would be 'the most surprised man in the world'. Early vote counts however, showed an unexpectedly high vote for opposition and independent candidates, who dominated the tally in Metro Manila and Cebu and won a number of seats in the provinces. Notwithstanding some implausible reversals of voting trends in the later stages of counting - particularly in Cebu, where demonstrations against ballot box stuffing and falsification of official tallies resulted in the death of some demonstrators - at the time of writing (August 1984) opposition candidates had won 60 of the 183 contested seats,

with independents winning another 13. Three ministers and
one deputy minister in the Marcos government failed to gain
re-election. The Minister for Political Affairs and the
deputy Minister for Human Settlements won by a slight margin
but under extremely dubious circumstances.

A naively enthusiastic international press generally
hailed the opposition 'victory' as (to quote Newsweek 28 May
1984) 'a stinging message to Ferdinand Marcos'; Ambassador
Jean Kirkpatrick (the most senior US official to visit Manila
after the cancellation of President Reagan's state visit in
November 1983) commended Filipinos for taking a major step
toward 'the perfection of [their] democracy'. The truth is,
however, that the 1984 election has done very little to
change the political situation in the Philippines, except
perhaps to weaken the personal position of Mrs Marcos who
campaigned actively, but in the event unsuccessfully, for KBL
candidates in Manila. Even if the Batasan elections had been
totally fair, and had returned sufficient opposition
candidates to provide an effective voice against the Marcos
regime, the fact remains that the 1973 constitution gives the
president power to veto Bills passed in the Batasan and in
effect to legislate by presidential decrees, letters of
instruction and executive orders which can be neither
repealed nor amended by parliament.

Moreover, even before the elections, Senator Ernesto
Maceda (the UNIDO campaign manager) was reported as saying
that if the opposition parties had fifty or so candidates
returned they would negotiate with Marcos 'for sincere
national reconciliation', and that if 60 per cent of them
were successful 'the opposition negotiating team may discuss
terms for a coalition government to make for a bipartisan
approach to work out solutions to the nations's ills'
(Bulletin Today 10 May 1984). Such a move could only
polarize further the already fragmented opposition since it
would certainly be rejected by the radical and intransigent
nationalist groups.

The president's health appears to have improved
(although as Wurfel's diagnosis suggests, temporary
improvements are to be expected) but the health of the
economy has not. With inflation running at an annual rate of
about 65 per cent in 1984, a recent analysis of government
figures by Business Day (a well respected economic newspaper
in Manila) showed that 70 per cent of Filipino families now
live below the poverty line and that more than half eat less
than the minimum nutritional requirements. An agreement with
the country's 483 foreign creditor banks to re-schedule
payments on its fantastic foreign debt is not expected
earlier than the first quarter of 1985 (Washington Post
(William Branigin) 12 August 1984).

Meanwhile, the stresses evident at the end of 1983 are
growing more acute. Demonstrations, some met with state
violence, have continued and there is a sharp rise in the
incidence of industrial unrest. According to statistics from
the Ministry of Labour and Employment, more than 28,000
workers were involved in strikes in the first half of 1984,

an increase of 80 per cent from the same period last year. President Marcos recently admitted that communist insurgency and the Moro secessionist movement have become a serious problem (<u>Washington Post</u> 12 August 1983).

Against this background we believe that the questions raised and discussed by contributors to this volume retain their immediacy.

ACKNOWLEDGEMENT

It is always difficult to get a group of specialists together and even more difficult to extract the final drafts from them. We are happy to acknowledge the co-operation with which this volume has been realized, and the tolerance of authors to our editorial persistence and license. Our task was considerably lightened, however, by the efficient help of Hilary Bek, Claire Smith, Charlotta Blomberg, Ellen Cordes, and Joanne Costin.

JOSE W. DIOKNO   Former senator;   presently   leader   of   the
        Movement for National Sovereignty and Democracy
        (KAAKBAY), one of the major opposition groups.

AMANDO DORONILA   Former editor, _Manila Chronicle_;   foreign
        news desk, _The Age_, Melbourne; graduate student
        in politics, Monash University.

BRIAN FEGAN   Lecturer, Department of Anthropology, Macquarie
        University, Sydney.

HAL HILL   Research fellow, Department of Economics, Research
        School of Pacific Studies, Australian National
        University, Canberra.

REYNALDO C. ILETO   Professor, Department of History,   De   La
        Salle University, Manila.

SISIRA JAYASURIYA   Research fellow, Department of Economics,
        Research School of Pacific Studies, Australian
        National University, Canberra.

ROBYN LIM   Lecturer, School of General Studies, University of
        New South Wales, Sydney.

ALFRED W. MCCOY   Senior   Lecturer,   School   of   History,
        University of New South Wales, Sydney.

R.J. MAY   Senior fellow, Department of Political and Social
        Change,   Research   School   of   Pacific   Studies,
        Australian   National   University,   Canberra;
        associate, Peter Gowing Memorial Research Center,
        Marawi City.

FELIPE MIRANDA   Professor of Political Science, University
        of the Philippines, Quezon City.

FRANCISCO NEMENZO   Senior research fellow, Department of
        Political and Social Change, Research School of
        Pacific Studies, Australian National University
        (on leave from University of the Philippines).

MICHAEL PINCHES   Tutor, Department of Anthropology,   Monash
        University, Melbourne.

DENNIS SHOESMITH   Lecturer, School of General Studies,
        Darwin Community College.

DAVID WURFEL   Professor of Political Science, University of
        Windsor, Ontario.

ABBREVIATIONS

A6LM	April 6 Liberation Movement
AFP	Armed Forces of the Philippines
AMRSP	Association of Major Religious Superiors of the Philippines
ATOM	August Twenty-One Movement
BCC	Basic Christian Communities
BLISS	Bagong Lipunan Sites and Services
BMLO	Bangsa Moro Liberation Organisation
BUSCO	Bukidnon Sugar Company
CBCP	Catholic Bishops' Conference of the Philippines
CC-MNLF-BMLO	Co-ordinating Council of the MNLF-BMLO
CHDF	Civil Home Defence Forces
CISA	Civilian Intelligence and Security Agency
CLT	Certificates of Land Transfer
CNI	Commission on National Integration
CNL	Christians for National Liberation
CPP	Communist Party of the Philippines
CRBDP	Chico River Basin Development Project
FBIS	Foreign Broadcast Information Service
FEBC	Far East Broadcasting Co.
FIES	Family Income and Expenditure Surveys
HYV	High Yielding Variety (of rice)
IBP	Interim Batasang Pambansa
IBRD	International Bank for Reconstruction and Development
ICFM	Islamic Conference of Foreign Ministers
JAJA	Justice for Aquino, Justice for All
JUSMAG	Joint Military Advisory Group
KB	Kabataang Barangay
KBL	Kilusang Bagong Lipunan (New Society Movement)
KKK	Kilusang Kabuhayan at Kaunlaran (People's Livelihood Program)
LABAN	Lakas ng Bayan (People's Power Party)
LP	Liberal Party
MBC	Makati Business Club
MHS	Ministry of Human Settlements
MILF	Moro Islamic Liberation Front
MLGCD	Ministry of Local Government and Community Development
MNLF	Moro National Liberation Front
MNLF-RG	Moro National Liberation Front - Reformist Group
MSPC	Mindanao-Sulu Pastoral Conference
NAPOCOR	National Power Corporation
NASSA	National Secretariat for Social Action, Justice and Peace (of the Roman Catholic Church)
NCSP	National Christian Socialist Party
NDC	National Development Company
NDF	National Democratic Front
NFSP	National Confederation of Sugarcane Planters
NGA	National Grains Authority

NIC	Newly Industrializing Country
NISA	National Intelligence and Security Authority
NP	_Nacionalista_ Party
NPA	New People's Army
NPDSP	Nagkakaisang Partido Demokratiko Sosyalista ng Pilipinas (United Democratic Socialist Party of the Philippines)
OLT	Operation Land Transfer
PANAMIN	Private Assocation for National Minorities/ Presidential Assistant on National Minorities
PC	Philippine Constabulary
PDP	Pilipino Democratic Party
Philex	Philippine Exchange
Philsucom	Philippine Sugar Commission
PKP	Partido Komunista ng Pilipinas
PTF-RAD	Presidential Task Force for the Reconstruction and Development of the Southern Philippines
ROTC	Reserve Officers Training Course
SPARE	Special Program for Assistance for the Rehabilitation of Evacuees
SPDA	Southern Philippines Development Authority
UNIDO	United Nationalist Democratic Organization

Chapter 1

THE PRESENT CRISIS

Jose W. Diokno

We have been brought together to discuss the Philippines after Marcos. This was conceived as an exercise in futurology, but it seems that events have caught up with us. The post-Marcos era has in fact already begun. It began on 21 August 1983 when an assassin's bullet shattered the skull of Senator Benigno S. Aquino. That bullet, we now know, did more than kill the leader of the opposition; it also shattered the regime of President Ferdinand E. Marcos. What we witness today are its death throes. True, Marcos still occupies the presidential palace, but his control over men and events has dwindled.

The assassination of Senator Aquino touched everyone. It destroyed the apathy and fear that had immobilized so many, particularly among the affluent. It united people of all social classes for the first time since martial law was declared. It evoked from all - the rich, the middle class, the poor - an unprecedented outpouring of grief for the fallen leader, shame of their past submissiveness, and outrage at the government that, if it had not itself perpetrated the crime, had by its neglect permitted it.

After the initial shock was over, grief, shame and outrage hardened into an unrelenting demand for change. The demand has come at a time when Marcos is peculiarly vulnerable. His health is apparently failing. The economy is in shambles, the result of bad policies badly implemented. His inept handling of the Aquino assassination and the arrogance with which it was perpetrated destroyed the little credibility he still had, both at home and abroad. Local capital has fled the country. Foreign investments have stopped. Foreign creditors have refused to grant new loans or roll over old ones. Marcos has had to sue for a suspension of payments, to devalue the currency twice in three months - depreciating its value by more than 50 per cent in 1983 - and to install a rigid system of controls. As a result, the rate of inflation has leaped. Workers and employees in government and industry have become restless; lay-offs have increased; consumers are angry; frustrated and militant.

The United States government, Marcos's staunchest ally, has begun to waver in its support for him. President Reagan cancelled a state visit that Marcos had worked very hard to get and which he badly needed to prop up his regime. The US House of Representatives, by a nearly unanimous vote, imposed two new conditions for continuing to support him: an impartial probe of the Aquino assassination, and the holding of free and fair elections. These are conditions that Marcos cannot hope honestly to fulfil without risking further loss of control. Politicians and businessmen whose loyalty Marcos believed he could count on are beginning to desert him, if not turn against him. Persons close to him have been booed when they have dared to appear, and sometimes even when their names are mentioned in public gatherings. Marcos himself dare not, or cannot, leave his palace to mix with the people.

In short, the once-feared dictator has been reduced to little more than a lame-duck president. He is still fighting to hold on, but his options are limited, both by the financial crisis and the political milieu. His political end is now clearly seen as inevitable, as merely a matter of time. Politicians and pundits worry more about what will happen when he finally goes than about what he might do next. And well they might, for while we know that Marcos will go, we cannot know for certain how he will go, or when. Will he die from natural causes before his term ends in 1987? Will he be assassinated? Will he resign soon - either of his own volition because of failing health, or under pressure? Will he be defeated in the 1984 parliamentary elections? Will he be ousted by a coup d'etat or overthrown by a revolution?

All these scenarios are possible, but two seem more probable than the others: death from natural causes, or resignation because of failing health or under pressure. Assassination seems unlikely because Marcos rarely ventures outside the palace grounds; in fact he has not left Malacanang, except to go to the hospital, since June 1983. And he is, in and out of Malacanang, protected at all times by tight security measures. Equally remote are chances of a coup d'etat, because Marcos does enjoy the personal loyalty of his generals (all of whom owe their appointments to him) and because both General Fabian Ver, who controls the Presidential Security Command, and General Fidel Ramos, who heads the Philippine Constabulary and Integrated National Police, are related to him by blood. The chances are also slim that the opposition could wrest the majority of the seats from the Marcos party, the New Society Movement (KBL) in the parliamentary elections set for May 1984. Given Marcos's power over the press and over the military, the natural desire of his party's candidates to retain their seats, and their combined control over the electoral system and the officials who administer it, the opposition would have to be more united, better organized, and better funded to win the elections than to force the Marcos government to resign.

With respect to the probability of a successful revolution: two rebellions have been going on in the Philippines for more than ten years, one led by the Moro National Liberation Front (MNLF) and the other by the

Communist Party of the Philippines' New People's Army (NPA). The first appears to be waning. The second is gaining ground, but its own leaders admit that it will take several years or more - some say about ten years - before the revolution could gather such force as to become a real threat to the regime.

Let us consider what might happen if one of the two more probable scenarios came to pass. What would happen if Marcos were to die soon? So many things _could_ happen that it is foolhardy to try to foretell what _would_ happen. If Marcos's constitution were followed precisely, the executive committee (chaired by the prime minister) would exercise the powers of the president, hold a free and fair election within ninety days to fill the unexpired portion of Marcos's term, and then turn over the government to the newly elected president. But the demands of the business community, that the office of a vice president be created and filled as soon as possible, indicate that they do not believe that this procedure would be workable. Few people believe it would, and with reason. There is no certainty about who would be prime minister at the time that Marcos might go. Mr Cesar Virata holds the position today, but under the Marcos constitution Marcos could remove him by the simple expedient of sending a new nomination to the parliament, the Batasang Pambansa. Even if the financial crisis were to dictate that Virata continue as prime minister, Mrs Marcos, supported as she undoubtedly would be by General Ver, could count on more votes in the executive committee than Virata could. If conditions made an election propitious, she would probably become a candidate. If conditions were not propitious, martial law could again be declared - or enforced without a formal declaration, the elections postponed, and government by the executive committee prolonged. Fair and free elections would seem to be remote; chaos and disorder more imminent possibilities.

Perhaps the one fairly certain result of Marcos's death in the near future would be that the country would become more unstable and volatile than it is today. Deprived of Marcos's firm hand, latent rivalries would surface within and among the three components of his political machine - the KBL (the political party), the technocrats, and the military. Would-be successors to Marcos's throne, either from his own party or from the opposition, would jostle each other (or perhaps worse) for political advantage or even for survival; they would form cliques and alliances and seek the support of factions within the military; some might even seek the support of the US government. In any case the situation would be an open invitation to either the military or the US government, or both, to intervene. Such intervention might produce the semblance of stability, but it would be an inherently unstable stability. It would not help solve the national problems, but only aggravate them, for it would lead to more militarization and less dialogue, greater repression and fewer chances of peacefully redressing the just grievances that spawned the Muslim and NPA rebellions, more poverty and exploitation of labour and less equality and justice, increased dependence on the US government and foreign capital, and diminished Filipino control over our economy, our future, even our very survival.

From these gloomy prospects let us turn to the second likely scenario: that the opposition could exert enough pressure on the Marcos government to cause it to resign. Since I am involved in the effort to exert that pressure, I think it would be neither proper nor prudent for me to try to explain how the opposition hopes to attain this objective. But if the objective is obtained, what will the Philippines be like after Marcos has resigned?

There will have to be a transitional government. A transitional government could assume power in a number of ways: perhaps through dialogue with Marcos or the executive committee; perhaps simply by seizing power and declaring itself the government. Acceptance of a transitional government would depend on the efforts of the opposition to seek public support. Once a transitional government is in power, the opposition is committed to perform the following tasks. Its first commitment is to call for free and honest elections within a period of not more than four months from the date that the transitional government takes power. In addition to calling and supervising those elections, the major tasks of the transitional government would be to restore the privilege of the writ of habeas corpus throughout the country; to grant a general and unconditional amnesty to all persons charged, arrested or convicted of political offences, wherever they may be (inside or outside the Philippines); to scrap all laws, decrees and orders of Marcos that impair constitutional freedoms - particularly the rights of labour; to scrap all decrees that grant special privileges to the cronies and relatives of Mr and Mrs Marcos; to restore full freedom of the press; to restore the independence and integrity of the judiciary; to conduct an impartial probe into the assassination of Senator Aquino; to redress the more immediate problems of our Muslim and highland brothers; and to seek a restructuring of and better terms for existing foreign loans. That, of course, is an extremely tall order, and for that purpose a committee is being created now to prepare the way for the transitional government and to handle as many of these problems as possible, immediately.

Through all of these scenarios, I have assumed that the military would play a secondary role, merely supporting a candidate in the event of Marcos's death, or standing aloof from the political struggle in the event of an opposition take-over after Marcos's resignation. How reasonable is this assumption? Or to frame the question in another way, how likely is it that the military will not try to seize power for itself and govern the country, possibly with the assistance of technocrats, following the Brazilian model? I do not believe that a military take-over is likely after Marcos. For one reason, the military is itself divided.

4

Many, if not most, of its generals do not command the respect, much less the loyalty, of their troops. Many of them have attained their positions more through connections than by merit or seniority. There is no one faction in the military that can control the situation by itself. Add to this the fact that the training most of the younger officers have had requires respect for civilian rule, and the uncertainty of any faction as to what the other factions might do if it tried a grab for power, and the risks of taking such a grab would, I believe, deter its occurrence - except, and this is a big exception, in one case: if the US government were to abet, or at least to give the go-ahead signal to a military take-over. Without explicit or implicit US blessings, in my opinion, the dangers of a military take-over, even after Marcos goes, are remote.

What then are the chances of US approval of a take-over? Under other administrations I would have said that the chances of the US approving a military take-over in the Philippines are remote unless such a state of disorder prevailed that a take-over was necessary to prevent anarchy. Under the present administration of President Reagan, I fear that such restraints may not operate. Reagan's rather simplified view of reality makes almost anything possible whenever he may feel that the security interests of the US are even remotely threatened.

This brings me to the vital role of the US in the Philippines. Even before the end of the Second World War, US policy had been to see to it that the Philippines 'remain in hands we can control or rely on', 'to permit to the Philippine government a continued independence in all internal affairs, but to preserve it as a bulwark of US security' (these quotes are from a memorandum of George Kennan in 1948); that it provide a base from which to project US power and gain access to the riches of Asia, the Indian Ocean, and the Middle East. So long as American security interests in the Philippines do not feel themselves seriously threatened, the US could be expected to act with a certain forbearance, with a certain subtlety, a certain amount of quiet diplomacy, both with the government and opposition figures, to try and secure its ends. But the point that I wish to make is that any successor government to Marcos must, if it is to solve the problems of the nation, break away from the constraints of the predominant influence and control of the US government.

However Marcos may leave the political scene, whoever may succeed him, whatever role technocrats and the military play in the transition and afterwards, the successor government cannot ignore the basic problems of Philippine society: the inequity of its social system and the maldevelopment of its economy, which together have bred poverty, injustice, and the rebellions of the Muslims and the dispossessed. There is no military solution to these problems, except genocide which would in any case be self-defeating. There is no solution either in following the same presciptions of the World Bank and the International Monetary Fund that Marcos, Virata and other technocrats have been pursuing. It is clear that the successor government must find its own way to solve these problems. There is no pattern it can follow, no model it can copy. If experience has taught Filipinos anything, it is that every country is unique and must forge its own future in its own way. But the primordial condition for doing this is that we free ourselves from the control of the US government. We could restore freedom to the Philippines. We could re-establish democracy. But unless the successor government can transform our society and change the structure of our economy, freedom and democracy would count for very little.

When we think about the Philippines after Marcos, when we contemplate the different political scenarios, let us not forget that what counts most is what will happen to the people. Whether it be a successor to Marcos arising from his death or resignation due to ill health, whether it arise from the opposition, whether it be a military government, the Philippines after Marcos must be a country for the people. The task is not going to be easy and it is not going to be quick, and we are going to need the best help that we can get from all the talent that could be made available. We may well fail and fail miserably, but we have to try. We will try, and I am certain that however it ends we will be a better people for having tried.

Chapter 2

THE PAST IN THE PRESENT CRISIS

Reynaldo C. Ileto

The Philippines gives the image nowadays of a people suddenly galvanized into action by Aquino's murder. There have been demonstrations, boycotts, marches, and prayer rallies. As one would expect, these started in the universities and public plazas, recalling the student-dominated displays of pre-martial law days. But now churches are very much in the centre of protest. Add to that business districts like Makati, and the slums. The workers are moving; every day one hears of strikes by this or that union or association. Even at the village level there is much agitation.

While the release of mass energies is noted by the media, the usual explanations for it invariably lead away from the experience to the stresses presumably causing it and to the instability it threatens. Marcos's authoritarian rule and a deepening economic crisis, to cite _Time_, is fostering 'widespread apathy and cynicism and [driving] young Filipinos into the country's small but increasingly troublesome Communist movement' (_Time_ 5 September 1983). Implied here is that the crucial, non-violent centre is crumbling. This goes for the 'legitimate' opposition as well: the murder of Aquino created 'a serious leadership vacuum in the opposition'. This all raises the spectre of a military take-over on one hand, and communism on the other. _Newsweek_ (5 September 1983) summed up its distance from popular sentiments by lamenting that 'in the long run [Aquino's] death could only hurt the cause for which he had sacrificed himself'.

It is clear that for the Western press stability and order are the main concerns. Instability and disorder (both internal and regional) are threatened by the impending fall of the centre (Marcos) and so most scenarios dwell on his possible successors, hopefully the restorers of order. The assassination and subsequent mass actions are seen as aberrations, or interruptions best pushed to the background as soon as possible.

From another perspective, however - and this includes that of the participants in the rallies - a very different notion of what is 'normal' seems to prevail. To put it another way, recent events are very much part of a certain rhythm of Philippine history, comprehensible in its own terms

7

and not necessarily a minor partner to the assigned 'stable' order of things. The Aquino affair and its sequel provides us with a set of events to illustrate this point.

Probe into Aquino's background and you find no revolutionary. He was a politician, a member of the ilustrado political oligarchy that was nurtured under the American regime. Ninoy himself is said to have had connections with the CIA during his early career as a journalist. He was an exile in the US, the former colonial power that backed his rival, Marcos. His wife, Cory, is the first cousin of a crony from the Marcos camp and some have speculated that he was returning in order to bolster the faction to which he was connected by kinship (McCoy in Sydney Morning Herald 23 August 1983). Observers recognized that both protagonists emerged from the same scene, and were still playing the old game; thus the maze of contradictions surrounding the contest. According to a close Marcos aide: 'Marcos and Ninoy were the most able intelligent pair of political strategists. There was a contest of wills between them. It was like the arms race. No one thinks that either side is capable of pulling the trigger. But they keep pushing each other to the limit, and suddenly it explodes'. It was 'the tragic last act of a long, almost medieval drama' (Time 5 September 1983).

The medieval drama is, indeed, a fitting analogy. Trouble is, attention has been fixed on the supposedly 'real people' behind the masks and the costumes. What students of Philippine politics often miss are the readings of the play by the various sections of the audience. Controversies in Philippine history have arisen out of the practice of locking events and personalities to singular, supposedly true and factual, meanings. Thus Rizal, to cite a well-known example, was the intellectual of Chinese-mestizo origin who inspired nationalism through his writings but condemned the armed uprising against Spain (thus speaking for order). We do not see that Rizal was not always what he intended to signify, that he also was the magical curer and the Liberator returning from overseas, whose martyrdom inspired people to join the uprising. He is very much the emblem of disorder in this alternative reading of his life and work. Aquino is just the latest in a series of figures whose meanings (not origins) have informed and will continue to inform popular responses to the present crisis.

The fact that Marcos politics has been fundamentally decentred (or destabilized) by the Aquino figure is more 'normal' than it looks. Philippine history has generally been written in a linear fashion: it is the saga of a people coming into its own, discovering their identity through opposition to the various colonial powers. Marcos in his multi-volume history Tadhana (Destiny) has himself rewritten this history in order to install himself as the successor to the series of fighters for freedom from the sixteenth century Lapulapu on. However, for each nationalist figure that appears dominant (and to which Marcos links himself) in this history, one can put forth either a contrary reading of this figure or another figure in opposition to it.

For example, during the American period dominated by 'compadre colonial politics', opposition was represented by the schoolteacher and former revolutionary general, Artemio Ricarte. Exiled in Hong Kong, he promised to return as the Liberator; he preached independence through struggle, and criticized the dominant politics as false and deceptive. His opponent in the drama was Manuel Quezon, the American protege who succeeded in 1916 (with the passage of the Jones Law) in displacing Ricarte as the Liberator who would gain independence. Historical writing, however, largely suppresses Ricarte, the radical 'other' of Quezon. So too it suppresses other figures who emerged to succeed Ricarte, some of whom were executed or given long gaol sentences for 'banditry'. The net effect is a coherent history dominated first by nationalist rebels, then by parliamentary politics, and progressing from the first or Malolos Republic to the Philippine Assembly, the Commonwealth, and on to the New Society.

How does the Aquino affair relate to all this? It has thrust into the foreground a meaningful politics which previously appeared only in the gaps of this linear history. This politics represents an alternative to 'pulitika' or the jockeying for positions among the old political oligarchy. To assert itself today, it has had to co-opt a traditional politician, Ninoy himself, and turn him inside out. Death made this possible. The old suspicion that somehow a politician's fine words are not matched by sincerity and action, has melted in Ninoy's case. One columnist viewing Aquino's body recalled what Ninoy had said to her in New York: 'And you doubt it?' She had doubted that

> because [Aquino] was a politician, he may not have had the interests of the Filipino at heart; that he may not have loved his country and our people. I looked at his ashen face, the bullet wound, and the blood all over his shirt. No, Ninoy, I said to myself. I have no more doubts. You loved your country and your people. God be with you, always, wherever you may be (N.C. Olivares in Mr.&Ms. 9 September 1983).

Words like these are usually thrown out by analysts because they belong to the realm of the sentimental or religious rather than real politics. But if the history of the 1896 revolution is at all useful as a guide, this is where the break with Spain began - a tearful, sentimental dialogue between mother Spain and daughter Filipinas over the bodies of three executed reformist priests. Spain, in the end, was no longer the mother (Ileto 1980a). And in like manner Aquino is no longer the whiz kid of the old politics: the switching of signs was made possible by the assassination and the surge of rumours and alternative media publications

9

giving details of the killing, recreating Aquino's last days, publishing his letters to friends, his funeral and so forth. 'It's time', Aquino is quoted as saying 'to be home with our people and suffer with them. And if you'll remember, when I left home, I promised to return. I'll be keeping that promise'. Then came his now-famous remark: 'I would rather die a glorious death than be killed by a Boston taxicab', said in jest, followed by a charismatic smile' (Olivares in Mr.&Ms. 9 September 1983). A week later, the same magazine published a personal letter Aquino wrote in June 1973, while in solitary confinement, to ex-Senator Francisco Rodrigo, containing such passages as:

> ...the mysteries [of the rosary] started me on my meditation. It was the life of Christ from birth to the ascension. Suddenly Jesus became a live human being. His life was to become my inspiration. Here was a God-Man who preached nothing but love and was rewarded with death. Here was a God-Man who had power over all creation but took the mockery of a crown of thorns with humility and patience. And for all his noble intentions, he was shamed, vilified, slandered and betrayed.

In this letter, Aquino seems to thrive in a discourse that enables connections to be made between the Christ story and that of Rizal, and on to the present crisis (imaged in terms of a suffering Mother Country), the new tyrant, and himself:

> I now realize why Rizal reserved the little book by Thomas a Kempis, 'The Imitation of Christ', for his beloved Josephine .... It was from this little book that he drew the strength of his spirituality and inner peace. He bequeathed his talisman to Josephine ... I have no doubt Rizal would have been the first to be picked up were he alive today and, maybe, re-enact his martyrdom at Bagumbayan (lit. "New Land", the public execution site at the Luneta). He was a victim of the New Land. Surely, his fate wouldn't be better under a New Society/Bagong Lipunan ... If I have been too harsh in my judgement of our colleagues, I pray for their forgiveness. If I, however, understand the truth of our tragedy and have been wanting in my denunciation of the tyrant who dragged back Mother Filipinas to her dungeon in chains, I hope God will forgive me for failing to rise up to the occasion (Mr.&Ms. 16 September 1983).

And so on; the public is now familiar with accounts. Aquino said the right things, provided all the signs that pointed to the past. The promise to return and the readiness to die, they made perfect sense - just as in the past they have. How can one understand the failure of the Japanese to subjugate the populace in the Second World War without reference to MacArthur's promise to return? Quezon, Ricarte and Rizal and Bonifacio before him played to the same sentiments. The language of Aquino's undelivered arrival speech is unmistakably patterned after the past - the idea of return, risk, sacrifice. Cardinal Sin had no difficulty latching on to such when he described Aquino as 'a Filipino pilgrim whose journey home had cost him his life' at the hands of 'the forces of darkness'.

The construction of Aquino the martyr was almost too easily done. Quite common are passages like the following:

> Mourners comment on his smile and the sweetness of the face and the kindness there. That face with its singularly haunting look and the smudges that the final violence left on it will haunt the Filipino people for a long time. Like Jose Rizal's final act of trying to defeat his killers by turning towards the sun and their bullets just before death, Ninoy's enigmatic look may well be his final victory (H. Paredes in Mr.&Ms. 9 September 1983).

In a way this is literary overkill. But the reference to Rizal is not at all forced. For all the anting-anting (magical power) stories woven around him, Marcos has never aspired to Rizal status. Aquino has succeeded on this point. The juxtaposition is clear in the portraits of Rizal and Aquino carried side by side in street demonstrations, and underscored by the words 'Great Men Sacrifice their Lives for Freedom'.

Rizal, through his novels and other works, managed to undermine the prestige of the friars and thus incur their hatred. Why did he return in 1892 despite warnings from his family and friends? His argument, repeated often by Aquino in a conscious reference to the past, was that if the ilustrados in Europe wanted to do anything worthwhile for their people, they must return and face death calmly. So he returned, and was greeted enthusiastically everywhere he went as a Redeemer. A few days later he was arrested, exiled, and eventually executed. His public execution in December 1896 was the real 'beginning of the end' for Spanish rule. For this was bringing the anti-colonial struggle to the level or the language which the ordinary Filipino understood.

Rizal's death was also a re-enactment of a familiar story. 'We are walking the way to Calvary', he was heard to say, 'Now Christ's Passion is better understood. ... He was nailed to a Cross; the bullets will nail me to the cross formed by the bones on my back'. The events surrounding his death were comprehensible in terms of a universally held reference myth: the story of an innocent man's death. Thus was born the notion of Rizal as the 'Filipino Christ'. The most popular songs and rallying cries of 1897 spoke of the martyr Rizal, the innocent man killed by the friars, whose death must be avenged by an act of separation from the bad mother Spain. The Katipunan appeal in 1897 was as follows: Rizal has shown the way, now it is our turn to prove our love of country by being willing to die. Even gangs of bandits and religious communes in the hills recognized the message, adopted Katipunan emblems and made 'Viva Rizal!' their rallying cry (Ileto 1982).

Similarly, the Aquino affair has enabled a good proportion of the populace to meaningfully organize their experience of hardship, anger, frustration, and hope, and to situate events in a scenario that might involve violence and death. Says one letter writer in the alternative press: 'If we are not willing to die, I am afraid we will be responsible for the death of another, and still another, Ninoy. For God's sake, for once in our lives, let's be Marcial Bonifacio' (R. Contreras in _Malaya_ 15-18 September 1983).

Marcial Bonifacio was Aquino's alias or pseudonym, and it is also a reference to the instigator of the 1896 uprising against Spain. We could be sceptical of such brave pronouncements by a member of the intelligentsia if it did not resonate with something familiar to the popular mind. The Aquino affair has been textualized, and it is not just the Rizal execution but Bonifacio's call to arms in 1896 made meaningful to the present. The silent dissenters of the past are now the majority, writes H. Basco, 'just because of Marcial Bonifacio (no relations with Andres Bonifacio). And, to think that the guy even failed to give out the cry the way the other did at Balintawak. Mind you, that bitch of a magnum is not only cruel but a killjoy. But that is History. But don't you ever realize that history repeats itself?' (_Philippine Times_ 12-18 September 1983). Even the former chairman of the Communist Party has installed Aquino in the line of martyrs beginning with Rizal.

Today the equivalent of 'bad mother Spain' is probably the Marcos regime, for like Spain it made a lot of promises and covenants - such as a democratic revolution, the emancipation of the peasant, a new society, and so on. Now it is all recollected as glitter, deception, empty form rather than substance. The inner-outer (_loob-labas_) dichotomy, a familiar theme in religion and poetry, has become the prism through which Marcos politics is perceived. It is fascinating to see repeated these days practically all of the arguments brought out in 1888, 1896, 1911, 1934 and so on. To top it all, an innocent man was killed and people have come to their own conclusion about who was ultimately responsible. When Marcos on television repeatedly tried to dissociate the palace from the affair, the almost universal outcry was: 'Pontius Pilate!'. A spokesman for the church said 'it is the HYPOCRISY of the regime that is so unbelievable. They are looking for the people who killed Ninoy, as if they didn't already know'. This is what was widely said about the Spanish government and the friars, and we know that it was convincing to the masses. The question is not what really happened, or who the culprit really was, but that a familiar drama involving familiar themes is being re-enacted.

The consequence of such an event on a national scale has been to enable a thorough inversion of the sign system imposed by the present regime - all the symbols of greatness and promises of bliss which could be mocked or ignored but not quite turned against itself. 'The Marcos administration loves you', cried Mayor Yabut before his foiled counter-rally. Shouts of 'Ninoy' drowned him out. Banners reading 'Marcos means hope' were torn down to be replaced by 'We love Ninoy' (AP-AAP 21 September 1983). 'Ninoy MEANS democracy', one placard said. Or as one columnist put it, Ninoy said what he meant, meant what he said, and died for what he believed in - a comforting unity of words and meanings after years of their alienation (Contreras in _Malaya_ 15-18 September 1983). It seems like a fresh discovery, but it is somewhat of a replay of the conflict beginning in the 1890s over the true significance of Spanish rule. Were the friars good or bad? To the revolutionaries, the friars were fake Christs; Spain was a mother whose love was false. The death of Rizal settled the issue. In like manner the death of and public outpouring for Aquino has become 'a stark reminder to all those who aspire to be "loved by the people" that true love can neither be bought nor forced' (L. Panaligan in _Mr.&Ms._ 30 September 1983). This Ninoy, whatever he really was, is the body to which all of those subversive meanings which used to float aimlessly around or were displaced into the religious realm have now adhered, thus making it a potent centre to challenge the old, which is precisely what Rizal became.

What we are talking about is not exactly an intellectual or mental process. In the past I have tried to show how _awa_ (pity), _damay_ (empathy) and other manifestations classified (and therefore dismissed) as 'emotional outpourings' are culturally and socially encoded, and to provide one explanation for the uprisings and rallies that are a constant feature of Philippine history (Ileto 1980b). It is important, then, to investigate the function of grief in the present crisis. Could the popular slogan _Ninoy, hindi ka nag-iisa_ (Ninoy, you are not alone) be another form of _damay_ for the suffering Christ? The function of grief at present is unmistakable. In his funeral homily Cardinal Sin said that Aquino's death had brought about a tremendous outpouring of grief because it 'personified Filipino courage in the face of oppression'.

> [To Ninoy's challenge] our people are waiting for a reply [from the State]. They wait, no longer as timid and scaztered sheep, but as men and women purified and strengthened by a profound communal grief that has made them one.

The image is familiar. We recall Mabini's comment that, in spite of the fact that the martyrs Gomez, Burgos and

Zamora 'had striven for the rights of a class and not of the people in general', their execution brought about 'deep pity and pain for the victims. This pain wrought up a miracle; it caused the Filipinos to think for the first time of themselves' (see Ileto 1980b: 166-167). The function of grief is overwhelmingly clear to anyone who investigates popular sentiments during the revolution - Katipuneros and peasants weeping for suffering mother country; grief (dusa, lunos, habag) over Rizal's death; grief imaged as a storm that sets the whole country in turmoil.

Mabini's observation of 1899 is in fact another one of those ancient themes that has sprung back to life. Why were the people so deeply affected by Ninoy Aquino's death, asks one observer?

> Gazing at his blood-soaked chest and his wounded face still bearing its bullet-marks, ... a grief stricken people were actually gazing not only at Ninoy Aquino but at themselves, bloodied and wounded by a long history of colonial domination, still suffering from foreign and native oppression (Panaligan Mr.&Ms. 30 September 1983).

Grief has made possible the generation and transmission of patriotic and radical meanings which are at the same time intensely personal. Thus, it is not simply the reference to the historical figure behind 'Marcial Bonifacio' that is so potent, but the effects of Bonifacio's poem Pagibig sa Tinubuang Lupa (Love for the Land of One's Birth), sung in the style of the kundiman (love song) and a big hit today (Malaya 9-18 September 1983). It evokes memories of a lost childhood happiness. So also has the 1930s song Bayan ko (My Country), that evokes pity for a suffering Motherland, become the second national anthem (Mr.&Ms. 30 September 1983). What matters is not the talk of love, pity, unity and struggle, but the experience of such in the public demonstrations of recent months. Even the Cardinal could not keep his composure:

> At last Sunday's mass at the Manila Cathedral, the Cardinal wept. He had been overcome by an excess of love of country and had succumbed to his emotions. He had asked the people to sing. No mas Amor que el tuyo, they sang, O Corazon Divino, El pueblo Filipino te da su corazon, and the Cardinal began to weep (Paredes in Mr.&Ms. 16 September 1983).

Analytical practices invariably relegate the above phenomena to the transitory and superfluous; the crucial questions appear to have to do with organization, guns and economics. Everyone will recognize, however, that recent events have seen the release of a tremendous amount of energy from below. Politicians have an instinct for what is meaningful to their audience, and so one expects them to play a rather traditional role in relating to this ground-swell. Laurel, LABAN, UNIDO, NDF, JAJA, etc.: are they organizing the rallies or trying to channel popular sentiments, giving it an organizational focus? Again the scene is familiar: 1897, 1906, 1911, 1921, 1934, 1945 and so forth - times when the populace was agitated by something: Rizal's death, war with Japan, Halley's comet, the Great Depression, MacArthur's return. For radical organizers and electoral politicians these were times to further stimulate mass action through oratory, to gain votes, followers, or members.

But the fear, always, has been that things would get out of control. The Aquino affair has released meanings which the intelligentsia (and the middle class) confidently feels it can control, but past experience does not lead to this conclusion. People do form their own opinions. Quezon, in the years when he had to outdo the appeal of the exiled Ricarte, used to wax eloquent on Rizal or Bonifacio day, speaking of shedding blood to gain independence from the US. But when the rallies and conspiracies seemed to get out of hand, especially under the leadership of non-ilustrados, Quezon worked closely with the US administration to silence them.

The leader of the local UNIDO chapter in Negros Occidental warned: 'The situation is volatile. Marcos may come up with a solution to the killing, but what Aquino had stood for and died for will always remain. I hope the ranks of the students will not be overrun by the hysteria of the moment, because we are in a situation that is inviting chaos'. Such fear of 'things getting out of hand' must be in many people's minds today. But to attribute the problem to a hysterical studentry is an anachronism. In 1971 this assessment would have made sense. At that time, I was observing two phenomena which had little to do with each other. In Manila and major cities students inspired by the Chinese cultural revolution were marching in the streets. Righteous anger and the clenched fist, the little red book and Chinese acrobatics; it was like the time in ancient history when liberalism and masonry radicalized the ranks of the principales and the ilustrados. Outside Manila, however, I discovered a marginalized, almost forgotten radicalism which centred on the veneration of the dead, particularly the heroes of the revolution, and which defined a rally as a time to be swept away (in grief, of course) by the sounds of Rizal's poem, Huling Paalam (My Last Farewell).

What has happened in recent months is a public display of the 'other politics', the one which has occasionally asserted itself in the past but which more often has remained the minor partner of a politics defined as colonial, national, central and elite. The form this 'other politics' takes is strangely reminiscent of the one I observed in Laguna twelve years ago. But now it is ex-Communist Party Chairman Sison who speaks of martyrs and Cardinal Sin who weeps after reciting a funeral homily that more than

resembles Rizal's _Huling Paalam_. Aquino's death, quite apart
from Aquino's own limited intentions, has brought the two
radicalisms together, effectively displacing the Marcos-
centred politics. As for how this combination is actually
going to win, or capture power: I have not given that much
thought. The fact is, the 'other politics', apart from a few
moments like the capture of a town or a march to the Luneta,
has never experienced being the centre, the state. If this
were ever to happen, it would constitute either a total break
with the past and thus a significant advance for Third World
socialism, or (which is more likely) it would mean the old
forms appearing in a new guise, the inner versus outer, light
versus glitter problem all over again.

Chapter 3

THE SUCCESSION STRUGGLE

David Wurfel

The fatal shooting of Senator Benigno Aquino at the Manila airport brought the succession struggle in Philippine politics to world-wide attention, but behind-the-scenes jockeying for power in anticipation of President Marcos's departure from the scene had been going on for some time. It is a process which reveals the strengths and fissures in any political system. In the Philippines, as in other poorly institutionalized systems, it also raises the basic question as to whether the existing political coalition which constitutes the regime can survive the succession struggle. Short, medium, and long-term consequences may be quite different. Regime change seems likely to be greater in the short than in the medium term, but less than in the long run.

Influences on regime change may be from external as well as from domestic sources. The Philippines, the second largest country in Southeast Asia, with more than fifty million people, has long been taken for granted by its mentor and former colonial ruler, the United States. This was because the Philippines enjoyed greater political stability than most Asian countries, first under constitutional democracy until 1972, and then under martial law and its indistinguishable aftermath. That stability protected US interests and was, in turn, protected by them. But as the prospect of severe instability grows, concern for approximately $2 billion in US investment and for the largest American military base complex anywhere outside US territory has focused both media and governmental attention on the 'Philippine problem', defined as how to maintain a friendly regime in power. In the long run it certainly will not be an easy task, as our analysis will indicate.

In the short run, however, we must remember that the struggle for succesion is intense only because the power which Marcos has focused in the presidency is very great, that is, there is something worth fighting for. Yet the longer the struggle lasts and the more heated it becomes, the more it threatens the unity of the regime coalition and thus that power concentration. In fact, events since 21 August indicate a near collapse of that coalition already. It is to be explained primarily in terms of the configuration of domestic attitudes and forces.

First, in order to understand the background of the

present struggle within the elite, we must recall the origins and progress of the most important personal rivalry in Philippine politics for considerably more than a decade. Then we will assess the strategy of 'normalization', by which some institutional changes took place from 1978. After that we can examine the impact of Aquino's assassination in proper perspective and go on to outline probable future developments.

Marcos-Aquino rivalry

At the centre of the Philippine political dynamic for the past seventeen years is a man who has been widely recognized as the most brilliant of the seven presidents since independence in 1946, and unquestionably the most forceful. In fact, Ferdinand Marcos, who was freely elected in 1965, re-elected in 1969, and has ruled with martial law powers since 1972, is probably one of the most skilful politicians in the Third World. Throughout his career, however, a man fifteen years his junior has dogged his footsteps. Benigno Aquino, the youngest elected mayor in the Philippines in 1955, was also the youngest senator in 1967. Thereafter he was generally believed to be the prime contender for the presidency in 1973 (when Marcos could not constitutionally run). In the meantime he was the sharpest critic of the Marcos administration.

Aquino had declared his intention to become president on the day he was elected mayor, but Marcos was elected first. The rivalry continued, producing tragedy and pathos. On 21 August 1971 a bomb exploded on a Liberal Party election platform in Manila, killing some and maiming others, but missing the tardy Senator Aquino, one of its intended targets. Though the crime has remained officially unsolved, the popular belief is that Marcos was responsible; he blamed it on 'the Communists'. It was not surprising, therefore, that when martial law was declared in 1972 Benigno Aquino was one of the first to be arrested, remaining in custody for more than seven years, much longer than any other major opposition figure. But he did not remain politically inactive. His eloquent rebuke to the courts martial trying him for subversion and related crimes and his subsequent hunger strike against the utter injustice of the proceedings were well reported by foreign journalists, and through them news filtered back home to the Philippines. Aquino was even allowed to become a candidate for parliament from gaol, an exercise apparently conceived by the president to deflate the prisoner's charismatic appeal by the experience of failure (he had never before lost an election). In 1978 Aquino indeed lost, but the fraud needed to insure his defeat was so obvious that the incident probably backfired on Marcos.

'Normalization'

That 1978 election was the first step in the process of

'normalization' as conceived by Marcos. For six years he had ruled without benefit of legitimation either by election or through a legislature. The results of his frequent referenda were so predictable that no-one took them seriously any longer. Then in his address to the inaugural session of the new parliament, the Interim Batasang Pambansa, the president declared that its establishment was a 'big step toward the full restoration of the representative system' (Marcos 1978:41). The reality fell far short of that proclaimed goal, however, with the handful of moderate opposition legislators themselves referring to the Batasan within a few months as a 'puppet parliament' (Canoy 1980:179-180).

'Normalization' was really designed to co-opt wider support without jeopardizing Marcos family control. It was supposed to prepare for a smooth succession. This strategy, which has not been basically altered since, was the result of at least three influences.

First and perhaps most important were intimations of the president's mortality. As in any authoritarian regime, the true health of the ruler is a well-guarded secret. The Shah of Iran successfully hid the fact of his cancer even from the prying eyes of the CIA until after he left Iran, undoubtedly prolonging the life of his regime in the process. The Philippines, however, is a place where secrets are very hard to keep. In 1978 visitors to Malacanang reported that the president found it difficult to rise from his chair without assistance. In 1979, signs of ill health became obvious even to TV viewers: the rash was explained as allergy; the puffy face, the awkward fingers were explained not at all. Numerous rumours of diagnosis floated in elite circles, populated by many physicians, including some who had communication with colleagues inside the palace. The dominant school of medical observers came to hold that he suffered from systemic lupus erythamatosus, a degenerative disease that may have acute episodes and spontaneous remissions at irregular and sometimes prolonged intervals. (Thus those who claimed from time to time that Marcos possessed full health and vigour could have been accurately reporting what they observed.) It is also widely believed that the president's kidneys have been sufficiently affected by his illness to require dialysis; in 1983 there were rumours of one being removed. Lupus is a disease which starts like arthritis, then gradually inflames more and more organs, including the brain, but with proper medical care is more often a cause of impaired functioning than an independent cause of death.

Thus, though it could not become the basis for confidently predicting regime collapse in the very near future, by 1978 the autocrat's health had become an important calculation in the assessment of his political longevity, by well-informed enemies as well as friends. Signs of the succession struggle began to surface from time to time. And there were hints in extemporaneous speeches that Ferdinand Marcos himself was thinking more about the image he would

19

have in history. Thus he gave more attention to the mechanism of succession. From the earlier, and quite unsatisfactory, arrangement of a secret committee that would succeed to power, the speaker of the Batasan was named in June 1978 as the president's interim successor. (But his political weakness made the arrangement hardly more satisfactory.)

If the president's illness had stimulated interest in the succession, it is understandable that his wealthiest supporters, both the Filipino economic elite and foreign bankers, were especially concerned that the process be smooth and legitimate, no threat to social or political stability. 'Normalization' was, secondly, at least in part a result of their pressure. The Carter administration also urged liberalization as a means to facilitate passage of Philippine military aid through congress.

Thirdly, the domestic opposition to martial law was itself demanding, with rising voice, a return to free, representative government. For Ferdinand Marcos, Machiavelli's most successful protege in Asia, these were demands not to be ignored. And what more ingenious way to make the opposition look like nattering nabobs than meet those demands, nominally, while filling the media with democratic rhetoric yet retaining all the mechanisms of firm control?

Players in the succession struggle

A continuing obstacle to any real loosening of the political process was the imprisoned Benigno Aquino, both an international embarrassment in gaol and a potential political threat if released. The president was unwilling either to enforce the death penalty that the courts martial had imposed, because of the international outcry against it, or to grant Aquino amnesty, even though he apparently promised at one point that he would. An easier way out was provided by Aquino's development of a severe heart condition that required by-pass surgery in early 1980. Perhaps fearing foreign condemnation if there should be surgical failure within the Philippines, and having resolved that Aquino abroad would lose his political relevance to the Philippine scene, Marcos gave permission for Aquino's surgery to be done in the US. (US pressure to the same end must also have been present.) Aquino himself, who had once been Imelda Marcos's most caustic critic, was fulsome in his praise of the First Lady for assisting his departure in May. He left promising to return when he recovered.

By August, Aquino seemed to have recovered fully from a triple by-pass and was speaking out so forcefully against the martial law regime, and was being heard so sympathetically in the US, that Marcos undoubtedly had second thoughts about having let him go. Aquino explained that his promise to return had no more force than a 'pact with the devil' (Chicago Philippine Times 16-31 July 1980). He also warned that failure of Marcos to launch genuine liberalization could push even moderate oppositionists toward violence. Within weeks bombs began to explode in Manila; the most strategically placed one succeeded in halting the conference of the American Society of Travel Agents in October. The group which claimed credit for such consternation was the 'April 6th Liberation Movement'. Its leadership within the Philippines was not clearly identified, but Marcos implicated Aquino - among other leading politicians - ordering his rearrest. This confrontation seemed likely to delay any further 'normalization' for the time being. Yet events moved at a surprising pace.

In December 1980, during a visit to the UN, Mrs Marcos invited Aquino to meet in her Waldorf-Astoria suite, after he had requested the opportunity. He described the conversation as 'long, friendly...quite useful' (Psinakis 1981:25). At first he admitted only to an agreement with her to help facilitate dialogue in Manila between the president and the opposition, but later revealed that Imelda had suggested that he might become prime minister (Asian-American News 16-30 April 1981). Clearly 'normalization' and the succession struggle had become intricately intertwined.

Madame Imelda Romualdez Marcos, despite occasional coy expressions of disinterest in the presidency, had not dampened her ardour for that high office since 1971 when political soundings about her prospects of winning an election were so discouraging. She also enjoyed hobnobbing with the world's social and political elites, whether in Persepolis, Westminster Abbey, Peking or the United Nations. The utter extravagance of her jet-set life style became an increasing liability to the president, even leading him to an occasional public condemnation of it. But he nevertheless co-operated from time to time in the extension of her power base. In 1975 she was appointed governor of Metro Manila, the boundaries of which have since expanded by hundreds of square kilometres, while the position remains uniquely exempt from electoral review. Then in 1977 she was named Minister of Human Settlements, heading a new department which seemed quite deliberately to have no bureaucratic boundaries and was sometimes refered to as a 'government within a government'. In the meantime she headed several diplomatic missions as the president's 'special envoy'. Her energy seemed to match her ambition.

But if his wife was an embarrassment, why did the president give her so much power? It is a puzzlement. The relationship between them is itself a curious mix of collaboration and conflict. Malacanang insiders often describe it as a stand-off between 'campo ni mam' and 'campo ni sir', the unique Tag-lish way of stating that His family and friends, and Hers each constitute a warring camp, in which the battlegrounds are appointments, government contracts, investment opportunities, media treatment, and priority in the allocation of funds. It appears that Mr Marcos would sometimes yield to Madame's demands, for example to fire his executive secretary, Alejandro Melchor, in 1975, and perhaps also his chief economic advisor, Gerardo Sicat, in 1981. But why?

It may be his belief that her management of his campaign to capture the Nacionalista nomination for president in 1965 was the key to his subsequent success, and he is forever grateful. Certainly she is his most loyal ally. And she does have a certain amount of political savvy. Others believe, however, that he recognizes that to thwart her ambition too completely could mean disaster for him. The power and wealth that the Romualdez clan already have, plus the information they retain about the manner in which Marcos acquired his power and wealth could, if turned against the president, be very damaging indeed. He sees, according to these observers, that her political satisfaction is the best way to keep family skeletons buried, to preserve his good image in history.

Aside from the crucial information that Mr Marcos holds on the Romualdez clan, the limitations on Imelda's power include the stern opposition of a major segment of the army and technocrats, fear of her irrational extravagances and her antipathy to economic discipline by the World Bank/IMF and dismay at her constant demand for 'donations' from the economic elite. After all she did not succeed in her 1981 campaign for appointment as prime minister. Nevertheless, she was named in mid-1982 to the executive committee, which according to a 1981 constitutional amendment was to succeed temporarily a disabled or deceased president. In sum, despite limitations her star has risen steadily, though not as fast as she might have liked.

The other key figures in the succession struggle within the regime are the Minister of Defence, Juan Ponce Enrile, and General Fabian Ver, Chief-of-Staff of the Armed Forces of the Philippines, commanding general of the Presidential Security Command, head of military and civilian intelligence agencies, and the president's close relative. Both are Ilocanos, sharing the president's ethnic origin, as do most of the military high command. Both have also benefited financially from their political position: Enrile controls the coconut industry (the nation's largest export earner) together with his long-time collaborator, Eduardo Cojuangco, while Ver's holdings are more diverse. The two men have been rivals for some time, but their rivalry did not break out in the open until August 1983 when Enrile lost a running battle over military appointments and threatened to resign.

Enrile clearly regards himself as a candidate for succession – despite a formal expression of disinterest in the presidency in September – and is so regarded by some of his cabinet colleagues, as well as a few general officers. However, competition from the most powerful general severely limits Enrile's options. General Ver himself was not initially seen as an independent contender for the throne, but was viewed as simply an ally of Mrs Marcos. The president publicly suggested that the general's promotion to

Chief-of-Staff was the consequence of the First Lady's intervention on his behalf. But this seems a bit contrived, and may have revealed that Imelda needs Ver more than he needs her. In view of her widespread unpopularity within the military this is undoubtedly the case. During the president's lifetime Ver's loyalty to the First Family is probably unquestioned; for instance, during his trip to Saudi Arabia in 1981 Marcos ignored constitutional provisions to entrust Ver with the keys to succession. But Ver is widely regarded as being sufficiently pragmatic and ambitious that he would not sustain an alliance with Mrs Marcos if she became a political liability. Thus she must constantly seek other allies as well.

'Normalization' and succession: dilemmas and constraints

The next steps in the 'normalization' process were simply designed to legitimize the regime's power at home and abroad, and make it more efficient. After the cosmetic 'lifting' of martial law in January 1981, the 1973 constitution was again amended, abandoning the British-style parliamentary system, which had never really been implemented, and replacing it with something that closely resembled the French Fifth Republic. This permitted the presidency to retain predominant power, while allowing much administrative detail to be passed to a thoroughly loyal prime minister. Under these new constitutional provisions the president asked for a new mandate from the people in June 1981. But he so resolutely refused to reform the electoral system that the opposition had no chance of success and thus no credible opponent could be found. The constitutional amendment itself had eliminated Aquino by raising the minimum age for the president to 50; Aquino was then 48.

Perhaps the most significant gain in both legitimacy and efficiency was the appointment of Cesar Virata as Prime Minister. Virata, who had been Finance Minister since 1970, was highly regarded in world banking circles both for his competence and for his unusual reputation for personal honesty in the bosom of a corrupt regime. Some believed, in fact, that the constitutional revision was pushed by the IMF/World Bank to create a more prominent place for Virata. The prime minister was also to chair the executive committee which was given full responsibility for supervising any succession, thus easing fears of a crisis on that occasion.

Yet by 1982, after four years of 'normalization' manoeuvres, very little had actually been accomplished, even within the narrow definition that Marcos had set for himself. There had been no progress in the co-optation of the elite opposition; in fact, their alienation, or exile, was more complete than it had been in early 1978. The position of the Catholic Church, a major determinant of regime legitimacy, had become more hostile. Provisions for succession were still not clear-cut enough (with a deeply split executive committee) to assuage the anxiety of business and financial interests. Nor was stronger positioning of Imelda in the succession race, which had been accomplished, their concept of an ideal solution.

None of this is evidence of the president's incompetence as a political tactician, however. He faced the more fundamental problem of attempting the impossible. For one thing he was caught in a dilemma attached to the authoritarian character of his rule. If he attempted to strengthen institutional legitimacy (by sharing power with the opposition) for purposes of a stable succession he undermined the short-term protection of his own family interests, whereas if he aimed for the latter he jeopardized the former. Furthermore, a patrimonial regime, such as that of Marcos, in which legitimacy and power are derived from the personal loyalties of thousands of followers for the leader, is by the nature of the system institutionally weak, and thus finds succession especially problematic. The president himself recognized this point in a comment to the Asian Wall Street Journal in 1982 when he said, 'everybody believes that if I step down, the party [i.e. the government's New Society Movement] will break up' (Asian Wall Street Journal 11 February 1982). The super-patron cannot pass on his role without allowing someone else to assume it, that is without succession actually taking place. And Marcos is clearly not ready for that, even though he has given his wife more and more opportunity to become super-patron in her own right, so that she has control of far more funds for the purpose of expanding clientage than any other cabinet member.

Marcos was reluctant to clearly name a successor partly because of his fear that designation would further inflame the succession struggle. (A casual naming of Virata as 'likely successor' in February 1983 had to be withdrawn six weeks later when brickbats began to fly. See Times Journal 22 February 1983; Canberra Times 8 April 1983.) Imelda complements her husband's refusal to make a designation with comments like, 'I never had political ambitions'. No-one really believes her, but she probably hopes that such statements will help diffuse efforts in the cabinet and the military to coalesce against her. (She announced in September 1983 that she was 'quitting politics' to continue her work in the private sector without taking concrete steps in that direction (Foreign Broadcast Information Service (FBIS) 20 September 1983, quoting Far East Broadasting Co. (FEBC) 19 September 1983). In any case, 'normalization' as Marcos conceived it could not ensure a smooth succession.

To the extent that the president became conscious of these dilemmas, he must have looked for new sources of regime legitimacy and reflected on the opportunities created by a new occupant of the White House who was strongly anti-communist, pledged to military build-up and less particular about human rights. Both Mr and Mrs Marcos had been seeking a White House invitation since 1972, unsuccessfully. To receive one from President Reagan was thus both a personal and political triumph. Marcos has been able to manipulate Filipino nationalist sentiments more effectively than his predecessors, but he has not abandoned a practice of Filipino politicians since the colonial era of seeking American blessings. Judging from the coverage in the controlled Philippine press of the First Couple's state visit to Washington in September 1982, it was regarded by the regime as a great success. The endorsement of the US president could not have been more fulsome. And through it all Mr Marcos was reported to be in good health. All of this seemed to bestow the boon of legitimacy without any of the pitfalls present in trying to earn it domestically. Yet in direct as well as indirect ways the triumphal return from Washington contributed to the brutal tragedy of last August.

The Aquino assassination: who's and why's

The lesson that Benigno Aquino took from the Marcos state visit only reinforced his experiences ever since Reagan took office. His hope of American backing as an alternative to Marcos – typical of the elite opposition – had been dashed. His Washington connections had been largely swept away by the Reagan tide. Thus he was thrown back on his own resources: good rapport with the world press, a crowd-pleasing charismatic appeal, a strong sense of his political destiny, a streak of bravery, and his Filipino friends. His timing was not significantly delayed by his second meeting at the Waldorf-Astoria with Mrs Marcos, in May 1983. After a renewed effort to buy his co-operation had failed, Ninoy later told friends, Imelda took on a vehement, bitter tone. She warned him gravely of plots against his life even 'beyond the control of the president'. Ultimately Aquino chose to return home in August, despite considerable contrary advice, because of an almost naive faith in the prospect of rational dialogue with President Marcos. Reports of his rapidly deteriorating health made the need for dialogue more urgent to Aquino, who hoped that a man who felt closer to the end of his life would be more philosophical. Tragically, however, Aquino failed to recognize that lupus could also cloud its victim's judgement.

The bloody scene on the tarmac of the Manila airport is all too vivid in our memories. But the true nature of the event remains behind so many screens that it may be years before we understand it. Still, informed speculation about what happened, and why, is a necessary prelude to assessing present and future consequences of the shocking murder.

It was a shock even to those familiar with Philippine politics, not because there were no fears for Aquino's safety but because the manner of the killing was so brazen, and so calculated to focus blame on someone in government. Marcos himself was believed to have eliminated several of his political enemies since his youth, and the military was widely believed to have 'salvaged' hundreds in recent years. Settings for those evil deeds, however, were remote or confused, and traceable tracks few. But to have done this in a blaze of world-wide publicity! Who? Why?

The Filipino opposition now blames Marcos, while the US government absolves him personally. A compromise thesis is that an over-eager subordinate sought to please his patron, even without explicit instructions. But in the long and sad history of Philippine political violence this is outside the cultural pattern. In any case, if Marcos did authorize the killing, it may not have been the same man with a well-earned reputation for tactical genius in politics. The impact of lupus on the brain does produce paranoia, which would also help explain some of the president's unusual statements. This is a possibility that cannot be ruled out. It would have created a frame of mind in which a motive would have emerged; and no-one has doubted the president's capability to initiate or have carried out an assassination. One quote from his 22 August news conference has never been clarified; said Marcos, 'No matter what explanation we make now, there will be some kind of shadow over the government, and this was never, never our purpose. We had hoped the matter could be handled with a little more finesse' (FBIS 24 August 1983, quoting RPN Television Network 23 August 1983).

The most dramatic revelation regarding the assassination is code-named 'E.T.' or 'Exterminate Totally' (see Liberation, the publication of the National Democratic Front (NDF) 30 August 1983). The documents and verbal accounts reporting on a plot by this name are still of doubtful authenticity in the view of most informed observers, but their contents are widely known in Manila, and often believed.

The president's own version of the assassination was that it was 'the communists', faceless culprits who have played a useful role for him in the past. (Prime Minister Virata, however, admitted that 'some elements of the government' may have been involved (AFP, Hong Kong, 9 September 1983).) Yet if he were to admit they had the capability, it would require the admission also of a terrible, unparalleled breach in military security. This is not impossible, but most unlikely. The argument for motive is also inconclusive. While it is true that the removal of a popular, pro-American critic of the regime would tip the balance of opposition forces more toward the Communist Party of the Philippines (CPP) by weakening the moderate voice, it must also be recalled that the party in recent years has had a generally cautious policy of avoiding provocations, especially moves that would rapidly enhance the power of the military, as this event has. (In late August student organizations friendly to the NDF condemned violent demonstrations (FBIS 2 September 1983, quoting FEBC 1 September 1983). And if the 21 September violence had been planned by the communists, there would have been militant follow-ups, which were absent. In fact, some friends of the CPP believe its leadership has been able to develop no consensus on how to deal with the entire post-Aquino crisis.) Ultimately what makes one most sceptical about the official version is that after three months the awesome power of military intelligence has not been able to come up with a credible witness.

In any case, whatever the fascination with various details of timing, ballistics, identification of bodies, and disappearing witnesses, about which a society with a superabundance of lawyers is particularly curious, the overwhelming fact was that most Filipinos believed that their president was responsible for the shooting of his major rival. Thus they could not imagine that any investigating commission appointed by that president would reveal the truth about the incident, expectations so far confirmed by events. Indeed, the inability of the first investigation commission to either gain legitimacy or begin its work - and the still shaky prospects for the second - are major indicators of the damage which the assassination has inflicted on the regime.

The political and economic impact of the assassination

The untimely death of a political hero, especially in circumstances that might justify the term martyrdom, would be a major event in the history of any nation. And the less institutionalized the political process, the more prominent the role of strong personalities, the more important such an event becomes. The execution of Jose Rizal by the Spaniards in 1896, on the basis of false charges against him, is now recognized by historians as having been a crucial stimulus to the Philippine Revolution against Spain, and the ongoing linkage of nationalism with folk Catholicism (Ileto 1982). Even though Filipinos now, nearly four generations later, are less likely to place political happenings in the framework of religious imagery, it should be noted that the death of Aquino may have a more profound impact on the national psyche at the mass level than such 'martyrdom' would at the level of the Westernized middle class or elite. Comparisons with Rizal have already appeared in the press.

In the short term Aquino's bloody sacrifice may have gone further toward undermining the authoritarian regime than any contributions he could have made in the complex compromises of life. The anger at this brazen killing has spread to segments of the population which were never before politicized. For instance, the immediate past president of the University of the Philippines, Emanuel Soriano, called for the resignation of President Marcos (Business Day 5 September 1983) and the normally apolitical Philippine Social Science Congress issued a scathing indictment of the regime in November. When an ageing regime has already been perceived by the relatively well-informed as suffering from increasing corruption and ineffectiveness, this mass emotional release rapidly creates a wider acceptance of that perception, even as it is radicalized and becomes more intense. An indicator was an escalation in the language of protest. Furthermore, large demonstrations are a welcome form of political expression for masses who have had no way

27

of voicing their dissatisfaction since the declaration of
martial law. A more rapid erosion of regime legitimacy and a
sudden acceleration in the growth of political participation
are thus the most immediate consequences of the
assassination, setting a new stage for the succession
struggle.

Changes of mood have a direct impact not only on
politics but on economics as well. The increasing prospect
of political instability shatters the confidence of investors
and creditors, both domestic and foreign. The actual flight
of capital in the first two months after the assassination
was estimated over $US 1 billion (Far Eastern Economic Review
(Guy Sacerdoti) 20 October 1983; Asian Wall Street Journal
21 November 1983). The devaluation of the peso in early
October by 21 per cent (which followed close on the heels of
a nearly 8 per cent devaluation in June) may have been an
adjustment to reality, but it only slowed the flight of hard
currency. And in the atmosphere of crisis foreign banks were
slowing proferred credit, though no-one would admit by how
much. A communication from Prime Minister Virata to the
president about the extent of the Philippines's international
financial crisis is said to have been so devastating as to
cause Marcos to switch almost immediately (on 3 October) from
attacking to cajoling the Manila business community, though
the good rapport did not last long.

The shift in mood in the Philippine business community,
and its behavioural consequences, was one of the more
dramatic developments after 21 August. This is not to say,
however, that Filipino businessmen were without long-standing
grievances. They had prospered under martial law in the
1970s, thus their bitterness against favoured Marcos cronies
or discomfort at the inroads of foreign corporations was
muted. But in 1981 the world-wide depression began to wreak
havoc in the Philippines. The GNP growth rate fell sharply
to 2.6 per cent in 1982 and was expected to reach zero in
1983. The cut-back in markets and in available credit
sharpened whatever lines of conflict already existed. The
old economic elite was angered by the generous bailout for
the failing corporations of Marcos cronies, while
manufacturers who had enjoyed tariff protection were shocked
and embittered by the prime minister's acceptance of World
Bank conditions on its 'structural adjustment loan', which
required a 30 per cent drop in import duties by 1985.

In 1981 the most articulate representative of business
interests became the newly-formed Makati Business Club (MBC),
headed by the ambitious and dynamic Enrique Zobel, president
of Ayala Corporation, one of the major concentrations of old
wealth. The MBC eclipsed the long-established Philippine
Chamber of Commerce and Industry in debating and critiquing
government policy and in proposing alternatives, which
sometimes extended beyond the purely economic sphere to
include restoring a free electoral process or reforming an
inefficient bureaucracy (Far Eastern Economic Review
(Sacerdoti) 24 September 1983). In another realm of his busy

life Zobel was at the same time challenging the management of the San Miguel Corporation, the Philippines's largest, in a board room fight that also had profound political overtones. He was defeated in his bid for control by the president's most aggressive crony, Eduardo Cojuangco, who replaced Zobel as Vice-Chairman.

Thus, it was not surprising to see Zobel's name surface in September. Ex-Senator Salvador Laurel, president of the moderate opposition alliance, UNIDO, has his law offices close to Zobel's headquarters in Makati. There seemed to develop between them the kind of co-operation that Laurel only dreamed of before Aquino's death. In retaliation Marcos arrested and briefly detained an Ayala Corporation vice president, ostensibly for his backing of a banned newspaper. Business support for the frequent anti-Marcos demonstrations in Makati became widespread extending by November to provincial cities. Some observers are predicting for Zobel, who has since retired as Ayala Corporation president, a more active political role in the future. Jaime Ongpin, president of Benguet Corporation, primarily a gold mining firm, and brother of a Marcos cabinet member, has been an even more articulate Marcos critic, calling for free elections, immediate choosing of a vice-president, and the resignation of Imelda Marcos from all offices. The shift among the economic elite from predominantly covert to more overt opposition to the government will surely have profound consequences in the near future. Already it has complemented the protests of UNIDO and thus helped compensate for that group's organizational weakness.

UNIDO was formed in January 1980 as the United Democratic Opposition (only in 1982 changing its name to United Nationalist Democratic Organization, without changing its acronym). It is an alliance of several opposition groups: remnants of the Liberal Party, regional organizations that had sprung up since 1972, such as the Mindanao Alliance, ·and the Laurel branch of the old Nacionalista Party of Ferdinand Marcos (new recruits to opposition ranks). It has yet to be transformed from an alliance into a single party, though there has been such talk. It was generally assumed that Senator Aquino would return to the Philippines to become chairman. In the meantime Salvador Laurel, son of the wartime president of the Philippines under Japan, who was elected to the Batasan in 1978, acted as head of UNIDO while making frequent trips abroad to consult with Aquino. He had neither the personality nor the reputation, however, to command the respect of UNIDO members to the extent Aquino could, though in September he resigned from the Batasan to emphasize the strength of his opposition to the regime. Thus while Aquino's sacrifice has altered the national mood, it may have been a blow to the organizational strength of the group he would have led. UNIDO does not have a local level structure in most provinces (and when it does the integration of local affiliates and national leadership is poor), nor is it organized down to the neighbourhood level in the metropolis as is the government party, <u>Kilusang Bagong Lipunan</u> (KBL). From November, however, UNIDO was expanding provincial political activity.

The Liberal side of UNIDO leadership - decimated by an assassin's bullet in August - could be substantially bolstered, however, if the senior remaining political exile, Jovito Salonga, were to return, a rumoured possibility. He left in 1980, partly for health reasons and partly because he had been falsely charged for complicity in the September and October bombings. Successor to the title of president of the Liberal Party when ex-Senator Gerardo Roxas died, ex-Senator Salonga has a reputation for nationalism, intellectual integrity, and social progressivism that makes him much more in tune with the times than the Liberals' elder statesman, ex-President Diosdado Macapagal (the predecessor of Marcos). More acceptable to important segments of the business community than ex-Senator Jose Diokno, Salonga might even emerge as the leading figure in the non-Communist opposition, if his health, permanently weakened by the 1971 Plaza Miranda bombing, would permit.

The role of the Church

In addition to the support from the business community, UNIDO protests have been augmented by the vocal role of Jaime Cardinal Sin, Archbishop of Manila. Indeed the Catholic Church has been growing in political importance ever since the declaration of martial law, as is often true in societies where legal political opposition is suppressed.

This is a valid parallel with Iran, though the long-standing and often emotionally intense identification of Shiite Islam with Persian nationalism does not have an exact analogue in the Philippines. To be sure, Fathers Burgos, Gomez and Zamora, as a result of their fight for the rights of Filipino clergy, were the first martyrs of the Philippine Revolution. But the Roman Catholic hierarchy was a target, not a part of that revolutionary struggle.

In the present situation also the church is rift by deep cleavages. Cardinal Sin's political leadership is designed in part to hold the church together, as well as to reform the government. As a good shepherd of his flock he voices the discontent that they cannot, but also maintains political dialogue with the regime to decrease the likelihood of a thoroughly damaging attack on the interests of the church, such as full taxation of church property. By attending to the concerns of both progressives and conservatives he helps prevent further cleavage. By professing sympathy and understanding for clergy who, because of their identification with the plight of the poor, actually co-operate with the communists, he is trying to reduce the vehemence with which the theology of liberation will be turned by its adherents against the hierarchy, with something less than complete success.

But in general the hierarchy is increasingly concerned about Marxist influence in the church. Until a few years ago there was still a number of bishops who not only sympathized with the inclination of some of their priests to work with communist-led organizations, but were themselves capable of dialogue and autonomous co-operation. Since then the impact of experience and the impact of the Vatican appear to have polarized views on this subject. Perhaps as many as 2 to 5 per cent of priests and nuns are committed to the NDF or the NPA and in one way or another are working with them. Dialogue with their bishops on their position has become more and more difficult, however. Testimony from an arrested NDF priest in Samar shocked moderates and conservatives. Several of the progressive bishops went through experiences in which they felt that Catholics working with the NDF had deceived and misled them. At the same time they were receiving messages through the hierarchy urging disengagement. In a more fundamental sense the incompatibility of Christian teaching on violence, to which many progressives have tried very hard to be faithful, and the Marxist line have become more evident as the armed struggle heats up, as guerrillas as well as soldiers more frequently succumb to the temptation for revenge (see, for instance, Bishop Francisco Claver, 'An Option for Peace', address to PDP convention, Cagayan de Oro City, 5 February 1983). (For some conservatives in the hierarchy their 'abhorence of violence' has been a double standard, a convenient tool with which to flog only communists. They must have welcomed the president's July appeal for an alliance between church and state against communism.) By February 1983, with a variety of motivations, the Catholic Bishops' Conference of the Philippines (CBCP) agreed unanimously, for the first time, on vigorous criticism of the excesses of the regime, coupled with a condemnation of the use of violence for political ends and of the subordination of Christian to atheist ideologies which provides a firmer theological basis for clerical anti-communism. NDF recruitment of and co-ordination with Catholic clergy is unlikely, therefore, to expand at the rate it has in recent years, unless military abuses escalate further.

In any case, despite its dual thrust, the February pastoral letter did mark an escalation in official church attacks on the Marcos regime. Since then Cardinal Sin, who was a personal friend of Aquino, has lent dignity and force to the protest over Aquino's death. On 27 November, Aquino's birthday and the beginning of Advent, the CBCP issued another pastoral letter - still more cautious than the cardinal - urging 'reconciliation' as a way to avoid the 'bloodbath of revolution' and asking those who espouse violence to reconsider in light of 'the unique demands of a gospel of love'. It also called for an 'end to graft and corruption', honest elections in May, and the restoration of people's basic rights (New York Times 27 November 1983). The church retains a much better communications system than does the secular opposition, having added a business-backed weekly newspaper, Veritas, in November. Church bodies could become more important informal allies of the UNIDO, and especially the Jesuit-backed Pilipino Democratic Party (PDP), in the near future.

The Left and broadening coalitions

UNIDO's greatest rival in the campaign to unseat Marcos is, and has been, the Communist Party of the Philippines (CPP), which at its founding in 1969 tacked on to its name '(Marxist-Leninist-Mao Tse Tung Thought)'. This awesome handle was, of course, designed to distinguish the organization from its predecessor and bitter competitor in Marxist circles, which usually still goes by the Tagalog name, Partido Komunista ng Pilipinas (PKP). Since 1972 the PKP - now a mere remnant of the potent leader of armed rebellion in the 1950s - has formally co-operated with Marcos, with a few of its former members co-opted into the regime. But in the last few years, aware of its loss of a mass base, the Party has attempted to organize peasant and worker protests. It is still not a significant element in the opposition movement, but the demise of Marcos and a shift in the Soviet line could alter that.

Since Mao halted modest material aid to the CPP in 1975, after hosting Mrs Marcos, the Maoist element in Party thinking has been weakened, but not without some vigorous debate, it is reported (Nemenzo 1982). Party strategists have been forced to rethink their plans more carefully in terms of Philippine reality. The Party preaches a sophisticated mix of guerrilla warfare with a mass base in the countryside and united front political activity in the cities, all carried out in the framework of a decentralized decision-making structure accommodating to the geographic fragmentation of an archipelago and the effectiveness of military intelligence. The central committee recognizes the need for 'protracted struggle' and is not over-optimistic about the timing of ultimate victory. Even friendly critics would question the realism of the faith in ultimate success, however, in view of the combination of the strength of American military and economic interests and the lack of a nearby friendly sanctuary. The counter-argument holds, of course, that neither of these factors is immutable.

But whatever its longer-term goals, the CPP has been able to build on the rising discontent with the regime much more successfully than the earlier somewhat comparable attempt of the PKP. The communists have Marcos repression to thank for creating favourable conditions.

The New People's Army (NPA), formed shortly after the Party, was present in thirty-three municipalities, all in Luzon, in 1972. The Party claimed 'guerrilla fronts' in four hundred towns spread over forty-seven provinces in almost all major islands by 1981 - and all reports indicate even more rapid growth in the last two years. In early 1983 the

military situation in Mindanao became so bad that the
president had to announce the airlifting of reinforcements.
(In August the PC admitted that NPA was active in 17 per cent
of barangays, which would be a higher percentage of rural
villages. Times Journal 1 August 1983). Since the Party
line argues that 'emphasis on political work has kept
military operations at a low level', the regime may have
cause for even greater apprehension in the near future. A
tapering-off of NPA military activity since 21 August was
probably only tactical.

Given the urban focus of the political reaction to the
murder of Aquino, however, the work of the National
Democratic Front (NDF) and its affiliates becomes more
important. Formed in 1973, the NDF is open to all 'patriotic
and democratic forces'. Its 'organizational base' is claimed
by the Party to be the Kabataang Makabayan (Patriotic Youth),
revived in 1977; an underground workers' federation formed
in 1975; an organization of the urban poor; and Christians
for National Liberation, which pre-dated the NDF (South-east
Asia Chronicle No. 62 May-June 1978; No. 83 April 1982).
Presumably each of these named organizations is
Party-controlled; but the NDF has also had temporary and
mutually autonomous alliances with a great variety of other
organizations. If any of these others are Party-controlled,
that, understandably, is a well-kept secret. But given the
fluidity of political organization in the Philippines
generally, it is unlikely that many are.

As early as 1981, when Marcos created conditions under
which the only logical response to a rigged presidential
election was boycott, a coalition was formed to promote
electoral abstention which spanned the entire opposition
spectrum, 'People's MIND'. In addition to UNIDO and well
established church, labour and student groups, there were
thoroughly independent peace and human rights organizations
led by ex-Senator Diokno, along with newer ad hoc formations
reputed to receive some inspiration from the NDF. These last
were best at organizing crowds. In 1982 there were efforts
to initiate such a broad coalition on a more permanent basis,
but they failed.

The killing of Aquino has created a new crisis in which
it is relatively easy to find common ground regardless of
ideological differences. JAJA ('Justice for Aquino, Justice
for All') is a coalition formally headed by the elderly, but
still vigorous, ex-Senator Lorenzo Tanada. More active
leadership seems to come from Diokno, JAJA secretary, now
probably the most widely respected nationalist and human
rights advocate, who has strong support in the church and
close connections with Amnesty International. The Aquino and
Laurel families have also been represented in JAJA's planning
sessions, along with representatives of more radical groups.
It has co-ordinated most major demonstrations, surpassing the
importance of UNIDO in that regard. But as in 1981,
effective co-operation over such a broad spectrum may not
survive.

The launching of another organization in November 1983, the Nationalist Alliance for Justice, Freedom and Democracy, also under the chairmanship of ex-Senator Tanada, may have been designed to survive for a longer period. Its structure is based on individual membership rather than group affiliation. (Diokno is not involved.) The language of the voluminous secretariat publications would seem to imply that the orientation toward the NDF is considerably closer than in the case of JAJA (see, for instance, Nationalist Alliance Secretariat 1983). But there are also some key UNIDO and PDP-Laban figures in its national council. The incentive to build bridges between left and right remains strong as long as crude military repression persists.

The Military and the President

The behaviour of the military since 21 August requires us to consider that possibility. The shooting down of demonstrators, as on 21 September, has fortunately been a rather rare occurrence under 'martial law Philippine style'. But the illness of the president could leave the military more and more under General Ver's direction without any moderating political guidance. Another profound consequence of the assassination may be an intensification of factionalism within the armed forces. More messages of dissatisfaction at middle levels are filtering through the opposition. And signs of Ver taking an upper hand will deepen the plotting by his rivals. The superficial calm within the military in the first few months after the assassination was not, therefore, necessarily reassuring for the future.

If major changes in the military's role depend on the ability of the president to exercise political direction over them, then, as in so many other respects, it is the top office on which we must focus. Next to Aquino himself Marcos has probably suffered more than anyone from this most dramatic episode of his presidency. Though the popular perception of his right to rule, his legitimacy, had been eroding rapidly in recent years, with rigged elections, declining living standards for nearly half of the population, and deteriorating peace and order, the events of August produced a nose-dive in the public's image of both his right and his ability to rule. For either one must conclude that the president is a murderer or that he has lost control over his own armed forces. And whichever explanation one chooses his medical condition figures prominently in the calculation.

Until August many observers of the Philippine scene, including some hard-bitten journalists, could discount 'rumours about the president's health' and proceed with their analysis on the basis of other information. Now that is no longer possible. For those few persons who saw him during his period of seclusion in August the advanced symptoms of lupus, whether or not immediately recognized as such, were dramatic. Since this was only a month after Manila was abuzz with talk of 'miracle cures' to explain how good the president looked, unpredictable fluctuation in his condition now has to be accepted as given. Speculation about his retirement or demise, which in June was measured in years, quickly shifted to measurement in months. Now even if his health does last another few years the undermining of confidence in his condition speeds regime ageing and thus factional infighting. The president may be able to recover some lost ground by emerging with balanced judgement, diplomatic language and careful political manoeuvre which characterized the 'old Marcos' that we knew. Though Cardinal Sin still described the president as 'troubled' and 'rattled' in late September (AFP, Hong Kong, 25 September 1983), he seems to have had some success in October. In November he again sounded quite paranoid. Awareness that his illness can affect his brain is now widespread; it will influence more and more political decisions of his subordinates.

US-Philippine relations in a new context

Changes in US-Philippine relations that have been brought about by Aquino's murder may still be largely under a classified security blanket, as is true of those within the military. But some outlines have already emerged. Both Congress and the State Department seem to be more willing to distance themselves from Marcos than they were when this year's renewal of the Bases Agreement was signed, with a price tag of $US900 million in military and economic assistance over a five year period.

Immediately after Aquino's murder the State Department called it a 'cowardly and despicable act'. A few weeks later the deputy assistant Secretary of State for East Asia and the Pacific, J.E. Monjo, testifying before a House of Representatives sub-committee, went further, saying, 'Many Filipinos, and not all of them opposed to the current government, suspect the complicity of elements of the government in the crime. It raises very disturbing questions that demand answers'. He concluded with the assertion that the May 1984 parliamentary election had become 'more important than ever' since 'a free and fair electoral process in which Filipinos can place their confidence is the key to the resolution of the political problems left in the wake of the Aquino assassination' (Sub-committee on Asian and Pacific Affairs, House Foreign Affairs Committee, 13 September 1983). How weighty these statements were in Manila, however, in view of the fact that every assurance was also given that the new situation would not jeopardize US security assistance, remains to be seen; payments have actually been accelerated to alleviate the dollar crisis. (Even the major congressional expression of concern, the Solarz-Kennedy resolution, failed to make a link with aid appropriation decisions.)

The planned presidential visit to Manila in November

became, of course, the key indicator of any shift in US policy. Despite the numerous editorial advisories in the US to cancel, both on the grounds of Reagan's safety and because it would send the wrong message to the Philippine government and people, few thought the White House would change its plans. But it did. The reason given only thinly disguised real official thinking, but the indefinite postponement to other ASEAN countries softened the blow to Marcos. Clearly the visit would have triggered a political explosion of primary benefit to the Left which Reagan's advisors sought to avoid. Ironically this postponement may thus have helped to prolong Marcos's power rather than weaken it, as some argued earlier.

The next important American policy decision will of necessity be a product of private/public sector consultation - on how to respond to the urgent plea from Manila for more credit. In the next few months that will prove to be more crucial than the question of a presidential visit.

It may be that the broad thrust of American policy was reflected in a speech by Ambassador Michael Armacost to the Makati Rotary Club on 17 November 1983. While describing new and accelerated American assistance to alleviate the Philippine 'financial crisis', he also insisted that Philippine problems were 'precipitated by questions concerning social and political stability' (Philippines Daily Express 19 November 1983; Veritas 27 November - 3 December 1983). At the same time he mentioned that additional US aid awaited the final decision of the IMF on credit for the Philippines. The December decision of the committee of twelve leading private creditors of the Philippines to offer $US 1.4 billion in new funds, plus a rescheduling of old debt, implied the same two-track policy: enough aid to avoid the 'worst-case' scenario but much less than hoped for in order to maintain leverage for political change. Most economists believe $US 3-4 billion in new money is needed to make possible real growth.

One would assume that in the midst of crisis, American leverage - in concert with the IMF - would be especially effective. But at the same time the very size of the Philippine debt made the US-centered international banking system in some sense dependent on Philippine developments, since they could not tolerate a complete default. Ineffectiveness of government to government leverage could draw the US into more direct sub-rosa involvement in Philippine politics.

Succession scenarios

The Aquino assassination has, as we have noted, produced a dramatic change of mood in the Philippines. But the flight of capital and the temporary halting of credit has probably been the most concrete consequence of the tragedy so far. The rapid deflation in the legitimacy of President Marcos is at least as important, but its practical impact may take a while to manifest itself. This creates so many uncertainties that there is a strong temptation for the analyst to try to look a bit into the future. And all such gazing forces a focus on the accelerated succession struggle. It is a risky business when secret plans, acts of God, and well-concealed private ambitions can hardly be made part of the analysis. The president himself warned in mid-September: 'Things are changing very quickly; with all these occurrences, all bets are off' (FBIS 12 September 1983, quoting RPN Television Network 9 September 1983). But what we do know about key persons, groups and institutions, and about how their counterparts have interacted in other societies facing succession, helps us at least to suggest the probable alternatives.

Certainly the preferred option for most Filipinos, and for most foreign friends of the Philippines, would be the electoral scenario. A new parliament is to be chosen in May 1984 and if those elections should be entirely fair and free, participated in by all legal parties, the National Assembly and by extension the whole government would gain new strength and legitimacy. The most stable transition might take place if the present opposition gained enough seats so that it should logically be taken into a coalition. The appointment of a prime minister who had the support of this new majority would allow the president to resign even before his term was up in 1987 without threatening effective administration or encouraging intra-elite factionalism or social upheaval. A more legitimate regime would certainly make it easier for the technocrats to orchestrate economic recovery. US pressure for free elections in May 1984 seemed to be geared toward this goal.

A variant on the electoral scenario, which has less support in Washington, has been proposed by UNIDO. Holding no faith in the ability of President Marcos to ever preside over a free and fair election, and denying the legitimacy of the 1973 Constitution, this plan calls for Marcos's resignation and his replacement with a council of elder statesmen to organize voting for a new parliament-cum-constituent assembly. Such a scenario includes the danger of a weak, confused interregnum, and even UNIDO leaders have not been consistent in interpreting or supporting its provisions. (In November 1983 they switched to declaring that Fernando Lopez, elected Vice-President in 1969, was the rightful successor to Marcos.)

Many observers would retort that any electoral scenario was 'the stuff that dreams are made of'. It is, of course, risky. Still, with strong, united, moderate opposition leadership, military tolerance of free debate and organization, and good health for the president for another year, it might work. These conditions would be difficult enough to secure, but economic recovery would also be needed to make the plan succeed. This listing makes one aware that reconstituting constitutional democracy after more than a decade of dictatorship is a bit like trying to put Humpty

Dumpty together again. Above all it requires a military willing to relinquish some power in favour of democratic forces - a condition which probably only tough, persistent US pressure could create.

But what conditions in the Philippines are most likely? There is an opposition rife with mutual suspicion and bereft of its most charismatic figure. Questions of electoral participation next year will surely split opposition forces if the president does not resign first. Concessions offered by Marcos in October to change the election law and the composition of the Commission on Elections would have been substantial in the context of past debate. But whether in the context of the new militancy they are adequate to induce general participation is exceedingly doubtful. The military appetite for power is growing, not diminishing, and seems even less likely to be moderated by a strong political hand in the near future. The most powerful General, Ver, appears to be the leading hardliner. A year's good health for the president is not impossible, but very chancy. Economic recovery, dependent as it is on the world's economy, wise Philippine economic policy, and both creditor and investor confidence, is even more problematical. In fact, inflation rates are likely to rise and real incomes for the majority to fall even further. Negative growth of as much as 10 per cent is predicted for 1984. Distributive injustice, which leads to political polarization and confrontation, will thus be more deep-seated.

In essence, the solution most compatible with this observer's values, and probably with the values of a majority of politically active Filipinos, is too delicate to have much chance of growing in the existing hostile environment. It is too threatening to those who now control the dominant institution, the military, and perhaps to others in the elite because many demands voiced in the electoral process would be for fundamental change. Furthermore, while Marcos has clearly shown greater political wisdom than most of his uniformed supporters, to base a scenario on the expectation that he can be persuaded to resign is very flimsy planning. It did not happen in the most comparable recent instance in Kenya and it is incompatible with the personality traits that have made Ferdinand Marcos a powerful leader - even more so when he is paranoid.

One of the most respected Filipino intellectuals, Renato Constantino, has argued that Marcos will resign in favour of a technocratic regime because it is desired by the World Bank/IMF and US financial interests, and they can persuade him (WE Forum 20-21, 22-23 September 1982). (He has long held that that foreign combine was the most potent force on the Philippine scene.) Certainly in the wake of Virata's appointment in July 1981 as Prime Minister under a revised constitution there seemed to be some weight to this contention. Constantino's thesis appeared to be substantiated again by the president's announcement on 31 October that 'the incumbent Prime Minister' would assume 'all powers and duties of the President ... in the event that the President cannot perform his duties'. This was clearly a further IMF/World Bank-inspired effort to bolster the position of the technocrats, but specifically avoided any hint of resignation.

Yet Constantino failed to deal adequately with the military as an autonomous power centre. Nor did he recognize that in a crisis situation the influence of money may be less useful than the power that flows from the barrel of a gun. Neither are there common interests between that large segment of the military enmeshed in bureaucratic capitalism and technocrats allied with the IMF/World Bank to support a cut-back on wasteful subsidies to Marcos cronies or to reduce tariff protection for favoured, inefficient manufacturers. Constantino discounted the prospect, which some take seriously, that Ver, Imelda, and friends would refuse to allow the control which is now so nearly theirs to slip from their grasp through free elections or early resignation. Ver is not tired and over-experienced like the Argentine generals. While he already has vast interests to protect, he has not yet savoured the exhiliration of 'absolute' power, nor known the frustrations of its limitations. The failure of the late November move to name Virata Vice-President is the best evidence of Ver-Imelda intentions.

Ex-Senator Arturo Tolentino had long proposed the restoration of the office of Vice-President as a way to clarify succession and thus help restore political stability. In October and November 1983 his views gained increasing support in the business and professional community. Tolentino and others filed a Bill in the Batasan for election of an interim vice-president during the May 1984 parliamentary election (Philippines Who (Cielo Buonaventura) 23 November 1983). But in the KBL caucus the president was strongly opposed to the idea. Said one KBL assemblyman, 'He just doesn't want to have a second centre of power'. Marcos escalated his opposition when he claimed that 'foreign interests were behind the move to restore the office of vice-president'. A columnist in a Marcos-controlled newspaper more plainly called it 'American sponsored'. The president later described pressure for a vice- president as 'a conspiracy' (New York Times 4 December 1983).

Some were surprised, therefore, when Marcos allowed the matter to be referred to a committee of seven including both proponents and opponents. The recommendation of the committee was less surprising: that the constitution be amended so that a vice-president not be elected until 1987 and that in the meantime the speaker of the Batasan should temporarily succeed the president, pending new elections. (This latter provision was the same as that which existed before the 1981 constitutional amendments.) Former Vice-President Pelaez brought to the full KBL caucus a 'minority report' which recommended that the prime minister be named interim vice-president, but nationalist responses to the perceived foreign origin of this idea resulted in its overwhelming defeat; the committee proposal was adopted. The amendment will probably be 'ratified' in a referendum in January.

Though Mrs Marcos on the same day dramatically resigned from the soon-to-be-abolished executive committee and renounced any intention of seeking the presidency, she probably improved her chances of succeeding her husband, since the present speaker is quite malleable, since he could be replaced any day by the Batasan (which the KBL controls), and since Mrs Marcos is fully qualified for the office. Her dominance of the executive committee may have been slipping in any case.

A more probable scenario recognizes the uncomfortable fact that it is a dominant segment of the Armed Forces of the Philippines, under General Ver, that is - at least in the short run - the most powerful political force in the land. Furthermore, in alliance with Mrs Marcos, Ver has a good chance of taking complete control on the death of the president with some semblance of legality. At least until January, the executive committee 'shall exercise the powers of the President' in case of 'permanent disability, death, removal from office or resignation'. Prime Minister Virata and two other cabinet technocrats, plus the Minister of Defence probably now constitute one voting bloc, having in common their dislike of the First Lady and fear of her allies. The First Lady, herself a member of the committee until late November, appears to have had at least four supporters: Deputy Prime Minister Rono; a youthful assemblyman and former presidential assistant, Ronaldo Zamora; and two provincial Governors, Eduardo Gullas of Cebu and Ali Dimaporo of Lanao del Sur. Former Vice-President and Minister of State Emmanuel Pelaez, comfortable with neither Enrile nor Mrs Marcos, was a swinging vote.

Presidential incapacity, possibly an earlier problem than demise, is determined (under provisions of a legislative enactment - Batas Pambansa Blg. 231, 11 September 1982) by a three-quarters vote of the cabinet. Even though the cabinet, with a generous representation of technocrats, now has a predominant political colour rather different from that of the executive committee, since Ver is more powerful the prospect of a successful 'cabinet coup' is not great. An undeclared but actual incapacity would favour those personally closest to the president, which includes Ver and Imelda, but few in the cabinet. It may have been an attempt to stem this drift, especially for the benefit of anxious foreign creditors, that in late October the president pre-empted the legal right of the full cabinet to declare and the executive committee to exercise by announcing that Prime Minister Virata could act on his behalf should he become 'disabled'. But the announcement had no legal effect, and Virata, whose power has derived from the patronage of the president, as well as IMF/World Bank backing, has shown no independent skill at intra-elite intrigue. While his chance at the succession was thus enhanced, it was by no means

40

ensured, as the November defeat in the Batasan for the naming
of the premier as vice-president reminds us. Only effective
American intervention in intra-military factionalism,
designed to undermine Ver, could do that, as the US
government seems increasingly to recognize.

Neither of the leading figures in a Ver-Imelda successor
regime would have competence in economics, though the First
Lady has a close friend in the governor of the Central Bank.
It would certainly be more corrupt than the present regime,
wracked with factionalism, and probably much less consistent
in the framing of policy. The response of the international
financial community would be a new test of Constantino's
thesis. If a Ver-Imelda entente proved to be as repressive,
as indecisive, and as devastating to the economy as most
observers now predict, foreign bankers would find common
ground with workers, peasants and intellectuals in wanting to
change it, though perhaps with different ideas about
appropriate alternatives. And the US government, only
recently unwilling to use talk of aid suspension as a weapon
to press for free elections, would probably find sufficient
threat to its interests to become much more involved in the
Philippine political process. That is to say, William
Sullivan's recent advice to Washington to do just that
(Sullivan 1983-84) would be more persuasive under conditions
of greater pain. (Some believe the commitment to involvement
has already been made.)

A worsening of conditions is probably necessary also to
activate and coalesce a group within the military more
inclined toward probity, democracy and economic rationality
than is General Chief-of-S has often been remarked that
General Fidel Ramos, deputy chief-of-staff of the armed
forces and also a relative of the president, who apparently
stands for those goals, is so imbued with the doctrine of
civilian supremacy that he could not be persuaded to lead a
coup except in the most dire straits. But if the dreary
prediction about a Ver/Imelda regime should prove accurate,
Washington would probably find that it was in US interests to
support a coup ostensibly devoted to those three
above-mentioned goals about the same time that Ramos or
like-minded officers decided to plan one. Given the
ambivalence of so many Filipinos about US intervention, under
those circumstances it would probably be tolerated by most if
the change was regarded as clearly for the better and if the
American role were not too obvious - though nationalist
protest would be loud. (A nationalist reaction within the
military might even frustrate US efforts).

Sadly it seems difficult to imagine such a development
sooner, but at that point many leaders of the present
opposition would probably be invited to take part in a
restoration of constitutional democracy. But will it really
be possible to restore constitutional democracy in the
Philippines within a few years even with military endorsement
and support? If by this is meant a limited opening of the
political process - with screening of candidates to keep out

the Left and some continued executive restrictions on
legislative power, including retention of a broad right to
reimpose martial law, all in the context of modest social
reform (probably, but not certainly, including a continuation
of the present type of land reform) - then the prospects are
good. A regime led by an alliance of military, technocrats
and reformist politicians, following policies not
incompatible with the interests of the existing economic
elite, could undoubtedly agree to implement such an
arrangement, and it might last for as much as several years.

But in the long run the fate of such a regime would not
be too different from that of the present one; widespread
unrest would revive. The political mobilization of Filipino
peasants and workers, as well as of the middle class, has
been broadly accelerated by the impact of martial law, quite
contrary to its intentions. In large sections of the country
it is not possible to return to the electoral politics of
patronage which sustained elite interests for a generation
after independence. Some radical voices would reach
parliament. Yet restoring free elections without allowing
for representation of a full range of views and interests,
including the Left, would lead to a reaccumulation of
political frustrations and rejustification of violence as a
strategy for change. Neither the limited social reform nor
the muted nationalism of such a regime could satisfy major
sectors. And as long as the socio-economic interests of the
elite remained relatively unchanged they would be frightened
by that frustration and that violence into a reimposition of
heavier controls. If, on the other hand, the opening of the
electoral process were unlimited, again without a basic
change in the elites controlling policy, the participation
explosion would bring a fearful reaction from those elites
even more quickly - unless the Left continued to opt for
boycott. (A kind of self-marginalization is often a
temptation for revolutionary movements.)

The response of dominant Filipino elites generally to
domestic political threats in the post-war period has been
twofold: to export their wealth - as happened again recently
on a massive scale - and to limit political participation as
a means of controlling the threat. A middle-class component
in the corridors of power that welcomed basic change has
never been very influential. As long as mass participation
and control over policy were unconnected, as was typical of
the 1950s and 1960s, stability reigned, but occasional
attempts to link up the two stages of the political process
have been destabilizing. And the trend toward increased
conflict between elite interests and mass demands is likely
to continue.

The prospect remains great over the longer run,
therefore, that revolutionary forces will not be dislodged,
but will, rather, grow in strength. If factionalism in a
military regime intensified to the point of hampering
effective rule, or of producing a group of 'young turks'
favourable to fundamental change, a new revolutionary

42

coalition would grow even more rapidly. Some activists dream of a coalition in which church progressives and frustrated 'national bourgeoisie', along with nationalist politicians, would join forces with the Left and nationalist elements of the military to quickly overthrow a dictatorial regime, obviating the need for a long-armed struggle. The model of Nicaragua is very attractive. But in the 1980s it seems unlikely to be followed; both constraints (especially US bases) and opportunities are different from what they were in Nicaragua. The NPA/NDF now seems geared to a long-term strategy.

If US response to growing insurgency should be as in Vietnam, or even in El Salvador, the guerrillas could be provided with the mantle of 'national liberators' that they have so far never quite managed to seize. Pro-Americanism is a colonial legacy which gives US policy in the Philippines greater leeway than it has almost anywhere else in the Third World. But it would quickly dissipate with the presence of American counter-insurgency forces, whether called 'advisors' or 'combat troops'. Filipino nationalism can be volatile under the proper stimulus. Nevertheless, if revolutionary forces prospered, the American temptation to intervene could be great, partly because the legal basis for the entry of US forces is clear, provided in the language of the 1979 amendment to the Military Bases Agreement under the rubric of 'off base security'.

Surely one consequence of intervention would be to produce a type of change in the environment of revolutionary war which in Washington today is thought to be <u>most</u> undesirable, namely Soviet involvement. Though the Soviets have so far maintained an 'unholy' alliance with Marcos and the CPP ideology has prevented an overture to them anyway, more direct US action against NPA guerrillas would likely produce a change in that situation. And the dimensions of the subsequent tragedy for those caught in the cross-fire could hardly be overestimated.

Conclusion

Our scenarios for political succession have various implications for the composition of the ruling coalition or regime. In the short run an attempt to broaden that coalition by bringing in a large number of civilian politicians through the electoral process, and making them the dominant element in the regime, seems destined to lose because of the power and the perceived self-interest of a major segment of the military. In fact, it is that dominant faction in the officer corps, headed by the Chief-of-Staff, Ver, which is most likely to assume power in the short run; there are signs the process may already have begun. Ver's take-over would constitute a narrowing of the ruling coalition assembled by Marcos. Certainly the technocrats and civilian politicians in the <u>Batasan</u> would be substantially downgraded, and there would be no replacement for the accumulation of political experience and skill which Ferdinand Marcos himself brought to what he likes to call 'constitutional authoritarianism'. It would be a regime primarily of the more corrupt elements in the military and some of the 'crony' entrepreneurs, plus - perhaps - Mrs Marcos.

Our medium-term projection, however, was for a regime more like that of the late 1970s than like the one controlled by Ver. The technocrats, with IMF/World Bank backing, would be reinstated, perhaps to a more prominent role than ever. Civilian politicians would also be back, with a much enhanced position, but weaker than in the 1960s. A different set of military officers would be in power, and probably with less influence and less tendency to abuse what remained than was the military in 1983. Furthermore, the economic elite would, at least at first, enjoy closer co-operation with the regime, until perhaps a new set of 'cronies' emerged. The basic thrust of economic policy would not change.

Long-term expectations must be less precise, of course. Yet one can be fairly confident of growing political mobilization of the populace and its impact on regime character. Social discontent in 1984 could escalate rapidly. If an influential segment of the ruling coalition should welcome growing mass participation and find in it a reinforcement of their own interests, then basic change in the character of the regime could come non-violently. Strong, legitimate institutions and imaginative leadership are necessary to make possible that scenario. But if the nature of mass demands on policy-makers is too threatening to the interests of the dominant faction within the elite (and its foreign backers), as seems more likely, then any thoroughly new regime is likely to be imposed through violent struggle.

Certainly most Filipinos, looking toward the future, would prefer to avoid that violent struggle. But if dramatic steps are not taken quickly to broaden political participation and to improve distributive justice, frustration and hatred will grow, making violence seem like the only choice for a larger and larger segment of the population - including many who would today consciously choose the non-violent path.

Chapter 4

THE LEFT AND THE TRADITIONAL OPPOSITION

Francisco Nemenzo

Beneath the legalistic reasoning of conservatives and the ideological pronouncements of radicals, Filipinos are basically political realists. Whether they support President Marcos or oppose him, they expect the highly personalized system he created in twelve years of authoritarian rule to collapse with the passing of its creator but, at the same time, they find it difficult to envisage a smooth return to constitutional democracy. This has given rise to a pervasive sense of uncertainty which in turn evokes grim visions of the immediate future (Diliman Review (A. R. Magno) November-December 1983).

In this paper, I speculate on how the Left and the traditional opposition might respond to three possibilities: the establishment of a full-blown military dictatorship, an attempt to modify the authoritarian system, and the restoration of constitutional democracy. I also assess the probable consequences of the ensuing struggles and realignments. To spell out the bases of my conjectures, I begin with an analysis of the interests and the strengths and weaknesses of the forces behind current regime.

THE MARCOS STATE

In half a century of 'political tutelage', the US superimposed democratic institutions upon a grossly undemocratic Philippine society. Marcos therefore had good reason to disclaim that he destroyed a functioning democracy (Marcos 1977 and 1978). Indeed, the elections before martial law were widely perceived as a rich man's game rather than a structure for popular participation. The major parties - Nacionalista (NP) and Liberal (LP) - represented volatile alliances of landowning and bourgeois families who had amassed enormous wealth through colonial patronage. Consequently, in between elections the representative bodies were inaccessible to ordinary citizens. This instilled a cynical attitude, especially among those who grew up in the post-independence period, that often expresses itself in vigorous boycott campaigns. I argue, however, that martial law aborted a process of democratizing this patently oligarchic system.

The Americans

Between the first quarter of 1970 to September 1972 the Philippines witnessed an extremely interesting development. Spurred by the Left, the hitherto mute and powerless masses were learning to organize themselves and intervene in state affairs. Finding the representative institutions unresponsive, they had to devise new channels for interest articulation: what the militants called the 'parliament of the streets'. This democratizing process did not last long enough to bring about substantive reforms, but in shaking the ruling class solidarity, it eventually compelled even the established institutions to heed the pressures from below.

Paradoxically, the primary target of democratization was the US, the erstwhile colonizing power and self-proclaimed mentor in democratic politics. Policies prescribed by the US-dominated World Bank and International Monetary Fund (IMF) could not get through the the Philippine congress, despite the strong endorsement of Marcos. The dockets of both houses of congress were filled with legislative proposals which categorically assailed American interests. The ongoing constitutional convention was working out a draft of the new constitution which also reflected these nationalist and reformist sentiments. In 1972 even the traditionally conservative Supreme Court rendered two precedent-setting decisions which placed in jeopardy the status of US investments upon the termination of the Laurel-Langley agreement (Shalom 1981).(1)

These developments were particularly disturbing not only to the US government but also to the local American business community. The Laurel-Langley agreement was due to expire in 1974 but the nationalist upsurge made its renewal seem improbable. Moreover, the Philippine-US military bases treaty was up for renegotiation while the Vietnam War was still in progress (Shalom 1981). In a remarkable display of political dexterity, Marcos turned these anxieties to advantage, invoking them to neutralize possible US resistance to his assumption of absolute power.

It is, of course, an accepted principle in American jurisprudence that states which believe themselves imperilled by war or insurrection have the right to declare martial law in order to save democracy. But Marcos in September 1972 used martial law to destroy what the Americans regard as essential to a democratic system. He disbanded congress and endowed himself with sole legislative authority. He also reduced the judiciary into a legitimizing instrument of the presidential will (del Carmen 1979). All this ran counter to the principles of separation of powers and checks and balances which are central to American political thought, and violated the 1935 constitution which the US government approved as the basis of Philippine independence. Marcos resolved the constitutional issue in a manner that the Americans would normally find offensive: he coerced the constitutional convention to adopt a draft which vested him with the power to govern by decree and submitted this to a rigged plebiscite (Muego 1976).

To placate the US, Marcos unilaterally extended 'parity rights' and the military bases treaty. He also reversed by decree the two Supreme Court decisions. In line with World Bank and IMF policies, he shifted the thrust of national development from import-substitution to production for export (Bello and Rivera 1977). Reversing the nationalist tendencies in 1970-72, he opened up the Philippine economy and gave all sorts of incentives to multinational capital which even Taiwan and South Korea do not offer in their export processing zones.

The Left-wing publications assert that the US ordered Marcos to declare martial law. This is obviously an overstatement. In fairness to Marcos, there is no convincing evidence that he actually solicited prior US approval. What is incontrovertible is that the US did not raise a whimper of protest as Marcos dismantled the legacy of US colonial rule. Quite the contrary, US military and economic aid (not to mention the massive loans) multiplied several fold in the years immediately following the declaration of martial law (Bello and Rivera 1977).

The Military

To enforce these unpopular policies, Marcos had to build up the coercive apparatus. The Armed Forces of the Philippines (AFP) was enlarged from 55,000 men in 1972 to 164,000 in 1977 and something like 250,000 today. The defence budget accordingly swelled from $136 million in 1972 to $420 million in 1977 (Diliman Review (Carolina Hernandez) January-February 1984; see also Far Eastern Economic Review (David Jenkins) 10 March 1983). Marcos also transferred control over the police from the local governments to the Philippine Constabulary (PC), one of the four major branches of AFP. Furthermore, the village bullies were armed and trained into para-military units called the Civilian Home Defence Forces (CHDF) under AFP supervision.

There is no way of calculating the size of two very important components of the coercive apparatus - the National Intelligence and Security Authority (NISA) and the Civilian Intelligence and Security Agency (CISA) - whose budgets and personnel are kept from public knowledge. Although technically independent of the AFP, both are placed under General Fabian Ver who is also the AFP Chief-of-Staff and the effective commander of the Presidential Security Command. Ver is Marcos's most trusted henchman, being a close relative and long-time bodyguard (Far Eastern Economic Review 10 March 1983).

The multiplicity of Ver's functions indicates the extent to which Marcos distrusts the military, while using it to suppress real and imaginary foes. He has devised various means of keeping the military in check. For example, he requires them now and then to pledge allegiance to civilian supremacy. (In the current context, however, this means allegiance to Marcos alone because military commanders are not obliged to heed the civilian officials at the sub-national levels.) This ritual is, of course, undependable. When generals and colonels plot against their Commander-in-Chief, they will take any number of oaths until they find a chance to move.

A more effective method is that of infiltrating NISA agents in all military units to spy on their superior officers. These agents report directly to Ver in his concurrent capacity as NISA director-general. Another control device is that of packing the AFP with 'integree officers'(2) who owe personal loyalty to the president. Many of these 'civilians in uniform' come from the Ilocos (the home region of Marcos and Ver), are members of the Vanguard Fraternity (graduates of the University of the Philippines Reserve Officers Training Corps of which Ver is the perennial president and Marcos is the most distinguished alumnus), or belong to political clans with a record of unflinching loyalty.

When there is widespread unrest and the legitimacy of the regime is questioned, these devices could backfire on the president. There are already signs of dissension among the 'regular officers' (i.e. professional soldiers who earned their commissions by graduating from military academies or scaled the ranks through sheer military prowess). The 'regulars' complain that the military profession is being degraded and 'politicized' by the influx of 'integrees'. While they must bear the burden of fighting the communist and Moro guerrillas, the 'integrees' get promoted faster while sitting on their swivel chairs. They are often stuck to the rank of colonel until they are just about to retire (interviews with a retired general, a retired colonel, and two colonels in active service whose names cannot be disclosed for obvious reasons).

The Technocracy

Another notable trend in the Marcos state is the emergence of the technocracy as a serious political force. This consists of former university academics and corporate executives whom Marcos has been recruiting as special assistants and advisors since he first became president in 1966, a practice which implies his innate distrust in the competence of career bureaucrats. While constitutional democracy was the prevailing system Marcos could not afford to make his fellow politicians feel insecure by admitting upstarts to the corridors of power. It was only with the advent of martial law that he elevated the technocrats to positions previously reserved for politicians. Today the cabinet - from the Prime Minister down - is filled with technocrats. He even created new agencies especially for them, like the Development Academy of the Philippines and the Ministry of Human Settlements. These technocrat-dominated agencies which he endowed with generous budgets duplicated and later displaced the established government bureaux. Marcos needs their expertise to design 'fundable projects' and relies on their credibility to negotiate with foreign entities.

At the outset observers sneered at the technocrats as politically inconsequential experts with whom any dictator could feel safe. Hardly anyone considered them a threat to Marcos or a potential factor in the post-Marcos rearrangement. It seems, however, that they have since learnt the Machiavellian art while serving in Marcos's court. This emerged in abundant clarity in April 1983 when Prime Minister Virata (the most senior technocrat in the government) masterfully parried the blows from the First Lady, the New Society Movement (KBL) and the crony-owned mass media, not only to preserve his own position but also to enhance the power-status of the technocracy in general (Far Eastern Economic Review (Ocampo-Kalfors and Sacerdoti) 5 May 1983; and (Bowring and Sacerdoti) 9 June 1983).

What the technocrats lack in popular support is compensated for by the trust of the IMF, the World Bank and other international lending and aid agencies. It has become more evident since Aquino's assassination that they are the main conduits for international capitalism. As long as the Philippines retains its neo-colonial character, and especially if the debt problem goes from bad to worse, they will always be indispensable to a successor regime of whatever form.

Their significance owes to the fact that they are the natural allies of the regular officer corps should a power vacuum emerge after Marcos's departure. There is a marked ideological convergence and functional overlapping between the military and the technocracy. Colonels now sit with technocrats in government panels. Some technocrats have actually been integrated into the AFP and, at the same time, regular military officers are acquiring technocratic skills and values through the National Defence College. The two have more in common than the fact of serving the current authoritaran regime. Both are believers in a strong executive and disdainful of politicians. Their loyalty to the regime is institutional rather than personal. Both seem to be uneasy with Mrs Marcos's irrational priorities and overtly hostile to the crony-capitalists whose ill-managed business ventures thrive on presidential favours.

Cronies and Politicians

The status of the 'crony-capitalists' in the Philippine power structure is so dependent on Marcos's political fortune for them to be considered a serious factor in the post-Marcos reckoning. They are too implicated in corruption and mismanagement that they could just be the convenient scapegoats for a successor regime. With the exception of Eduardo Cojuanco, Roberto Benedicto and Antonio Floirendo, they are too preoccupied with wealth accumulation that they have not bothered to build independent power bases. Rumours are rife in Manila that they have been investing abroad or smuggling their money to Swiss bank accounts, ready to evacuate the moment Marcos's regime crumbles.

Habitual opportunists, the majority of KBL politicians deserted the NP and LP when they realized that Marcos would have a monopoly of patronage for a long time. But their political allegiance is so mercurial that, should anything happen to Marcos, they will probably scamper like rats in a sinking ship. Some are beginning to make critical noises, and a few have actually joined the moderate opposition. They are unlikely to stand by Mrs Marcos or any chosen successor. Having lost their credibility with the masses and as thoroughly immersed in corruption as the crony-capitalists, it is doubtful if they will count in the politics of the post-Marcos period.

A sizeable part of the KBL rank and file, especially in the Ilocos region, are genuinely loyal to Marcos. There are also ordinary people, especially in the rural areas, who feel a genuine sense of gratitude for his social amelioration projects, no matter how limited their beneficent impact. It is not possible at this juncture to assess their readiness to fight for a legend, but we cannot exclude the possibility that they will evolve into a movement similar to Peronismo in Argentina.

To sum up, the Marcos state is analogous to what Marx called 'Bonapartism' (Marx 1977). It achieved 'relative autonomy' from the ruling class with the support of the army and a pliable mass organization. The circumstances which allowed Marcos to assume total power were remarkably similar to what created the opportunity for Louis Bonaparte to pose as the saviour of France: intense contradictions in the ruling class and a mighty challenge from below, resulting in the paralysis of the old state machine. It is therefore reasonable to ask whether the breakdown of this personalized regime will also usher in a Filipino Paris Commune.

ENEMIES OF THE MARCOS STATE

While the legal/underground dichotomy is convenient for describing current opposition activities, it is unsatisfactory for speculating about their future roles. Many opposition groups, while operating legally, define their roles in the context of armed struggle; in other words, they perceive themselves as ancillary to the underground movement. In this paper I distinguish the 'Left opposition' (whether legal or underground) from the 'traditional opposition' whose goal is limited to the restoration of constitutional democracy. But it is necessary to stress the latter's growing ambivalence because, as the struggle gains momentum, those who initially clamoured for restoration could veer towards a radical posture.

Marcos himself is largely responsible for blurring the difference between the Left and the traditional opposition by indiscriminate repressiveness. Alleging that a 'Rightist conspiracy' abetted the 'Leftist rebellion' (Presidential Proclamation no. 1081, 21 September 1972), he ordered the arrest and detention of politicians, businessmen, landowners, and church people whom he perceived as potential objectors to authoritarian rule.

Had they the will to fight, this should have been a sufficient provocation. In the first few years of martial law when Marcos himself was uncertain of his control, they could have led the mass resistance. They had the financial capability, the political machinery and, above all, the aura of legitimacy. But they wavered. But they chose to sit idly by, while their peers were being persecuted and Marcos abolished the positions to which they were legally entitled.

The most plausible explanation for default was a deep-seated fear that the masses, once aroused and accustomed to extra-legal modes of struggle, would eventually assail the social system of which they are a privileged part. They may have applauded and perhaps even colluded with the fledging Left soon after the fraudulent 1969 elections, but by September 1972 the Left had grown into such a formidable force that the traditional oppositionists themselves became apprehensive. Knowing this, Marcos capitalized on their apprehension just as he capitalized on the anxieties of US imperialism.

Instead of putting up a resistance, the traditional oppositionists hoped for the US to restrain the vindictiveness of Marcos and pressure him to restore the representative government. Senator Manglapus, for instance, sought political asylum in the US and devoted his energies to delivering lectures in Ivy League universities and lobbying in Washington. Ex-President Macapagal published a book wherein he raised the preposterous charge that Marcos was handing over the country to communism and insinuated that the US had a moral duty to rescue democracy in its former colony (Macapagal 1976).

With Jimmy Carter in the White House waving the human rights banner, the traditional oppositionists entertained illusions of the US liberating the Philippines for the third time in history.(3) All this fell to pieces with the ascendancy of Ronald Reagan. Only then did they start mending their political fences, a belated effort which culminated in the founding of the United Nationalist Democratic Organization (UNIDO) in April 1982.

UNIDO collected the remnants of the LP, the Laurel faction of the NP, and ten regional parties and sectoral associations. It is essentially a loose coalition with no unifying principle other than a common hostility to Marcos. Its acknowledged leader, Senator Laurel, supported Marcos in the early phase of martial law and even won a parliamentary seat in 1978 as a KBL candidate.(4) Having been out of power since 1966, the once formidable LP machine had been steadily eroded. The other affiliated groups regard UNIDO as an ad hoc structure from which they are free to withdraw at any time.(5)

Apart from UNIDO there is the People's Power Party (LABAN) that was hastily formed in 1978 to contest the Metro-Manila seats of the National Assembly (Batasang Pambansa). Since the LP then took the ambivalent line of officially boycotting the elections while allowing its members to run in their individual capacities, Senator Aquino (the LP Secretary-General) chose to campaign from his prison cell under the LABAN banner. The truth, however, was that the active apparatus of LABAN in 1978 consisted of communist and social democratic cadres. What remained after the latter withdrew were just a few high society figures with no visible following. Especially after his assassination, LABAN tried to capitalize on the Aquino mystique; obscuring the historical fact that, while exiled in the US, the slain senator judiciously dissociated himself from any particular opposition group.

Potentially the most significant organization of the traditional type is the Pilipino Democratic Party (PDP), founded in 1982 by the controversial mayor of Cagayan de Oro city Aquilino Pimentel. It has a more tangible machinery than LABAN. With a coherent programme that embodies some of the radical concerns, it is attracting the young militants of the non-communist Left. There is the possibility, however, that when the politicians in its central leadership begin to take a more pragmatic course, PDP (like LABAN after the 1978 elections) will lose its mass activists to the social democratic underground.

In 1983 PDP coalesced with LABAN, forming what is now popularly known as PDP-LABAN, the second major component of the traditional opposition. To a lesser extent than UNIDO, this coalition suffers from the disability of failing to adapt to the changes over the last decade. They are still oriented to the American style of politics which rely on theatrical antics, patronage and unprincipled alliances. The last elections proved that this is still effective for winning votes, but it is unsuitable for prolonged extra-parliamentary struggle. Moreover, it is repulsive to the young people who grew up under the dictatorship - the so-called 'martial law babies' whom Marcos tried but failed to depoliticize.

It is too early to write off the traditional politicians. The failure of the boycott movement last May indicated that they have a mobilizing capability for electoral purposes, even if the final outcome also demonstrated their incapacity to protect the ballot box. But one should be careful before drawing the conclusion that people still look for an electoral solution to the current crisis. A sizeable number voted for UNIDO and PDP-LABAN as a demonstration of protest, rather than an expression of faith in the electoral process. The real test of strength between the Left and the traditional opposition will come after the elections. It is interesting to observe how effectively the Left can foment and sustain extra-parliamentary resistance to the IMF-imposed conditions which Marcos most probably accept.

The Left opposition

In this paper the term 'Left opposition' denotes an assortment of groups and individuals who can be distinguished from the traditional opposition by the following criteria: they want to get rid of US military bases and abrogate all 'unequal treaties' with the US; they oppose the massive and unregulated inflow of foreign investments and the heavy reliance on foreign loans; they advocate structural reforms, especially with regard to ownership and control of the means of production; they demand the dismantling - not just the modification - of the Marcos state; and they believe that these ends can be attained only through the mobilization of the masses and that armed struggle is a legitimate mode of political behaviour.

Sectarian elements on the Left may object to such a broad definition which lumps them with groups and individuals whose views deviate from their narrow conception of 'the correct line'. I believe, however, that to understand the inner workings of the movement and forecast its response to future crises, it is more useful to stress the 'polycentric' character of the Philippine Left rather than reiterate the legend of its 'monolithic solidarity'.

The Philippine Left today is divisible into three ideological streams: Marxist, Christian and Islamic. The Marxists represent pro-Chinese, pro-Soviet and a variety of independent tendencies. Christian radicals whose 'liberation theology' approves of collaboration with the Marxists are called the 'Nat-Dems' (National Democrats) as differentiated from the 'Soc-Dems' (Social Democrats) who distance themselves from Marxism while agreeing with the Marxists on all points enumerated earlier. I understand that the Islamic radicals are also divided into at least three recognizable factions. These trends clash and converge in the course of struggle, building up a body of common experience that serve as a basis and impulse for occasional dialogues. Beneath the appearance of diversity, however, there is consensus on a wide range of issues (Nemenzo 1984).

A major reason for this mixture of cohesion and plurality is the indisputable pre-eminence of one group, the new Communist Party of the Philippines [Marxism-Leninism-Mao Zedong Thought] (CPP). Of the various groups that profess Marxism-Leninism, the old Partido Komunista ng Pilipinas (PKP) is the only one which challenges the CPP's claim to the vanguard role. The rest acknowledge it as the effective leader of the revolutionary movement, notwithstanding their criticisms of its theoretical and strategic-tactical formulations. They generally choose areas of activity which the CPP has neglected and they hope to prove in practice the correctness of their own ideas. The reluctance of these organizations to call themselves a party signifies an open attitude toward eventual unity, with the CPP as the core (People's Liberation Movement 1980; Solidaridad Dos 1980; and Socialist Republican Union 1982).

The PKP - the oldest Left-wing organization (founded in 1930) - has been literally consigned to the fringe of the movement it once led. It earned the contempt of other revolutionary groups by its brutal methods of handling internal disputes and its decision in 1974 to surrender and collaborate with the martial law regime (Ang Bayan 15 October 1979). Emasculated by a series of defections, the PKP now consists of a few dispirited veterans of the Huk rebellion. Even the pro-Soviet, pro-Vietnamese and Fidelista mavericks in the independent Marxist groups refuse to associate with the PKP.

In the days of Stalin and Pope Pius XII, the Filipino Marxists and Catholics regarded each other as implacable enemies. The Huks harassed the priests and the priests assisted the counter-insurgency operations (Pomeroy 1974). Even after the young Maoists broke with the PKP, they preserved this anti-clerical tradition. In fact, it was the CPP which popularized the term 'clerico-fascists' for the Christian reformers. The latter's efforts to 'contextualize theology' and redefine the social mission of the church in line with the new perspectives of Vatican Council II did not ease this historic tension (Yu and Bolasco 1981). It was Marcos who inadvertently radicalized this arch-conservative institution (Youngblood 1981) and made possible this odd marriage of clerics and cadres.

The indiscriminate repressiveness of martial law drove the Christian reformers underground. Since they were unprepared for this contingency, they had to seek refuge in the NPA areas. Many eventually reconciled with the CPP under the National Democratic Front (NDF) umbrella, while the rest formed their own underground network - the Philippine Democratic Socialist Party (PDSP) in 1973. At the outset PDSP was too weak and small to draw attention from the government or the CPP. It began to show signs of vigour only around 1978, when sympathetic bishops and religious superiors became worried about the growing number of priests, nuns and lay workers who joined the NDF in the absence of a Christian alternative to the Marcos dictatorship.

PDSP thus offered a third choice: revolutionary but non-communist. While renouncing the philosophy of dialectical materialism as incompatible with Christian doctrines, it borrowed liberally the Marxist analyses of secular problems as well as some Leninist organizational principles (NPDSP 1979). It also established its own military arm - the Sandigan - as the Christian equivalent to the communist-led New People's Army and Marcos's Armed Forces of the Philippines.

Alarmed at the prospect of competition, the CPP launched

a strident propaganda campaign against the PDSP, stigmatizing it as an 'imperialist trojan horse' and tracing its origins to the Jesuits and Jesuit-trained intellectuals in the 1950s who played an active part in the counter-insurgency operations (Philippine Resistance No. 2, 1980). But again, the indiscriminate repressiveness of the regime diffused this 'cold war' in the Philippine underground. A raid on the PDSP headquarters and the arrest of its leaders made the Soc-Dem activists realize that the struggle against the dictatorship must take precedence over the struggle against the CPP. In 1980 PDSP split on the issue of co-operation with the communists. One faction advocated affiliation to the NDF and another favoured the toning down of anti-CPP propaganda while maintaining organizational differentiation. Even the hard-core Soc-Dems have reportedly modified their rabidly anti-communist attitudes (Interview with the PDSP international representative).

The CPP itself is by no means monolithic. It accommodates divergent tendencies. While some remain unrepentant Maoists and others toe the Deng Xiaoping line, an increasing number of CPP members favour an independent stand on the Sino- Soviet dispute. Although the CPP official organ - Ang Bayan - still bears the phrase 'Guided by Marxism-Leninism-Mao Zedong Thought' in its masthead, it may no longer be accurate to describe the new communist party as Maoist. As Horacio Morales (the alleged NDF chairman and presumably a ranking CPP official) told the Far Eastern Economic Review (21 August 1981: 20):

> The communist members of the NDF resent being called Maoist because of the derogatory connotation that they are subservient to a foreign power. They prefer to be known as Filipino communists. While it's true that NDF members study Mao's writings on the Chinese revolution, we also study the Vietnamese, African and Latin American writings.

Privately some leading CPP figures express disenchantment with the current Chinese foreign policy and the 'four modernizations programme.' While they remain critical of the Soviet Union, the virulent anti-Soviet, anti-Vietnamese and anti-Cuban epithets have completely disappeared from Liberation, the NDF monthly magazine. They have also become rare in Ang Bayan and in the recent party documents.

Since the second half of the 1970s party-to-party relations with the Chinese has been reduced to ritualistic exchanges of banal greetings on historic dates. Beijing has scrupulously honoured its commitment to the Marcos regime that it would cease all material aid to the Filipino rebels. The CPP now subsists mainly on local support and, to a minor extent, on assistance from non-communist sympathizers abroad. This has considerably facilitated the process of indigenization. Its political line is no longer a monotonous

NPA ACTIVITY

Source : *Liberation*, September 1982.

rehash of Chinese policy statements, especially on foreign affairs. For instance, the CPP implicitly rejects the underlying proposition in the 'three-worlds theory' that the USSR, rather than the US, is 'the most dangerous enemy'. In bold contrast to the Thai and Malaysian communist movements, the CPP has not been weakened by this alienation from its erstwhile mentor; quite the contrary, the overcoming of ideological dependence is a major factor in its phenomenal growth (Nemenzo 1984).

The CPP directs the two most dynamic underground organizations: the New People's Army (NPA) and the National Democratic Front (NDF). When the NPA was born in March 1969 it was nothing more than a rag-tag army with twenty automatic rifles and fifteen handguns. It had a very narrow operational zone in the southern part of Tarlac province. By the time Marcos declared martial law, the NPA armoury had increased to 350 high-powered weapons. Its operational zone already extended to the Cagayan Valley in Northern Luzon, and it had a few armed propaganda units, Bicol, Southern Luzon, Western Visayas, and Mindanao (Umali 1983).

Crushing the NPA was the avowed purpose of martial law. The result was the reverse. By destroying at the same time the bourgeois democratic system, martial law radicalized the Christian reformers and created favourable conditions for armed struggle. Today the NPA has at least 12,000 full-time guerrillas and 35,000 part-time militias. It is operating in 56 out of 72 provinces, and in 400 out of 1,500 municipalities. Lieutenant-General Fidel Ramos, the PC chief, admitted that at least 20 per cent of the barangays are controlled or infiltrated by the NPA (The Age 26 September 1983). As the attached map shows, the NPA is widely distributed throughout the archipelago, unlike the PKP-led Huks in the 1950s who were confined to central and southern Luzon.

The number of villages under effective NPA control at night time or what the NPA calls 'guerrilla fronts' is a more meaningful index of rebel strength. As of the end of 1983 thirty-six of these were located in all the major islands. Each covers several adjacent towns where mass support is so broad and stable that NPA units can move freely and strike with impunity. Within a guerrilla front local NDF committees function as the de facto government. They collect taxes, regulate trade, determine interest rates, administer justice, implement a land reform programme, run adult education classes, organize public health and provide paramedical services, and so on. In these areas the officials and policemen are either active sympathizers or reluctant collaborators of the NPA.

In the cities and the big towns where government forces are firmly in control, NDF cadres work inside the open legal organizations. Even the barangays, the local units of the Civilian Home Defence Force, and the KBL party branches are reportedly penetrated by them. Having mastered clandestine techniques in twelve years of practice under the worst circumstances, they often succeed in steering these organizations along a radical course while leaving the formal leadership to non-party personalities. Whenever the government cracks down on the so-called subversives, the latter invariably get caught but the real NDF cadres often survive to resuscitate the mass organizations once the troops withdraw.

During that long period when the traditional political machines stayed dormant the NDF, PDSP and other Left groups had the field of mass organizing entirely to themselves. This is why the traditional opposition groups must call on the Left to provide the critical mass for the anti-Marcos demonstrations. Mass actions unilaterally called by the traditional opposition in which the Left did not participate attracted very few people. For instance, the UNIDO-sponsored airport rally to welcome Aquino on 21 August 1983 drew a small crowd of around 2,000 and the 'general strike' called by PDP-LABAN in November was a total failure (Nemenzo 1983).

The NDF is potentially the more powerful weapon of the communist party. Lacking an external supplier, the NPA's expansion is hampered by the arms it can procure through small scale encounters, supplemented of course by what can be purchased from drunken GIs in the American military bases. No matter how auspicious the political situation, the chances of military victory are slim. In the Philippine context the main value of guerrilla warfare is inspirational; without it the NDF and the national democratic movement as a whole cannot sustain the spirit of resistance. But the decisive struggles will most probably occur outside the battlefields. I therefore give little weight to estimates of the revolutionary prospects in the Philippines which are based on calculations of the military balance (e.g., Problems of Communism (Philip Dion) May-June 1982).

Unless the intelligence community can weed out the NDF cadres in all the key institutions and mass organizations, it is difficult to stage a repeat performance of events in September 1972. This is the basis for my assumption in this paper that the NDF will play a critical role in the post-Marcos rearrangement because it has the utmost capacity to destabilize the successor regime.

POST-MARCOS SCENARIOS

As argued earlier, what happens to Marcos will decisively affect the course of events because the present form of government is built around his person. This is not an institutionalized system in which the leader's physical and political health is of secondary importance. The Philippines's future depends, at least in the short run, on how and when Marcos leaves the presidency. Three possibilities may be considered in this connection: (1) he drops dead before a viable succession mechanism could be installed; (2) he is forced to resign either by coup d'etat or by popular pressures; and (3) he stays in power long enough to successfully institutionalize the system.

Despite vehement denials, rumours of his failing health continue circulating in Manila. People in business and politics act on the assumption that Marcos cannot finish his current term. Since he had shirked the task of building up a successor or establishing a structure for succession while his authority was still firmly rooted, his death in this period of uncertainty will set the country in chaos. In that case a military takeover is the likely consequence. Even the most ardent anti-militarist will have to admit that the AFP is to date the only force capable of filling in a power vacuum.

Until the NPA can develop the people's war to the 'strategic stalemate' stage, Marcos can rule the country even without popular support, provided the AFP stands solidly behind his government. So far there are no symptoms of an impending coup. Factionalism in the officer corps (which I noted earlier) does not necessarily indicate a mutinous tendency. The disaffected officers generally aim their criticisms at Ver and Defence Minister Enrile, and seldom at Marcos himself. The internal tensions in the officer corps will become a crucial factor only if the opposition gets strong enough to force his resignation but not sufficiently strong to seize and wield power, or if Marcos's death becomes imminent before there is a widely accepted succession mechanism. In either circumstance it is possible for a clique of ambitious officers to execute a coup, with or without the complicity of civilian technocrats and politicians.

The response of US imperialism is, of course, a factor to consider. Even after granting formal independence in 1946, the US has been able to make and unmake governments in the Philippines. This interventionist capability was further enhanced under martial law because, by opting for an export-oriented development strategy and relying heavily on foreign investments and foreign loans, Marcos made the country more vulnerable to external economic pressures.

The US will surely search for a course of action that would ensure greater stability for the neo-colonial state. But its options are increasingly narrowed down by the radicalization of Filipino consciousness and the growth of the national democratic movement. Within this context I shall examine the three scenarios which are most widely discussed in Manila today.

Scenario No. 1: a military government

Beset with graver problems in Central America and the Middle East, the US will probably stave off a military take-over in the Philippines. Unlike Iran under the Shah and Nicaragua under Somoza, where even the moderate opposition forces had been totally crushed, the Philippines has civilian alternatives to offer. For instance, the technocrats in the present government and certain elements in the traditional opposition are more than willing to accept vassal status. It therefore makes more sense from the standpoint of US economic and security interests to install civilian rulers. Military rule could further weaken the moderate forces and completely destroy people's faith in bourgeois democracy. If, however, the two circumstances cited earlier would suddenly create a power vacuum, the military may indeed intervene even without consulting Washington. The US may find this disagreeable but none the less accept the fait accompli as a short-term expedient.

In my first scenario the military stages a coup d'etat and decides to govern with an all-military junta. Depicting itself as a 'caretaker government', the junta promises 'free elections' as soon as normalcy is restored. Meanwhile, it imposes martial law to deal with the economic problems and the breakdown of law and order. Anticipating resistance from the Left, the church, the traditional opposition, and even the anti-militarist factions in the Marcos camp (e.g., the faction of Labour and Employment Minister Blas Ople), the junta enforces 'preventive detentions', night-time curfew, news blackout, and ban all strikes and demonstrations. To impress people with its iron will, it publicly executes the prominent dissenters.

Given the limited skill-structure of the Philippine military, the junta realizes it cannot govern alone. It needs the managerial skills and credibility of civilian technocrats who, at any rate, bear close ideological affinity with the professional officer corps. Its relations with the politicians are more problematic because militarists view them with contempt. The junta may wish to exclude them but the US will probably insist on their inclusion as a legitimizing factor.

If the military succeeds in normalizing the situation, the US (for reasons cited earlier) may pressure the junta to hold early elections and hasten the restoration of civilian authority. The regular officers who are anxious to keep their profession out of politics may also exert added pressures from within. Unless the junta has the nerve to purge the regular officer corps, it will be forced to make conciliatory gestures while stalling the actual transfer of power.

For example, it can start the process by holding elections for a constitutional assembly and allow the longest possible period for campaigning. The junta can rely on the politicians to quarrel on every minor matter in the convention. The longer and more vicious their squabble, the better for the junta. When a draft is finally adopted, there will be two more campaign periods - first for the plebiscite and then for the parliamentary elections. This whole process could drag on for years, giving the military ample time to entrench itself in the political structure. Unless a revolution overturns the entire system, the military will continue to wield power even after the junta is dissolved.

The process just described can only be smooth if the military is able to establish and maintain a firm grip of the situation. This is difficult to achieve because, over the years of authoritarian rule, the organized Left has acquired the capacity to destabilize any regime. The CPP and the other underground groups will surely intervene at various stages in this process to prevent the junta from consolidating itself. They will try to foment contradictions within the military-technocratic complex, and between the junta and other political forces.

In the countryside, NPA units may launch tactical offensives to divert troops from the cities. And in the cities, particularly in Metro-Manila, the NDF may dip its feet in the water with a series of 'lightning rallies' (a technique it developed to near-perfection in the early years of martial law).(6) If the popular response to such initiatives is positive, the NDF will try to escalate these into mass demonstrations. The military rulers will then have to face a major dilemma. If they tolerate mass demonstrations or fail to suppress them, people may lose respect for their most valued asset; i.e., a monopoly of violence. At the same time, a display of maximum force may trigger a nationwide upheaval reminiscent of the 'Bloody Sunday' in Tsarist Russia.

A mass demonstration is obviously more difficult to organize than a 'lightning rally', especially in a very tense and repressive atmosphere. Its success depends on the participation of the unorganized citizenry who are naturally cautious and more easily frightened. The martial law regime demonstrated in the early 1970s that crowds could be dispersed with minimum violence at the assembly points, but the radicals have also discovered ways to surmount this tactical problem. For instance, the demonstrations in Manila after Aquino's murder were mostly assembled in the three Catholic and one Protestant churches around the Quiapo area. They were usually preceded by a 'protest service' for which a sympathetic priest or minister devises an agitational liturgy. Once tens of thousands have congregated and their passions aroused, they will gain the courage to march out in open defiance of the riot police. It requires utmost violence to diffuse large and angry crowds. From the standpoint of the authorities, this poses an extremely delicate question: will the soldiers always obey an order to open fire? It is one thing to shoot peasants in some God-forsaken village and another to massacre middle class dissenters while the whole world is watching. But they can only prevent it by sealing off the churches and thereby risking confrontation with the powerful ecclesiastical hierarchy.

If the 'lightning rallies' elicit only a lukewarm response, the CPP will not push them any further. Filipino radicals today do not forget the 1950s, when the PKP urged the Huks to escalate the struggle before people were ready for an all out clash with the state. Hence, the Left will probably bide its time until a real revolutionary situation emerges.

They will continue to pursue the strategy of protracted war but their mass organizations will also intervene at the various stages of regime consolidation. For sure they will not put up candidates in the elections because that will contribute to the legitimization of the military regime, but they will certainly take advantage of the electoral campaigns for propaganda and organizational purposes. Obviously, such interventions will not be sufficiently destabilizing. But the Leftwing groups have good reason to expect that the junta will not be able to solve the severe economic problems left behind by Marcos. Provided they can sustain the struggle in the countryside, conditions for simultaneous insurrections in the urban centers will inevitably mature. The notion of protracted war could mean a long wait for this decisive moment.

Scenario No. 2: modified authoritarian rule

Pressured by the US and the international banking community to establish a mechanism for succession, Marcos and his supporters are now working out their own scenario for the post-Marcos era. This entails modifications of the autocratic system to allow a degree of power-sharing with the moderate opposition while retaining its essential feature of a strong executive. The National Assembly (Batasang Pambansa) with 183 elective is its basic participatory structure.

Under the 1973 constitution, as amended and reamended to suit Marcos's volatile political strategy, the president has the powers to veto National Assembly bills and issue decrees which the National Assembly can neither repeal nor revise. In effect, Marcos remains the supreme lawgiver. The National Assembly can legislate only for as long as the president permits.

Should anything untoward happen to Marcos before his term ends in 1987, the speaker of the National Assembly will act as the interim head of state but he has to call for a presidential election within sixty days. Marcos has already made provisions to ensure a KBL victory in that election. The most important of these is to pack the Commission on Elections (COMELEC) with his loyal henchmen. In a country like the Philippines where frauds and terrorism are time-honoured practices, control of the COMELEC and its network of poll inspectors is crucial.

Today all the major print and electronic media are owned by Marcos's cronies. Since the death of Aquino, however, the audience of Radio Veritas (the radio station of the Catholic Church) has grown and the government has tolerated opposition newspapers like Malaya, Veritas, and The Philippine Signs. The weekly magazines, including the ones owned by the cronies, have also taken a mildly oppositionist posture. But their editors, columnists and correspondents live under constant threat of detention since Marcos has not repealed decrees that were designed to curtail freedom of the press. Moreover, the government can always silence them by withholding the supply of newsprint. These anti-Marcos media exert an influence out of proportion to their circulation. They tend to be expensive because the big corporations find it imprudent to advertise in them, but those who can afford to buy usually pass them around to trusted friends.

Like all governing parties, KBL has the added advantage of access to public funds. It is to be expected that between now and 1987, Marcos will use all available resources to ensure his re-election or the election of his chosen successor. His immediate goal is to secure the political and economic future of his family, his cronies and his devoted followers after he leaves the presidency.

What are his chances in this endeavour? Mrs Imelda Romualdez Marcos is often mentioned as the strongest contender, but I doubt if she ever was a serious candidate (Nemenzo 1983). Marcos may have many faults, but we should recognize his acute sense of political realism. He must be aware that his capricious and extravagant wife will never earn the confidence of the US and the international banking community. The technocrats as well as the regular officer corps of the armed forces are also quite explicit in their rejection of her. She may have the initial support of the powerful General Ver, but it is doubtful that he could swing the entire military organization in her favour the moment Marcos departs.

Marcos has to explore other possibilities such as Eduardo Cojuanco, Defence Minister Enrile, Labour Minister Ople, UN Under-Secretary-General Rafael Salas, and Prime Minister Virata. Unfortunately, they all have tremendous disabilities. Despite the exposure of fabricated economic figures, Virata has retained his popularity in foreign banking circles, but his own people view him as the cause rather than a solution to the current economic crisis. In the tumultuous post-Marcos years, factions in the military will be manoeuvring for positions and popular support could then be a critical factor.

Since he resigned as Marcos's executive secretary, Salas has continued to command a following in the technocracy. He is probably as acceptable as Virata to the military, the US government and the international banking community. His ambiguous relationship with Marcos and his many years of absence from the country are both an advantage and a disadvantage. Marcos distrusts him but if the pressures for his resignation mount, Marcos may see Salas as the last hope for some continuity. Salas is more likely than those who were deeply involved in the regime to placate the radical opposition, or at least a segment of it.

Ople has been quite open about his presidential ambitions but he is the least likely contender. The military suspects him of Left wing sympathies while the Left despise him as an opportunist. His supposed power base is a sector of organized labour which is too weak and unmotivated to be an effective counterforce to the Left and the military, potentially the most destabilizing forces in the post-Marcos era.

Enrile, on the other hand, prematurely began his campaign for the presidency and in the process acquired too many powerful enemies. He has a brighter prospect if the first rather than the second scenario materializes. His best hope of acceding to the presidency is to rally the regular officer corps against Ver and his cohorts, but even this is improbable unless he can persuade Lieutenant-General Fidel Ramos (AFP deputy Chief-of-Staff and Commanding General of the PC) to stage in a pre-emptive coup.

Of the crony-capitalists, Cojuanco alone has exhibited political acumen. Taking a very low profile for the greater part of the martial law period, he had evaded the pernicious controversies that ruined the reputation of others. He quietly built a following in the armed forces with the help of Enrile, but when the latter's efforts backfired, he defected to the Ver camp and continued carving out his own power base with the sufferance of this faction (Far Eastern Economic Review 7 June 1984). While the corporate empires of the other crony-capitalists have collapsed, Cojuanco not only retained his grip on the coconut industry but recently also captured the San Miguel Corporation (the largest business enterprise in the Philippines which used to be the financial backer of his late cousin and political adversary Benigno Aquino).

The fundamental question, however, is whether the structure of the Marcos state will survive his death or forcible withdrawal. Until the early months of 1984 political observers were predicting his downfall. Reagan cancelled his state visit to distance the US from his tottering regime. The IMF was not eager to bail him out. Ungrateful protegees were joining the opposition. Some military officers were voicing dissatisfaction. Meanwhile, the economy continued sinking and the mass movement continued mounting.

For the first time in a decade Marcos appeared vulnerable. The US congress ordered him in unequivocal terms to hold elections and secure the participation of the opposition parties:

> It should be the policy of the United States Government to support genuine, fair and free elections to the National Assembly in May 1984 and, to that end, to urge the government of the Philippines to take the necessary steps to secure the full participation of the opposition parties in these elections, including the prompt reconstitution of an objective, impartial electoral commission and the restoration of full freedom of the press... (US House of Representatives,

Concurrent Resolution No. 187, 6 October 1983).

Realizing that Marcos desperately needed to make the elections credible to the US, all opposition forces from the CPP and PDSP on the one hand, and the UNIDO and PDP-LABAN on the other held a people's congress (KOMPIL) in January 1984. They all agreed to boycott the elections unless Marcos would abdicate his power to rule by decree and turn the National Assembly into a real parliament. That was indeed a rare chance to extract meaningful concessions from a beleaguered dictator.

Unfortunately for Philippine democracy, the UNIDO and PDP-LABAN broke the agreement. After a secret chat with the US Vice-President, UNIDO chairman Laurel announced his party's intention to participate in the expensive farce. PDP-LABAN took an irresolute stand which unbared its ideological confusion. While its opportunist leadership decided to participate, its militant rank and file opted for boycott. Once assured of 'full participation' as mandated by the US congress, Marcos resumed his adamant posture and refused to reconstitute the COMELEC or restore freedom of the press. The regime thus gained a lease of life not because of the legendary cunning of Marcos but because of the vacillation of his adversaries.

In the elections KBL lost massively in Metro-Manila and other urban centres, but managed to rectify the results in remote areas. Despite numerous instances of blatant frauds and 200 political murders, the foreign press declared the elections to be a historic landmark. Marcos is reported to have regained control while the revitalized opposition supposedly gained a stronger position to check the government party. On the other hand, the radicals are said to have suffered a major setback because a high percentage of voters ignored their boycott call (e.g., Newsweek 28 May 1984 and The New Republic 11 & 25 June 1984). Ambassador Jean Kirkpatrick even described the elections as a major step toward 'the perfection of your democracy'.

The celebration might have come too soon. One consequence of the elections was to alienate the traditional opposition from the militant masses. With the continuing decline of the economy, the symptoms of social unrest manifest themselves everywhere. Demonstrations now occur even in hitherto placid towns and industrial strikes are becoming more violent. Meanwhile, the traditional oppositionists who constitute one third of Marcos's rubber stamp parliament are dramatizing their own impotence. If this trend drags on and the locus of decisive battles shifts from parliament to the streets, there is good reason for the US to fear that the militant masses will rally behind the CPP as the only force capable of armed resistance.

Scenario No. 3: constitutional democracy restored

If the CPP can galvanize the extra-parliamentary

struggle and the National Assembly loses its last remaining credibility, the US might persuade Marcos to resign. He and his family will be offered asylum, with the amenities and protection normally accorded to fallen despots. A denial of loans by the IMF will help, and if all this fails, the pro-American officers of the armed forces can make a few threatening gestures. Being so dependent on the military, Marcos will have to yield rather than risk the dreadful consequences of scenario no. 1.

In this third scenario the military decides not to govern but asks the technocrats to constitute a civilian provisional government with acceptable members of the traditional opposition. This government tries to shake off the Marcos stigma and appeals for national reconciliation. The 1973 constitution and all presidential decrees are nullified. The most notorious Marcos henchmen are put on trial. The Bill of Rights is restored. A general amnesty is proclaimed and the underground organizations allowed to surface. A constituent assembly is convened and its draft submitted to a plebiscite without delay. Members of the provisional government inhibit themselves from running for elective office. Free and honest elections are held and the provisional government readily cedes power to the elected government.

Since this arrangement conforms to popular sentiments, it would be foolhardy for the Left to oppose it. The Left will probably reciprocate the gestures of reconciliation, even as it remains vigilant knowing that the military is lurking in the shadow of the provisional government. The NPA will refuse to disarm but agrees to a truce. The NDF will also preserve its clandestine network while taking advantage of every occasion for propaganda and organizing work. While abstaining from outright attacks on the provisional government, the CPP and its associated organizations will keep a political distance. Should the sectarian elements in its leadership foolishly oppose the provisional government at the outset, the CPP will be isolated and this will be the chance for PDSP to seize the initiative.

Like the modified authoritarian rule envisaged in scenario no. 2, the restored constitutional democracy will have to settle the dreadful legacy of the Marcos years: uncontrollable inflation, a staggering balance of payments deficit and a huge foreign debt. Unless the US will commit as much economic aid as it did in 1950 (an unlikely prospect in this epoch of global recession), the newly-elected government will have to keep wages down and enforce a severe austerity programme. Such measures, no matter how rational, will be difficult to bear by the millions who live below or close to the poverty line.

Once the euphoria of Marcos's downfall wears out, there will be a resurgence of industrial strikes. The students will return to the streets. Some members of parliament will champion their cause and constitutional democracy will again be reduced to a 'democracy of stalemate'. The contradictions of 1970-72 will resurface, perhaps in more vicious forms. These will be the cues for the NPA to resume the armed struggle. The politicized military officers will also find their backstop role increasingly intolerable. Then another Marcos, a new 'man of destiny' (iginuhit ng tadhana) will come forward to snatch the republic from the brink of disaster.

Conclusion

This exercise in political speculation presupposes a time-frame of seven years. It assumes that Marcos will not last until the end of the 1980s: either his government is toppled or his kidney is consumed by lupus erythematosus. But a revolution is unlikely to be the immediate outcome. Even the CPP, with its predilection for extravagant optimism, does not expect that to happen in the near future. The death or downfall of Marcos will only give rise to an extremely volatile situation wherein the military-technocratic complex and the traditional opposition will try to work out a mutually acceptable arrangement.

On its own, the traditional opposition is incapable of capturing power. Its mobilizing capacity is limited to gathering votes and does not even extend to effectively protecting the ballot box. Despite the outburst of anti-Marcos feelings after the Aquino assassination, there is little chance of the traditional opposition parties rebuilding their shattered political machines in time for the next presidential polls.

UNIDO is alienated from the young militants who are in the forefront of extra-parliamentary struggle. While PDP-Laban is somewhat more alluring, tension exists between its leadership and its militant rank and file. Thus, if Marcos hangs on for some more years the traditional opposition might be consigned to oblivion. At the moment their prime value is that of a legitimizing factor, but this too is dwindling as fast as the Philippine currency. The last elections reduced rather than enhanced their potential for constructive intervention. In the long run it is the historic confrontation between the Left and the military-technocratic complex that will decide the Philippines's future.

Although the Left will neither be a contender for power nor a participant in a ruling coalition in the next seven years, it can influence the course of events by the skilful use of its enormous capacity for political destabilization. Whatever the form it takes, the post-Marcos regime is going to be be more vulnerable than the Marcos state because it will inherit a severe economic crisis while consolidating itself.

The prospects for a national democratic revolution in the 1990s depend to a large extent on how correctly the Left analyzes and responds to the fluid situation in the next seven years. Imbued with an overwhelming self-confidence that borders on arrogance, some CPP leaders are not beyond committing fatal errors that could wipe out their phenomenal gains during the Marcos years. At the moment the CPP appears to be preparing only for scenario no. 1. It is interesting to observe if the CPP leadership can transcend its dogmatic tendencies and execute a strategic switch should scenario no. 2 or scenario no. 3 materialize. What happened in the 1950s (when the PKP plunged the Huk movement to a colossal debacle) may happen again if at a critical juncture in the immediate post-Marcos period the CPP misjudges the real situation and drives the movement along a disastrous line of march.

The non-CPP elements of the Left (Soc-Dems and independent Marxists) have much to contribute in this enterprise. Free from a centralized party discipline, they are exploring other dimensions of the Philippine reality and trying out alternative modes of action. Rather than regard them as foes to be discredited, isolated and eventually crushed, a mature vanguard party would encourage these tendencies and establish channels for continuing dialogues. Their reflections and experiments will probably help in evolving a truly Filipino radical perspective that grasps the present reality and the future prospects in their fullest complexity and dynamism. But an arrogant party leadership that claims a monopoly of wisdom and righteousness, a bureaucratic centralist leadership that stifles critical thinking and muzzles debate, is doomed to waste a historic opportunity.

FOOTNOTES

1. In a constitutional amendment extracted by the US from a fledging Philippine republic in 1947, US citizens and corporations were granted 'parity rights' in the exploitation of Philippine natural resources and operation of public utilities. This was spelt out in a treaty known as the 'Laurel-Langley agreement' that was due to expire in 1974.

2. 'Integree officers', as distinct from 'regular officers', obtained their commissions by going through a four-year Reserve Officers Training Course (ROTC) as part of their regular university education. During martial law thousands of these ROTC graduates were called to active duty and conferred high military ranks.

3. An allusion to the conquest of the Philippines in 1898 and the reoccupation in 1945 which the US justified as a liberation.

4. The bulk of the pre martial law NP politicians joined Marcos's KBL party, while another faction identified with Senator Roy played the role of 'loyal opposition'. When the traditional and Left opposition groups decided to boycott the 1981 presidential election, for example, Marcos asked the NP-Roy faction to put up a token candidate against him.

5. Interview with leaders of two UNIDO-affiliated regional parties who eventually broke with UNIDO just before the May 1984 parliamentary elections.

6. A 'lightning rally' is a technique developed by student activists in the late 1970s to embarrass the martial law authorities. Briefly, it consists of blocking the traffic at two points in a busy street (an easy thing to do in Manila at certain times of the day) so as to keep the police mobile patrols from moving swiftly to a preselected area. Several activists with their faces covered would then appear in this area, chanting slogans, waving placards and distributing leaflets. Before the policemen are able to reach the area on foot, the activists merge with the milling crowd. This usually provokes them to arrest the wrong people. Such forms of mass action proved to be very effective in reviving the spirit of resistance. Their immediate tactical objective is to demonstrate the impotence of the coercive apparatus against people who 'dare to struggle and dare to win', and their ultimate goal is to help the citizenry recover from the initial shock. Aside from testing the clandestine network's operational capability after the first round of arrests, these 'lightning rallies' also measured the people's readiness for higher forms of urban struggle.

Chapter 5

THE CHURCH

Dennis Shoesmith

The crisis provoked by the assassination of Benigno
Aquino has uncovered the underlying weakness of a regime
which has systematically dismantled the political and
governmental institutions it inherited but has failed to
erect credible institutions in their place. As the Marcos
government struggles simply to survive, the larger dilemma
confronting the regime and its opponents is how to restore
political processes atrophied over the past eleven years of
authoritarian rule.

The faction fighting around the president and the
present agonizing over succession are one symptom of this
political vacuum. Eleven years of personal rule have
seriously compromised the judiciary and the media. The
military has been drawn into the political arena and
entangled with the Marcoses, and is a new factor to be
reckoned with by any successor. The opposition, since 1972,
has not had a role in the political system. Its
demoralization is reflected in the present debate over
whether or not to participate in the proposed May 1984
elections.

The aftermath of the assassination has also uncovered
the wider consequences of the past eleven years in the
Philippine electorate. Mass demonstrations in Manila have
attracted prominent national business leaders and
professionals, marking the final disenchantment of the
educated urban middle class with a regime which is now
perceived as lacking not only the legitimacy of the rule of
law but the legitimacy of success. The political crisis is
compounded by an economic collapse which signals the failure
of the development strategy of the 1970s, a strategy which
President Marcos offered then as the justification for 'New
Society' authoritarianism. If the urban middle class is
suddenly disenchanted, the radicalization of Filipino
peasants and workers has been a slower but cumulative
process.

In the short and medium terms, the political options
have narrowed. Perhaps one or more of the factions competing
for the succession within the ruling circle will manage to
work out a formula with Marcos and reconstitute the regime.
It is unlikely that such an arrangement would last.

Perhaps elements in the present regime might negotiate a face-saving coalition with more moderate opposition groups under the guise of some kind of government of 'national reconciliation' but, again, opposition groups which accepted such a deal would risk losing support in the present climate. Perhaps, possibly with US support if Washington perceives such a course in its own interests, an independent opposition might find the means to challenge the regime but it is likely that such a challenge would be savagely opposed by a leadership with nowhere to go. The possibility of a reformist, 'middle way' regime succeeding Marcos is problematical. Such a regime would face fundamental problems of restoring political institutions, resolving the economic crisis and mapping out a new development strategy, putting the military in its place, renegotiating the critical relationship with the US and offering something to the mass of Filipinos who have lost out under authoritarian rule. A reformist regime would also inevitably be confronted by the revolutionary Left which has gathered strength in the present crisis.

In the coming months, the one national institution which was not co-opted or finally compromised during the past eleven years - the Roman Catholic Church - could play a significant and possibly even decisive role in determining which of the short- and medium-term options will prevail. The question is not only whether the church has the will and the capacity to effectively intervene but whether the church has any coherent position in the present crisis.

The political significance of the church

Traditionally, the Catholic Church has played a pivotal political role. During the Spanish colonial period the powers of the Archbishop of Manila rivalled and sometimes eclipsed those of the Governor-General. The church operated as one of the two institutions of colonial rule under the terms of the Spanish patronato real which recognised it as an integral part of government.

Since the Philippine Revolution and the separation of church and state under American rule, the political significance of the church has been indirect and harder to evaluate. Today, the church undoubtedly commands significant physical and moral resources. It claims the spiritual allegiance of more than 80 per cent of the population. Precisely how that allegiance translates into direct political terms is uncertain. On those very few occasions when the bishops have offered collective political advice in joint pastoral letters there is little evidence one way or the other that their pronouncements have had a significant effect.

But at the broader level of popular perceptions of the regime and its legitimacy, the bishops and clergy exercise real if diffuse influence. The abstract language of the official statements issued by the Catholic Bishops'

Conference of the Philippines (CBCP), while themselves the product of compromise between conservative, moderate and progressive bishops, offer theoretical grounds for a challenge to the state. Translated through the local priest or missionary to lay leaders and community groups, the bishops' pronouncements provide religious authority for social justice programmes.

The most effective presence of the church, however, is probably through individual activist bishops and priests working with their own communities. The church operates a national network of parishes, missions, schools and colleges, lay organizations and media. Church personnel in the religious orders and in diocesan social action centres are often articulate, trained professionals who can connect Christian activists in the barrios to the church's national and international resources. In the local community, the church worker is often the only alternative channel of action and protest to provincial politicans unresponsive since 1972 when provincial politics were frozen.

The political significance of the church goes beyond its physical and human resources. It is the only national institution which has retained its independence and credibility when political parties, the courts, the military, the bureaucracy and the media have all been co-opted or discredited by a regime intent on centralizing all power on the president.

In fact, the bishops have made substantial compromises with the Marcos government since 1972, compromises which seriously inhibit the ability of the hierarchy to challenge the regime in the present crisis. The policy of 'critical collaboration' with the regime pursued by the Archbishop of Manila, Jaime Cardinal Sin, on behalf of the hierarchy accepted the necessity for martial law and the legitimacy of the changes made to the political system by the Marcos government.

Fortunately for the church, its assumption of the role of conscience of the regime has obliged it to be more critic than collaborator. Individual bishops and on a few occasions, the CBCP collectively, have spoken out against the violation of human and civil rights, the treatment of political prisoners, military abuses, the exploitation of the poor, and even against structural injustices built into the authoritarian system.(1)

The regime itself has helped the bishops maintain a healthy distance by periodically mounting attacks against moderate as well as radical church critics, raiding church organizations, arresting clergy and lay workers, threatening church property and toying with the idea of introducing social legislation condemned by church teaching (Youngblood 1981).(2) Even conservative bishops have maintained a lively sense of corporate rights under state pressure.

A minority of bishops was uneasy if not hostile towards martial law from the beginning. By the mid1970s moderates as well as progressive bishops were increasingly disenchanted while maintaining the policy of critical collaboration. The hierarchy has also stressed criticism rather than collaboration to retain the loyalty of the hundreds of their own clergy and religious who would have repudiated church leaders who moved too close to the president.

Beyond its influence as a social institution, the church exercises profound symbolic power in the Philippines. It claims, and is widely accepted as possessing, a universal, divinely sanctioned spiritual and moral authority. It is the focus of deeply held Filipino values and beliefs. The bishops are not in full control of this symbolic presence but their importance as political actors reflects it. Aquino's death was interpreted by many of the millions who followed his coffin in the context of potent folk religious traditions which have surfaced at earlier periods of national crisis. Whatever Aquino's significance alive, dead he has been transformed into the folk tradition of national martyrs. Twice before, in 1872 and 1896, martyrdom signalled a fundamental shift in the direction of Philippine history.

In the aftermath of assassination, the church was highly visible. Cardinal Sin and twelve bishops conducted the funeral mass. From 19 September the bells of Manila's churches tolled every day, calling for five minutes of prayer for Aquino and 'for all who are oppressed because of what they believe or what they are'. Symbolically, the church's presence contributed to a change in the national mood which can only be fully understood in terms of Filipino political culture. Perhaps only half consciously, the hierarchy confirmed in the popular mind that the assassination marked a shift in the moral or even the supernatural order; that the regime had lost all moral authority.

Divisions within the church

While the bishops were unable to mount a united challenge to the regime after the imposition of martial law, they retain the independence and the prestige to exert strong pressure on the Marcos government in its present weakened state. That the church in the months since the assassination has been unable to mount such a challenge reflects divisions within the church itself, divisions which were widened during the martial law period and which have become possibly irreconcilable in the past two years.

The Philippine church, despite its institutional strengths, is organizationally clumsy and slow moving. Traditionally, the church has not been an innovator; rather it has been embedded in the status quo, resistant to change. In the nationalist movement of the 1880s and the revolution of 1896 the hierarchy spectacularly failed to come to terms with the movement of Philippine history. Despite the changes in social teaching and organization encouraged by the Second Vatican Council and a new emphasis on social action and involvement in the world, much of this inherited conservatism and inertia still characterizes the Philippine church, particularly in the larger, older dioceses of Luzon.

The bishops will decide the official church response to the present crisis but it is not certain that the clergy and Christian lay leaders will follow them. Bishops exercise full authority, individually in their dioceses and collectively through the CBCP, but the rigid juridical and ecclesiastical structure is deceptive. The Philippine church is no longer a monolith. The church reflects divisions within Philippine society and is caught up in the struggle between conservatives, moderates and revolutionaries. Bishops, clergy and laity are also caught up in competing theological and ideological movements committed to rival and sometimes incompatible understandings of the church's social and political role (Shoesmith 1979).

While the more than one hundred bishops in the CBCP represent only part of the spectrum of contending political ideologies in the Philippine church generally, they are themselves aligned into at least three factions. The CBCP includes a minority of traditionalists and conservatives, a moderate majority led by Cardinal Sin, and a progressive minority which asserted itself in a dissenting statement from the moderate response in the first week of martial law. The moderates articulate official church policy towards the state steering a wavering course between conservatives and progressives. The progressive minority has probably had a disproportionate influence on CBCP statements and joint pastoral letters but it does not determine the hierarchy's stance (ibid.).

Theological and political divisions within the hierarchy are real; they have limited the bishops' capacity to act decisively in the past and appear to be operating against a firm church stand in the present crisis. But it is also evident that the bishops hold together under attack, that they all share an overriding sense of their corporate character and interests. A Filipino bishop is a bishop first and a conservative, moderate or progressive second. The irreconcilable split within the Philippine church is not between bishops but between the bishops and Christian revolutionaries.

Tensions have also surfaced between the CBCP and the national organization linking the religious orders, the Association of Major Religious Superiors of the Philippines (AMRSP). The AMRSP has pursued a more activist, critical course since 1972 and has come into direct conflict with the regime through its social justice task forces and its media. The religious orders do not have the ecclesiastical authority of the bishops but they include hundreds of foreign missionaries and can draw on international support, control their own educational institutions and media and to an extent are less constrained by the bureaucratic detail and administrative problems which preoccupy the bishops of the larger dioceses.

The hierarchy is also inhibited by the extensive material interests of the church. On this point, the bishops' critics from far right and far left agree. A position paper by the Communist Party of the Philippines (CPP), 'Nature of the church sector, orientation of our political work and tasks of comrades within the sector', argues that

> The Roman Catholic Church has for centuries been aligned with the oppressor classes. As a result, this church is the wealthiest entity in the country outside of the state... It is public knowledge...that the Archdiocese of Manila is one of the richest world-wide and the Jesuits in the Philippines have assets running into hundreds of millions of pesos.
>
> In our semi-feudal, semi-colonial society, the clerical and lay leaders of the churches are themselves landlords or compradores, big bourgeoisie in various ways and they defend and promote their own bourgeois and feudal privileges and comforts (CPP n.d.).

Thinking within the regime, indicated by an article on 'Contemporary religious radicalism in the Philippines' published in 1979 in the Quarterly National Security Review, agrees that

> Within the parameters of the present social system and when all the chips are down, the Catholic hierarchy or the overwhelming majority and mainstream of it, can be expected to take a conservative or even reactionary stand on decisive issues... Apart from religious considerations, the Catholic Church in the Philippines has temporal interests that apparently fix it on the conservative or reactionary side. It has tremendous assets in capital and land. It would not risk these in violent revolution. The temporal interests of the church are derived from a long history of being an instrument of colonial domination and being a close ally of the ruling elite...it is bound by countless social ties to the incumbent social elite (Kintanar 1979)

The author recommends that the state look after the interests of the religious conservatives to maintain church support, but even in this area there have been serious conflicts. The struggle over church holdings in Philippine Trust, the threat to tax church organizations including schools and colleges, and the urban land reform policy, ratified in the January 1984 referendum, alarmed the bishops. Both analyses are undoubtedly correct in judging that the conservatives and moderates and probably most of the progressives in the CBCP regard a revolutionary government as

the ultimate threat to the church's material interests.
Efforts within some of the religious orders, for instance to
divest themselves of compromising financial ties, have not
altered this constraint on the church's freedom of action.

The most serious divisions within the church operate
between church leaders at the centre and parish clergy,
religious and lay organizers radicalized by their work among
political prisoners, the victims of military persecution and
the rural and urban poor. Robert Youngblood's
centre-periphery model of the Philippine church is a useful
way of conceptualising this division (Youngblood 1982).

The centre - Pope and Curia in Rome - is furthest from
the reality of Philippine politics in the barrios and most
concerned with the interests and institutional priorities of
the church as a supra-national entity. The CBCP and the
archbishop of Manila occupy the centre of the periphery,
intermediaries between Rome and the Philippine church. The
next circle is occupied by regional bishops' conferences,
regional social action centres, then the individual bishops
in their dioceses. The institutional church is in daily
contact with the people of God only at the furthest circle of
the periphery through the local parish, basic Christian
communities and local church self-help groups and
associations. The concerns, priorities, experience and,
increasingly, the theology of Philippine Christians shift
according to their place in this schema.

Ideological divisions

Ideological and theological divisions within the church
are reinforced by this varied exposure from centre to
periphery to the processes of change and conflict in the
Philippines, although distance from the poor does not always
neatly correspond to theological conservatism. The National
Secretariat for Social Action, Justice and Peace (NASSA), the
national co-ordinating body for the church's social
programmes, pursues a progressive activist line though it
operates from Manila and is responsible to the bishops.
Relations between NASSA and the CBCP have been tense,
approaching the point of rupture at least twice in recent
years. In Mindanao, the bishops have repudiated their
regional social action organization, the Mindanao-Sulu
Pastoral Conference secretariat.

Competing theological and ideological visions of the
political role of the church reflect the wider polarization
of Philippine society but have their own internal dynamic and
momentum. Despite its internal divisions, the CBCP has
presented at least the appearance of a united position which
draws on the progressive understanding of the church's
commitment to social justice spelled out in the early 1960s
by the Second Vatican Council and in the encyclical letters
of Pope Paul VI. The reorientation of the church's mission
in the world of the 1960s provided the model for the
substantial reworking of Philippine church programmes on the

eve of martial law. Post Vatican II social teaching precludes the kind of accommodation between church and state reached between the Spanish bishops and General Franco in the 1930s and 1940s.

An older, traditionalist understanding of the church's role as exclusively 'spiritual' survives with a number of the higher clergy but the social justice thrust of the 1960s is the new orthodoxy and is irreversible. In their statement on church-state relations issued in December 1982, the bishops collectively reaffirmed that 'action on behalf of justice and participation in the transformation of the world fully appears to us as a constitutive dimension of the preaching of the Gospel, of the church's mission for the redemption of the human race and its liberation from every oppressive situation' (Ichthys 10 December 1982:3-4).

Confusingly, the bishops have also stressed, most recently in the joint pastoral letter, 'A Dialogue for Peace', that Christ 'gave His church no proper mission in the political, economic or social order'. The church cannot and should not be 'identified with any political community nor bound by ties to any political system'. Rather, it is 'the sign and safeguard of the transcendental dimension of the human person'. (This pastoral letter, dated 20 February 1983, is published in Ichthys 25 February 1983.)

The distinction between commitment to 'action on behalf of justice and participation in the transformation of the world' on the one hand and the bishops' disclaimer that the church has any 'proper mission in the political, economic or social order' on the other, is peculiarly subtle. Pope John Paul II, during his Philippine visit in early 1981, told Filipino priests to stay out of politics. Cardinal Sin, in late 1982, as bluntly said it was the priest's right and duty as a citizen to take part in political activity and that one of his important roles 'is to guide his flock on the morality of human activity.' Politics is a human activity; ergo, it has a morality. And who would be best equipped to explain this morality than a priest' (speech given before the Manila Rotary Club, Manila Hilton, 21 October 1982, published in Events (Visayas Secretariat of Social Action, Justice and Peace) IV(2) 1982:4).

If the signals from the hierarchy are confusing, it is increasingly clear that a significant minority of Christian activists are no longer listening. From the early 1970s, the social justice teachings of the bishops have been challenged by radical and revolutionary theological movements which advocate the complete restructuring of Philippine society. The bishops claim exclusive authority to speak on behalf of the Philippine church but there exist significant rival centres of power beyond their control. At a time of growing national emergency, the bishops have been preoccupied by the effort to combat 'infiltration' by the radical left of church organizations.

This pluralism complicates church-state relations which can no longer be confined within the conventional formula of formal relations between two 'powers', the 'spiritual' and the 'temporal'. It is in this sense that the bishops find it difficult to articulate and enforce a coherent policy towards the regime which commands the assent of the lower clergy.

The moderate response

In the immediate aftermath of the assassination, Cardinal Sin played a highly active role. His public statements included some harsh criticisms of the regime. During his homily at the funeral mass for Aquino, he called for the restoration of 'the freedoms the people have lost' and for the government to 'recognize the people's right to participate fully in the political process'. 'The atmosphere of oppression and corruption, the climate of fear and anguish that the Philippine bishops spoke about have resulted in a truly tragic condition; [the Filipino] has become an exile in his own country...he must only whisper, never shout the truth; he must tremble before those who were sworn to serve him; he must hide his children if they refuse to bow down to tyranny' (Shoesmith 1983:1).

Cardinal Sin was appalled by the assassination, but another theme sounded more strongly through his public statements after 21 August. His overriding concern was to try to avert a bloody uprising. In repeated calls for reconciliation, he warned that Aquino himself represented reconciliation between the regime and its opponents and 'if we allow Aquino's death to fan the flames of violence and division, then Aquino will have died in vain'.

During the funeral homily and, later, during a half-hour interview with President Marcos at Malacanang, Cardinal Sin urged the president to convene a council of national reconciliation. As preconditions for such a council, Sin called for a free press, an independent judiciary, a thorough and impartial investigation of Aquino's murder and free elections. The council should include representatives of the government, the opposition and the church. The meeting with President Marcos on 23 September was unproductive and the cardinal was clearly dismayed by Marcos's apparent intransigence. Over the following months, Marcos grudgingly made some concessions but not enough to persuade leading groups in the opposition to accept the validity of the forthcoming May 1984 elections. They boycotted the January 1984 referendum on the crucial point that the president should relinquish his special emergency powers, making a transition to an opposition regime a real possibility through the May 1984 elections.

Cardinal Sin has urged the opposition to participate in the elections. Whatever his disillusionment with the Marcos regime, he is above all concerned with stability and apparently believes that this can be attained through a compromise between Marcos and the opposition. This is consistent with Sin's position since the mid-1970s. It is a position that is on the surface oddly inconsistent. He has appeared, especially in the foreign media, as an outspoken critic of the Marcos regime. In August 1979 he demanded that the president step down, warning of civil war. By November, he was rejecting an appeal from Aquino, then in prison, to lead opposition demands that Marcos step down. His statements following the assassination have taken a similar, puzzling, zig-zag course. A month after the assassination he celebrated a thanksgiving mass for the president's birthday. On 22 September, following major riots in Manila during which eleven demonstrators were killed and hundreds injured, he criticized the president's opponents for their 'seemingly uncontrollable desire to hurt or maim or destroy'.

> I do not want to see our streets converted into rivers of blood because our students, armed with nothing more than their idealism, will charge a tank manned by presidential security troopers. I want to see our people united and happy, securer in their belief that they have a government and a national leadership that is sincerely concerned about their welfare.

Yet, as he acknowledged in the same speech, the people were disenchanted with a regime that had to share the blame for the violence because of repressive policies which 'bring back memories of Mr Goebbels of Nazi Germany' (Asian Wall Street Journal 23-24 September 1983).

A prominent Filipino Jesuit once described Cardinal Sin to me as a shrewd tactician who lacked an overall programme. He is open, accessible, well informed by his own intelligence network, in touch with leading individuals in the government, the military and the opposition. But Sin's skills in the personalized politics of Manila do not add up to any long-term strategy.

The Cardinal's dilemma in the wake of the assassination is a dilemma which has faced the moderates in the hierarchy for eleven years. Sin explained the moderates' fundamental policy during an earlier crisis following the grossly manipulated 1978 election. Responding to an attack by Defence Minister Juan Ponce Enrile, against the 'Christian Left', Sin said:

> He doesn't know we are helping the government. If we were not here worse would happen. I am making a bridge between the left and the right. My duty is to be able to bridge this gap between those who are against and those who are in favour of Marcos. But this cannot be done without the basis of justice (Far Eastern Economic Review 21 July 1978:25).

Reconciliation

The Aquino assassination has confirmed the radical polarization of Philippine society. The moderates represented by the cardinal are a bridge whose right and left banks have receded, leaving them marooned in a rising tide of conflict. Sin is, in effect, still pursuing his policy of critical collaboration with the regime, while increasingly stressing the need for reconciliation. Committed to the defence of human rights and the need for social justice, he and the moderates in the CBCP are alarmed by the regime's capacity for violence but are more alarmed by the threat of violent opposition. Their deepest fear is that the confrontation between the regime and its opponents will encourage revolution. The moderates share with the conservatives among the bishops the conviction that it is revolution, not dictatorship, which poses the greatest danger to the church itself. The policy of critical collaboration, as Sin acknowledged in 1977, assumed that the church could live with dictatorship. The form of government was not important:

> It could be monarchical, it could be democratic, it could be a dictatorship, it could be authoritarianism as [we] have in the Philippines. What we are interested in is the freedom of the church to exercise her functions (Asiaweek 12 August 1977).

The significant omission from this list is any reference to a government to the left of centre.

The cardinal has been working to convince the opposition to take the May elections seriously and the government to offer enough concessions for this exercise to hold out the chance of national reconciliation. Church position papers urging reconciliation and enumerating its conditions have proliferated recently. (This is also the theme of the Protestant churches in 'NCCP Statement on National Reconciliation', signed by Bishop Abdias de la Cruz and La Verne D. Mercado, 26 October 1983; see Ichthys 4 November 1983.) They have also provoked criticism from within the church, condemning the demand for reconciliation as unrealistic and 'too passive, it tends to reinforce the illusion that Marcos can be removed without painful struggle on the people's part' ('In search of an effective and credible alternative to Marcos', Plaridel Papers No. 1, October 1983. These papers were prepared by a group of professionals in touch with progressive church groups). In an address on 'National Security and Reconciliation', given on 6 December, Bishop Antonino Nepomuceno, one of the few dissenting voices in the CBCP, argued that 'the oppressive structure of national security installed by the regime with the collusion of the US has to be dismantled for national reconciliation':

> The question to ask is: can there be real reconciliation between the people and the Marcos regime without confrontation and without him

resigning? I don't think so (<u>Ichthys</u> 30 December 1983:7).

The progressives

Bishop Nepomuceno is one of a fluctuating group of some ten to seventeen bishops who have been both systematically critical of the regime and advocates of a more prophetic, democratic church. The best known spokesman of what might be called the progessives in the CBCP is the Jesuit, Bishop Francisco Claver of Malaybalay, Bukidnon, in central Mindanao.

The progressives have gone further than the moderates in their critique of the political and developmental nature of the Marcos regime but they stop short of the Marxist-influenced structural analysis applied by the more radical of their clergy. The progressives distinguish between the church as a hierarchic institution concerned with the defence of its own, institutionally-defined, interests and the church as the people of God. Their theology takes up a re-emphasis of the nature of the church introduced during the Second Vatican Council. Authority is understood as flowing upwards from the community of believers as well as downward through the pope to the bishops, the clergy and finally, the laity. The church has a prophetic role in society, discerning the 'signs of the times' in the real lives of the people. Starting with the social, political and economic experiences of ordinary Christians, this understanding of the church's role in the world emphasizes the transformation of unjust social systems, a perspective included in official statements by the CBCP but not taken up by the moderates.

Actually, the more democratic model of church advocated by the progressives is ambiguous. It uneasily includes two competing views of authority and mission in one ecclesiology. The tensions between the traditionalist view of the bishop as the final authority within the local church and the prophetic-participatory idea of authority ascending from the people of God are left unresolved.

Tensions within the progessive programme for the local church have led to a series of confrontations over the past three years. Much of the controversy has been in the Christian areas of Mindanao whose bishops, signficantly, have mostly belonged to the activist vanguard within the hierarchy.

The first struggle has been for control of the basic Christian communities (BCC). The BCC were a church initiative to encourage local community organization, attracting ordinary Filipinos back to a closer involvement in the church (in the conservative view), or enabling the poor to organize themselves and more effectively assert their right to social justice (in the progressive view). What remained unclear in the case of progressive bishops was where the authority of the BCC and the authority of the local bishop met.

This issue was addressed recently by Bishop Julio Labayen, a prominent spokesman for the activist-progessive position. Bishop Labayen emphasized that while the 'prime actors in social change are the people's organisations' and 'the role of the church is to support these organisations', the church must remain 'free to suggest, criticise and even withhold support in extreme cases'. The church could not be identified with a particular people's group. 'Once it is a partisan supporter it is dragged into the world of half-truths, manipulation, scheming and dishonesty...' (speech at international seminar on development and justice, Galway, Ireland, 16 June 1983, quoted in Asia Link 5(September) 1983:2-3). It was the bishops' responsibility to guide and correct the lay leaders of the BCC. Archbishop Mabutas, president of the CBCP, in a letter warning against Marxist infiltration of church organizations, put this warning more strongly:

> It is...an injunction of the church that these small communities must remain attached to the local church in which they are inserted and to the universal church under the leadership of the Pope. They must not allow themselves to be ensnared by political polarisation or fashionable ideologies (quoted in Shoesmith 1983:1).

The regime's view of the BCC is probably that put forward in the Quarterly National Security Review article on contemporary religious radicalism:

> What is now emerging as the most dangerous form of threat from the religious radicals is their creation of the so-called Basic Christian Communities in both rural and urban areas. They are practically building an infrastructure of political power in the entire country (Kintanar 1979).

The progressive bishops, as alarmed by the danger of 'infiltration' of church organizations as the conservatives and moderates, and as unwilling to set aside their episcopal authority, can repudiate the BCC in their dioceses, but only at great cost. By doing so, they risk losing their credibility and authority in any case with the lay leaders of the more politicised BCC and with the significant minority of clergy and religious who support the popular struggle for social justice.

Bishop Claver, in particular, has been acutely aware of this dilemma. In the late 1970s, Claver was still arguing, despite the risks, that 'the notion of the Church of *the Poor' (expressed in the BCC) consists essentially of 'letting the poor think for themselves...of supporting them in the action they themselves define as leading to their common good...' (Claver 1976). But his experience in Bukidnon confronted him with the problem of 'a growing number of priests and religious, other Christians who - even in the context of 'Progressive Christianity' - are going more and more for a strictly Marxist option (Claver n.d.).

The controversy over control of the BCC pales in comparison with the much more savage dispute which again involved the bishops of Mindanao with their own Mindanao-Sulu Pastoral Conference (MSPC) secretariat, the co-ordinating agency for social action programmes in the south.

For two days, over 30 April-1 May 1981, the bishops of Mindanao interrogated Bert Cacayan, Executive Secretary of the MSPC secretariat. The lay staff of the secretariat were charged by individual bishops with espousing revolutionary violence and class war in MSPC publications, using Marxist-influenced structural analysis, having connections with radical underground groups, and denying the bishops proper control over the church's own organization. One bishop defended the secretariat, arguing that 'democracy is not working; therefore, people have no other choice left but revolution' (minutes of Mindanao Bishops Meeting, Malasag, Bethania Retreat House, Cagayan de Oro City, 30 April-1 May 1981). While most of the bishops were hostile, basic points of disagreement among their own understanding of the church's social mission emerged during the interrogation.

An exchange between the executive secretary and a number of bishops during this meeting is revealing for the theological confusion dividing the bishops themselves, a confusion which helps explain the apparent inability of the hierarchy to respond decisively in the present crisis:

Archbishop Mabutas: Bert, you talk about ecclesiology as the People of God. This is the problem because the Holy Father during his visit to Davao expressed that the ecclesial character of communities is under the authority of their respective bishops. Therefore, one's understanding of the church must be in accord with his bishop.

Bert: I learned my ecclesiology which is that of the People of God with co-responsibility and co-participation as attendant features from my own Bishop.

Archbishop Mabutas: Who is your bishop? Does he agree with this?

Bishop Morelos: Yes, this is the ecclesiological model of the Vatican II. And time and again we have tried to live the principles of co-participation and co-responsibility especially among our lay people.

Bishop Claver: There is no problem with the principle. It is in the interpretation of People of God where

the error could lie. There is an orthodox
interpretation and a wrong one such as people of
God that excludes the bishops. The Secretariat
and the Board cannot decide for the whole church
nor for each diocese. The autonomy of each
diocese must be respected.

The following year the bishops severed their connection with
MSPC and they boycotted the fifth MSPC conference in Davao
City in 1983, urging clergy and religious not to
attend - with little success. At that conference, MSPC
changed its name to the Mindanao Interfaith People's
Conference.

The 'infiltration' issue

The parting of the ways between the Mindanao bishops and
their own secretariat, a parallel if less decisive conflict
between the CBCP and NASSA, and controversy over the
direction and control of the BCC, all took place in an
atmosphere of internal crisis within the church. The
Apostolic Nuncio, in an address to the CBCP in 1979, called
on the Philippine bishops to confront the problem of radical
infiltration of church organizations (Archbishop Francisco
Cruces, 'Safeguards against leftist infiltration in the
Church', Commission on Doctrine and Faith, December 1981).
Two years later, the bishops came into possession of a
nineteen-page position paper, apparently drafted by the
Communist Party of the Philippines, which analysed various
groups within the church and put forward a strategy to
'neutralise and divide the ruling classes and reactionaries'
while 'winning over the middle forces to the revolutionary
cause'. Two key areas of working through church programmes
were identified: encouraging progessive church workers to
work among the masses and be radicalized by this experience,
and penetrating church social justice offices to mobilize
support for 'people's organisations and anti-fascist
protests'.

The ideal situation is to have at least one
national democratic collective within each
progressive mass organisation, justice-oriented
church office or project, religious congregation,
seminary etc. The collective would form the
underground network within the sector (CPP n.d.).

The Marxist 'infiltration' issue helps explain why the
minority of progressive bishops were perhaps louder in
denouncing the revolutionary option after 1981 than the
moderate majority. It was the progressives' social action
programmes which were apparently the target for communist
manipulation.
    Bishop Claver, in a series of reflections following the
Mindanao bishops' decision to withdraw from MSPC, defended

the decision because the MSPC secretariat 'has been following a definite ideological line - sympathy at least, outright support at the most, for the National Democratic Front option: the armed struggle'. The secretariat, without the knowledge of the bishops, pushed projects which advanced the NDF revolution. There was strong evidence that some of the staff were card-carrying members of the Communist Party, he claimed.

> The churches of Mindanao-Sulu are being used to further a political end that some in the Secretariat and Board have decided we must all support because, so their constant refrain goes, "the people have so decided". It is bad enough for us to be used, simply used. It is worse when we do not agree with the end for which we are used, and worst of all when those ends go against everything we hold sacred as Christians (Bishop Francisco Claver to Bishop Fernando Capalla, Malaybalay, 15 May 1982).

The struggle between radicals and progressives in the church is over real issues where, ultimately, compromise may not be possible. The bishops are defending what they see as the essential principle of episcopal responsibility and authority. All the bishops, including the progressives, reject the ideology of class struggle and revolutionary violence.

The costs of the internal struggle are great. The action of the progressive bishops over the past three years to repudiate the revolutionary left has left radical (but not Marxist) clergy and laity with no role in the official church. The bishops' move against infiltrators is becoming a self-fulfilling prophecy. The strategically crucial group of Christians between the progressive and revolutionary positions could be driven into the National Democratic Front.

Claver himself has recongized the bishops' fear that 'by our action we are forcing the formation of a 'parallel church'. This alternative church, rejected by the bishops, could not call itself Holy, Roman, Catholic and Apostolic but

> in the supposition that bishops are expendable in one's concept of Church - a Church of the People in the sense that it is being used today by sympathisers with the Left - we already have de facto such a Church...(Claver n.d.).

The internal struggle is also weakening the bishops' ability to act decisively at a time of acute national crisis. The two major statements issued by the CBCP in the past year illustrate their distraction with the revolutionary threat within the church, confusing their policy towards the regime. The joint pastoral letter, 'A dialogue for peace', of 20 February 1983, followed an escalation of regime moves against the church. Yet the letter (reprinted in Ichthys 25 February 1983) is more concerned with balancing criticism of the regime with criticism of the left than putting an unequivocal challenge to the Marcos government:

> we...reprobate any action or program that runs counter to the primary values of the Gospel: the torture and murder of citizens simply because they are of a different political persuasion from that of present or would-be powerholders; the silencing of people; the suppression of the media, merely because they speak the truth of our national situation; the increasing use of arms and violence, both by forces on the right and the left, in pursuit of their ends of power; and closer to home, the use of Church funds, the manipulation of Church programs, for the political purposes of ideological groups.

This divided message is repeated in the bishops' response to the Aquino assassination in the joint statement, 'Reconciliation today', of 27 November 1983. Criticism of the regime is stronger but again it is balanced by criticism of the revolutionary movement:

> Many events have pushed our country closer to the brink of chaos and anarchy. Among these events are numerous unexplained killings, the heinous crime of assassination at the Manila International Airport, the worsening economic insecurities brought about by inflation and devaluation, the widespread clamour for justice dramatised by all sectors of our society through rallies, demonstrations and strikes.

The bishops do not reject the legitimacy of the regime; rather, they call for 'reconciliation as an alternative to the continuance of present injustices and violence which would put brother against brother in a bloodbath of revolution where the gospel ethic of love would undeniably be sacrificed'. The statement directs 'Christians who believe in armed revolution to consider their option against the unique demands of Gospel love and the deepest feelings of our countrymen who yearn for a peaceful and non-violent solution to the problems of our country' ('Reconciliation today', a statement of the Catholic Bishops Conference of the Philippines, 27 November 1983, reprinted in Ichthys 2 December 1983).

The revolutionary option

Christian revolutionaries have their own history in the Philippines. A number of Filipino priests were active local leaders of the revolution of 1896-1898 and continued to act as officials of an alternative, underground government in some provinces into the early American colonial period.

The present Christian revolutionary movement had its origins in the late 1960s and early 1970s, a period of intellectual ferment and student radicalism preceding the imposition of martial law. Christians for National Liberation (CNL) was a founding member of the revolutionary coalition, the National Democratic Front, in which the Communist Party of the Philippines is the moving partner (Roekaerts 1981). Fr Edicio de la Torre, the inspirer of CNL, spent most of the martial law period under detention. His short-lived release in late 1981 may have encouraged CNL to revive its programme, after a period of relative inactivity.

The CNL ideology combines elements of Latin American liberation theology with secular Maoism. In the 'Program of the Christians for National Liberation' released in 1981, the CNL explains the Christian revolutionary's commitment to the struggle for national democracy as

> the historical expression of our vocation to help build God's kingdom. It is the political incarnation of our Christian faith at the present stage of Philippine history.

> Our belief in Jesus Christ calls us to incarnate our Christianity, to give it flesh and blood. This we seek in the passion, death and resurrection of the Filipino people - the people's democratic revolution.

The people's war 'takes the main form of armed struggle. But it fights on all possible fronts: armed and non-armed, secret and open, legal and illegal...' The CNL defines its task as helping to build a united front of all revolutionary and progressive forces under the leadership of the NDF (CNL n.d.).

As an organization of Christians, the CNL sees its particular work as involving the Christian churches on the side of the people's struggle. Historically, the churches have fought on the side of the counter-revolution but

> revolutionary and progressive Christians need to wage a disciplined and sustained struggle within the Christian churches if only to deny the people's enemies the full use of the churches' moral and material resources.

> We can struggle for even more. We must try to mobilise as much of the churches' resources as we can for the people's struggle. In the process, we create the conditions for transforming the churches themselves (ibid.).

The CNL understands its role as, first, to co-operate with other revolutionary groups in the 'overthrow of the US-Marcos dictatorship and the establishment of a people's coalition government', and secondly, to develop a revolutionary mass movement of Christians which will radically transform the churches themselves. The armed struggle also calls for a cultural struggle:

> Our enemies...use imperialist, feudal-comprador, and fascist culture to keep the people passive, confused and divided.... Hence our task: to promote a culture that would teach people to rely on themselves, on their collective efforts, to solve the problems that confront them...

> In a special way, religious culture is used by our enemies to mystify and domesticate the people... We want to deny to our enemies the religious legitimacy they possess. More positively, we want to offer the concepts and symbols of Christianity to the people: to help strengthen the resolve and sense of injustice as they struggle...(ibid.).

The CNL identifies the 'transformation of the unjust structures of the churches' as part of the revolutionary struggle. This will mean the transformation of the churches' political function as supporters of the counterrevolution into supporters of the revolution, a long-term objective which will be achieved only as part of the general revolutionary transformation of Philippine society. The short-term objective is to widen the rift between church leaders and the regime, preventing full collaboration.

The transformation of the churches will also mean radical changes in the churches' internal structures:

> We want more self-determining and more self-administering churches. We are against all forms of feudal and imperialist relations with foreign churches and bodies. We want more indigenous forms of religious expressions, a Filipino theology, liturgy and spirituality. We want more democratic church structures, with more democratic participation in choosing leaders, defining programs, shaping structures and sharing resources... Our understanding of the church as primarily people, the people of God, urges us to create more democratic structures in our churches (ibid.).

The revolutionary theology of CNL reverses the model of church authority held by the conservatives and takes ideas of participation, identification with the poor, and prophetic action on behalf of justice to a logical extreme unacceptable to the progessives. The CNL is undoubtedly correct when it judges that its programme for the church can only succeed after the revolution has succeeded but, just as the bishops have the power to deny the regime moral legitimacy in a Christian Philippines, the 'Christian Left' can reinforce the moral legitimacy of the National Democratic Front among Filipino peasants whose world view and values are rooted in their religious culture.

In this sense, Christian revolutionaries, though a minority rejected by church leaders, may play a central role in determining whether, in the longer term, the revolutionary option will succeed.

FOOTNOTES

1. The first major statement by the CBCP on the martial law situation was in the Joint Pastoral Letter, 'Evangelisation and Development', of 25 July 1973, where the bishops acknowledged the church's responsibility for encouraging 'internal colonialism' and 'the collective sin of unjust and anachronistic structures'.

2. An important struggle over church property took place in 1978 when Herminio Disini's Herdis companies moved to take over Philippine Trust Co., the financial institution with substantial church holdings (Asian Wall Street Journal (M.T. Malloy) 5 August 1978). Disini is a cousin through marriage of the president's powerful wife.

Chapter 6

THE MILITARY

Felipe B. Miranda

This paper attempts to define three alternative scenarios for post-Marcos Philippines and the role the military could play in each situation. All scenarios are set within three years, a constraint which nevertheless permits a wide latitude in political imaging.

Three assumptions are made. The first reflects the conviction that the Philippines is more enduring than its most durable president to date. The second is that the welfare of Filipinos is better served by political regimes where the role of the military is least synonymous with the rule of the military. The third assumption is that underground political opposition of the national democratic type, despite recent trends indicating its growing success in political organizational work, will not take over power in the Philippines within the next three years.

The role of the military is explored in various situations, where (i) <u>within a year</u>, there is sudden or dramatic termination of the Marcos government due to natural or political causes; (ii) <u>from a year to two years</u>, the president is ousted due to 'pressure politics' precluding national reconciliatory sentiments; and (iii) <u>from two to three years</u>, the president resigns as a result of the same politics but without precluding the possibility of a national reprieve.

The main propositions advanced in the scenarios are: (1) the military option to take over political control must be considered a distinct possibility within the next three years; (2) this option becomes more difficult to take the longer it is delayed; (3) such delay is facilitated by increasing the operational capabilities of civilian political institutions; (4) currently the most critical need is for the aboveground opposition to build up and exercise capabilities best wielded within mass political groups or parties with restrained ideological platforms; and (5) military take-over becomes less imminent as the radical left desists from adventurism and continues its organizational work basically within the limits of united front activities.

Finally, the set of scenarios indicate that foreign political pressure must not be discounted in any active excercise of the military option in Philippine politics.

These scenarios are certainly not exhaustive of the many possibilities open to a currently rather volatile political system. In a sense they are even unsatisfactory scenarios, for they beg the more urgent question of how the present Philippines, with Marcos very much around, could change into another Philippines, with Marcos very noticeably absent. Or to put it more directly, how Marcos would be displaced from political pre-eminence.

The military in Philippine politics: an overview

Among students of the post-war Philippine military, there is consensus that up to 1972 this sector had not actively involved itself in Philippine politics (Hernandez 1979; Niksch and Niehaus 1981). Even during Magsaysay's incumbency as Secretary of National Defence and President of the republic, when he undoubtedly enjoyed national popularity and the extensive support of men in uniform, military support did not translate into political action straining either the principle of civilian supremacy or the notion of military professionalism. Though the military figured prominently in ensuring relatively clean and peaceful elections in 1953 and undertook civic action programmes with extensive socio-economic projects in the 1950s, the military was not popularly perceived as having assumed politicized roles.

Up to 1972 civilian control over the military was effectively shared by congress and the executive. While the latter had primary control over military operations, with the president constitutionally identified as the Commander-in-Chief of the armed forces, congressional control was also considerable. Congress effectively defined the military's budget, passed on the promotions of senior military officers and conducted investigations when military activities could be prejudicial to the public interest.

Constitutional regulation of the military was facilitated by a strong historical tradition of military submission to civilian authority. This tradition was particularly strong among military officers, the most senior of whom were trained in the US where their ethic of civilian control was further reinforced. A related factor was a marked preference among Filipinos for civilian over military careers, a preference which served to mimimize the prestige of the military. This bias probably reflected on the meagre pay and the minimal benefits which military men endured.

With the rise of Marcos to the presidency in 1965 and up to the declaration of martial law in 1972, the military's traditional low profile and its non-participatory role in civilian functions changed. During this period, President Marcos was instrumental in identifying roles for the military beyond the traditional ones of maintaining peace and order, defending the integrity of the national territory and securing national sovereignty. On the basis of presidential delineations, an analyst has been moved to describe the

Philippine military as a 'catalyst of social change', a 'training institution for national leaders', the 'defender of the seat of government', a 'nation builder', and a 'model of national discipline and self-reliance' (Maynard 1976: 337).

Marcos's involvement of the military in Philippine politics was even more extensive after 1972. His proclamation of martial law in September of that year was made only after his 'Twelve Disciples' (every one a military man except Juan Ponce Enrile, the then Secretary of National Defence) had concurred. Under martial law, the expansion of military participation into civilian areas of operation was unprecedented in Philippine history. The record has moved a student of the Philippine military to remark:

> Under martial law, the military became the primary basis of regime support as well as the partner of the martial law regime in implementing governmental policies. Soon after the proclamation of martial law, Congress was disbanded, political parties were prescribed, the media was controlled and civil liberties were curtailed. In a country with no militaristic tradition, where the military was traditionally low keyed and had a low profile, the military became visible, performing an expanded security and law and order role, a new judicial role, greater management and administrative and development roles, and a new political role (Hernandez 1983: 17).

Elaborating on that 'new political role', Hernandez adds:

> Perhaps the most significant political role of the [military] since 1972 has to do with its replacement of the traditional politicians as dispensers of political patronage in the political system. Feeling the change in the distribution of political power, many petitioners transferred their locus of operations from the traditional politicians to the officer corps.

> ... a number of officers also act as officials of certain political subdivisions (towns, sub-provinces, etc.) where internal security is minimal. Like the military PRODs [Presidential Officers for Regional Development], they enjoy executive and administrative powers within their respective political subdivisions as well as political patronage and a political base (ibid.: 24).

The martial law legacy of military participation in Philippine politics has continued, with many military officials still actively functioning in civilian posts. The government indicated in October 1983 that a campaign to revert these military men to their original units was going to be pursued.(1) Less than a month later, however, a reversal appeared to have occurred. No less than the president himself, pointing out that civilian-military collaboration was critically indicated by the times, called in the armed forces Chief-of-Staff and the most senior generals to attend a full cabinet meeting for the first time (Philippines Daily Express 5 November 1983). Subsequently it was revealed that these senior military officers were also going to be welcome at the caucuses of the Kilusang Bagong Lipunan (KBL), the Marcos-led party in power.

A review of the military in Philippine politics cannot be completed without remarking on the current structure of command and control for such a critical institution as the armed forces. It has earlier been noted that in pre martial law Philippines civilian institutions like congress and the executive jointly exercised control over the military. With the declaration of martial law and the subsequent abolition of congress, command and control functions were effectively exercised only by the executive. Up to the 1981 lifting of martial law, the President and his Secretary of Defence were the only civilian officials to whom the military operationally reported.

On 31 July 1983, in a remarkable clarification of civilian lines of authority over the military, the president stressed the principle of unity of command over the defence and military establishment (Philippines Bulletin Today 1 August 1983). Without explicitly noting what incident might have triggered his clarification, the president emphasized that although the Defence Minister was his 'alter ego', the latter was not part of the channel of command and could only act as the president delegated authority to him. The Chief-of-Staff, General Fabian Ver, was explicitly acknowledged as the president's direct link to the military, making the Chief-of-Staff part of this channel of command. As a necessary implication of the principle of unity of command, the president stressed that in the Philippines only he or his subordinate, authorized in writing, can order the transfer or assignment of military men, move military contingents, or be responsible for decisions of an operational character as regards the military. Thus, unless he explicitly authorizes his Minister of National Defence in writing, the latter civilian official posseses no operational command and control functions over the military. It is of some historical interest that when the president left on a state visit to Saudi Arabia in March 1982 his written instructions, covering the situation should anything happen while he was abroad, were left with General Ver.

Effectively, in the last fifteen years, command and control by civilians over the military has moved from multiple institutional control (congress and the executive), to single institutional, multiple official control (the executive, with the president and his Secretary/Minister of Defence as the civilian control officials) and, finally, to single institutional, single civilian official control (the executive, with the president being the sole civilian official with operational control over the military).

The current situation is logically precedent to a subsequent stage where no civilian control is present. It bears stressing that a logical development need not actually obtain and in point of fact has not occurred in postwar Philippine history. Nevertheless, the very volatility of present politics makes the logical a veritable possibility.

This possibility could well depend on the ability of military men themselves to consolidate political control within their sector. If unified command and control could be effected by politically conscious military officers, the likelihood of a military take-over in the Philippines would be enhanced. Thus, analysts of Philippine politics would do well to be sensitive to developments which appear to concentrate operational control within the military in the hands of a few military men. Such developments could even be facilitated by civilian political leaders who may look at the military as trump cards in dangerously desperate plays for power.

It is my belief that up to now the military has enough officers and men who can make the institution a force for freedom and democracy. This belief appears to be shared by some civilians who have had extended experience with the military. For instance, the most credible aboveground oppositionist, former Senator Jose W. Diokno, a political detainee for several years, was reported as acknowledging the presence in the military of genuinely concerned [patriotic] military men. He implied that this type of man might be the majority in the services. The worst abuses by the military, after all, according to Diokno (as reported in The National Times 18-24 November 1983), could be attributed to some specific segments, military units like the Presidential Security Command and those concerned with intelligence work. Diokno's appraisal of the military needs to be borne in mind by those who desire and work for structural changes in Philippine politics. It will be a serious mistake for concerned Filipinos to give up on the military and incline it to assume, actively, political roles which pit it against the citizenry.(2)

The expanding military: manpower and finance

The military's increasing participation in civilian government has been attended by rapid growth in manpower and an impressive increase in its financial outlay. From about 58,000 men in 1971, the Armed Forces of the Philippines (AFP), grew to 67,000 in 1975 and approximately 113,000 in 1982. Para-military forces are currently estimated at about 110,500 (this includes 43,500 in the Philippine Constabulary, 65,000 in the Civil Home Defence Force, and another 2,000 in the Coast Guard). Reserves for all services are reported to be about 124,000. Thus, in 1982 about 347,000 men comprise the Philippine military and its reserves.(3) One out of every 145 Filipinos is either with the active military or could be activated to join it.

The national defence budget has increased from P367 million in 1970 to P8,212 million in 1983, accounting on the average for about 15.3 per cent of the annual national budget. (See Table 6.1.)

Table 6.1

Philippine national and defence budgets, 1970-1983

Year	National budget (P million)	Defence budget (P million)	Defence as percentage of national budget
1970	3,196	367	11.5
1971	3,462	413	11.9
1972	4,574	608	13.3
1973	5,639	842	14.9
1974	8,606	1,392	16.2
1975	20,169	2,962	14.7
1976	22,399	2,918	13.0
1977	23,759	5,381	22.6
1978	28,681	5,845	20.4
1979	32,236	5,579	17.3
1980	37,894	5,864	15.9
1981	50,320	7,108	14.1
1982	57,092	8,312	14.6
1983	61,838	8,808	14.2

Source: Annual National Budgets, 1970-1983.

In terms of constant 1979 dollars, Philippine military expenditures increased by 279 per cent, from $US 193 million in 1971 to $US 732 million in 1980. Among ASEAN counries, Philippine increases for the period cited are the highest, followed by Malaysia (193 per cent) Thailand (62 per cent), Singapore (53 per cent), and Indonesia (51 per cent). This phenomenal increase in military expenditures is noteworthy considering that from 1971 to 1980 Philippine GNP increased only by 75 per cent, compared to Thailand's 81 per cent, Indonesia's 85 per cent, Malaysia's 100 per cent and Singapore's 110 per cent (Pauker 1983:11-13).

Prospects for further military expansion:
stress signals

Some factors suggest that, unfortunately, the build-up

in military resources will probably continue. Philippine society is currently a highly stressed system, as indicated by the increased strength of the leading radical group, the communists; the nation-wide deterioration of peace and order conditions; the increased restlessness of labour and the growing tendency to public protest actions by increasingly large numbers of people from all walks of life. Where government's ability to politically manage and defuse social stress weakens, the temptation is maximized to strengthen the military and rely on it for stress confrontation.

The communist challenge

The expansion in military personnel and resources in the early 1970s was primarily occasioned by a strong Muslim secessionist movement (the Moro National Liberation Front) which required extensive deployment of AFP units in the south.(4) At this time the AFP did not have to contend much with the communists whose radical organization, the Communist Party of the Philippines (CPP), and its military arm, the New People's Army (NPA), suffered organizational and operational reverses soon after the declaration of martial law in 1972. In the second half of the 1970s, however, a resurgence in communist activity was most noticeable. Increasingly successful organizational work and enhanced operational military capabilities indicated the growing viability of communists in the Philippines. The strength of the CPP-NPA has grown such that in 1982 the NPA was reported as having penetrated, if not being in control of, 20 per cent of the country's 40,000 barangays and able to count on 180,000 civilian sympathizers. With 3,500 to 5,000 armed guerrillas, the NPA was also reported to have 30 strategic guerrilla fronts, with provincial revolutionary committees in all of the 71 provinces (Makati Business Club 1982, Appendix: 4-5). The communists themselves appear to be more modest in their claims regarding the extent of operations of the NPA. They acknowledge non-operation in Batanes, some provinces in southern Luzon, and three provinces in Mindanao (Ang Bayan 7 October 1983). Even higher estimates are offered by foreign analysts working with American intelligence reports. (For instance, NPA strength is estimated in 1982 by Larry Niksch to be about 6,000 armed regulars 'with a support base of from several thousands to several millions'. The same analyst notes that other estimates of NPA guerrillas go as high as 30,000 armed regulars operating in Central Luzon, Bicol peninsula, the Visayas and eastern Mindanao (Niksch 1982:69-70). Another analyst speaks of two million NPA sympathizers, or about 4 per cent of the population! (Niehaus 1982:11).)

The communist resurgence has been indicated by the increasing number of NPA encounters with the military. Reported military encounters with all dissident groups (NPA, MNLF, and unspecified elements) increased by 248 per cent between 1977 and 1982, with the NPA share of encounters rising by 417 per cent and the MNLF's by 113 per cent. For the same period, average annual rates of increase in reported encounters with the military are 60 per cent for the NPA, 27 per cent for the MNLF, 28 per cent for unspecified elements, and 31 per cent for all groups. Clearly, the NPA has become the primary group challenging the military. (See Table 6.2.)

Table 6.2

Reported military-dissident encounters, 1977-1982

Group	1977	1978	1979	1980	1981	1982
NPA	70	67	106	83	252	362
MNLF	38	32	34	76	117	81
Unspecified	137	152	128	218	319	409
All Groups	245	251	268	377	688	852

Sources : Bulletin Today, Daily Express, Times Journal, WE Forum, New York Times, and Far Eastern Economic Review

Peace and Order

The deterioration of peace and order, yet another factor that could point to the expansion of military resources and the intensification of military (together with police) operations in the country, is underscored by the increasing national crime rate for the period 1971 to 1981. As estimated from data provided by the Philippine Constabulary, the national crime rate showed consistent annual improvement from 1971 to 1976. In 1971 it was 247 crimes per 100,000 population. By 1976, the rate had dropped to 183. This trend was reversed starting 1977, rising to 212 in that year and to an estimated 313 by 1982. (See Table 6.3.) It is noteworthy that this deterioration in the national crime rate was recorded even as the Metro Manila crime rate registered consistent annual improvements from 1971 to 1981. (See Table 6.3.) The implication appears to be either that there was a significant underreporting of crime in the primate city, or else that the non Metro Manila areas had experienced truly dramatic increases in criminal activity. The latter possibility points to an ominous situation, one where traditionally peaceful, largely rural Philippines might have undergone a dramatic breakdown of peace and order in the period 1977 to 1981.

Table 6.3

Annual national and Metro Manila crime rates
(per 100,000 population), 1971-1981

Year	National	Metro Manila
1971	246.6	1706.9
1972	235.8	1675.6
1973	231.4	1498.8
1974	207.5	1566.7
1975	184.3	759.4
1976	182.8	583.4
1977	211.9	512.4
1978	243.8	460.0
1979	248.9	355.3
1980	279.0	304.3
1981	286.8	274.6(a)
1982	313.2(b)	n.a.

Source: Philippine Constabulary data. Originally provided
in monthly form, the PC data have been recast into
annual figures.

(a) PC data available only from January to June 1981;
multiplied by two to approximate a year's figure.

(b) 1982 estimate taken from Ramos 1982-83:110. Estimates
for all other years are based on official data provided
by the PC before the Ramos article was published.

Restless labour

Labour unrest has also picked up. Strike notices and
actual work stoppages have been on the increase at least
since 1979. By 1981 the number of strikes and workers
involved had reached the highest since martial law was
declared in 1972, indeed since 1957. Between 1980 and 1981
alone, strike notices increased by 117 per cent, actual
strikes by 337 per cent, workers involved by 383 per cent,
and man-hours lost by 656 per cent. (See Table 6.4.) The
lifting of martial law and, perhaps even more, the
deteriorating economic position of labour appeared to have
triggered this explosive mass activity. The worsening
economic conditions since then and in the immediate future
hold little hope of dampening this tendency towards labour
militancy.(5).

Protest Actions

Citizen protest actions erupted in September 1983, soon
after the burial of ex-Senator Benigno Aquino, the

assassinated opposition leader. In Metro Manila alone, from 1 September 1983 to 31 October 1983, seventy-seven anti-administration rallies were reported by pro- administration media to have taken place, involving well over a million people (Miranda 1983). Workers, professionals, businessmen, the religious, students and just about every group of citizens took part in these massive outpourings of national resentment in Metro Manila and other areas of the republic. There is no evidence suggesting that these forms of mass protest have run their course. On the contrary, one may anticipate a spill-over of these mass actions to other urban centres in the country.

Table 6.4

Number of new strike notices filed, actual strikes, workers involved and man-hours lost, 1966-1981

Year	New strike notices filed	Actual strikes	With notice (c)	With -out notice	Workers involved	Man-hours lost(d) ('000)
1966	612	108			61,496	6,050
1967	561	88			47,524	5,575
1968	569	121			46,445	4,676
1969	621	122			62,803	8,533
1970	819	104			36,852	7,958
1971	979	157			62,138	11,434
1972(a)	1,043	69			33,396	8,029
1973						
1974						
1975(b)	13	5	1	4	1,760	31
1976	305	86	40	46	70,929	1,713
1977	146	33	23	10	30,183	274
1978	295	53	24	29	33,731	1,250
1979	316	48	24	24	16,728	1,391
1980	362	60	31	31	20,902	842
1981	784	260	155	155	98,585	6,368

Source: Data from Bureau of Labor Relations and MOLE Regional Offices.
(a) Up to the month of September, since all work stoppages were prohibited due to martial law.
(b) December 1975 only
(c) Prior to martial law establishments were not required to file notices of strike.
(d) For 1966 to 1972 man-hours lost are computed by multiplying reported man-days idle by 8.

The scenarios

The first scenario envisages the sudden termination of the Marcos government due to natural or political causes. This contingency presents the greatest possibility for an outright military take-over, or at least the veiled control by the military in a modified political regime. Given the military's increasing ability to consolidate political control within itself, the current underdevelopment of possible countervailing civilian political institutions, and further given the incipient character of organizational work among aboveground oppositionists, the sudden demise of Marcos, either as a result of failed health or loss of political control over erstwhile subordinates, presents a great temptation for politicized military elements to take over directive functions in government. Such military control might be exercised in a regime where the military openly rules, amidst claims of temporary political dominance to ensure social order and until such time as civilian government may once more normally operate. Or military predominance might be exercised in a regime where civilian figure-heads are allowed to formally make decisions.

The second scenario is characterized by the persistence of 'pressure politics', a term popularized by a leading oppositionist to indicate sustained, concerted organizational work, underground or aboveground, focused on destabilizing Marcos's political control through a series of informational activities (e.g. 'truth forums'), mass sectoral and multi-sectoral rallies and demonstrations, and formal organizational build-up, increasingly directed towards creating national political opposition groups and parties. Pressure politics might be extended to include all efforts at eroding the political foundations of authoritarianism and building new bases for more democratized politics. Clearly not a new phenomenon, pressure politics has continued to gain critical mass in the wake of recent political events and the ensuing further deterioration of an economy gone critical even before the Aquino assassination.

In its earlier, renascent stage, that is soon after Aquino's murder, pressure politics was not systematically at work, most of its manifestations reflecting fairly spontaneous public outrage over Aquino's murder yet not quite able to mobilize citizens in organized, partisan political work. The rise of broad-spectrum associations like the Justice for Aquino, Justice for All (JAJA) movement, the August Twenty One Movement (ATOM) and recently the Nationalist Alliance points to the possibility that this initial, renascent stage is even now being transcended. Within the next two years viable aboveground national organizations, even political parties with much greater effectiveness and appeal than the United Nationalist Democratic Organization (UNIDO), could arise. The emergence of such organizations could be facilitated by more focused organizational work among various sectors of Philippine society, in particular urban and rural workers, businessmen, the religious, and youth. United front strategies within the next two years could be made more viable through collaboration of sectoral elements whose ideological differences would be much less pronounced than at present. Thus several united fronts might spearhead the process of pressure politics in the next two years.

Within this period, pressure politics would probably be attended by realignments, even desertions, by political actors hitherto supportive of the Marcos government. Political institutions could become increasingly responsive given a growing systematic impact of pressure politics. The Supreme Court and the <u>Batasan</u> might yet surprise the citizenry with progressively independent actions. Even the regime's KBL may show stress signs indicated by a growing list of deserters or, at least, party policy dissenters.

With national emotions still running high, largely propelled by sustained economic difficulties and outraged memories of the Aquino assassination, the will towards national reconciliation may not be sufficiently strong to permit a presidential resignation. Even if the formal act turned out to be a resignation, a belligerent national mood might dictate the operational dynamics to be one of presidential ouster.

The military's role in this scenario is challenging, for several options are open. As its more politicized elements continue to undertake internal consolidation work, the option to capture political power as in scenario 1 remains. Within the military, the politicized elements could rally rank and file to protect institutional or corporate interests gained during the Marcos period.

Beyond the military, these elements may point to the active organizational and mobilizing work in the various civilian sectors, as indicative of mounting social disequilibrium, necessitating firm action by the military to restore social order. To the extent that pressure politics is perceived as ideologically inspired and controlled by the radicals, there will be an increasing temptation for the military to take over political control. Again such control might be directly or indirectly exercised by a consolidated military.

The neutralization of this active military option would depend on the skill and effectiveness of civilian leaders of the political opposition. First, their organizational and mobilizing work could deliberately avoid a projection of the military as having been the sole or main support of the Marcos government. Instead the political opposition groups and their leaders in particular could work to alienate the politicized elements within the military. Campaigns could be launched to identify and publicize military men involved in graft and corruption, both within their own institution or beyond it. A similar campaign could isolate those who have abused the civil and political rights of citizens. Simultaneously, campaigns could be run seeking to build up military men with exemplary service records. Those with relatively well-developed professional, civilian-authority orientation could be publicly projected and their public image deliberately enhanced. This two-pronged strategy of isolating the politicized and enhancing the professional military men, specially at the higher echelons of military officialdom, to encourage rank and file perceptions of alternative loci of loyalty within the military, may well be one of the most crucial challenges of pressure politics.(6)

As part of this effort to curb the influence of politicized military elements, programmes could be publicized by the opposition guaranteeing military personnel at least their current material benefits, with clear commitments to significantly improving them should there come about a successful regime change.

Another move to help deactivate the option of military take-over is possible. It would depend for its success on the effectiveness with which pressure politics practitioners recruit and mobilize in language most of the military can identify with, or at least not be emotionally antagonized by. The military as a whole has a strong anti-communist orientation. Until such time as military men go through a programme of responsible 'brainrinsing', the lasting influence of irresponsible cold warrior programming, of 'brainwashing', cannot be simply wished away. If pressure politics aboveground is not to give up on the military, but instead prudently considers it vital to enlist military support, then appropriate means of communication which do not immediately disorient the military could be employed.

A significant depreciation in the influence of the politicized elements on the military activates a more prudent option for the military in this second scenario. Given political opposition groups and leaders which do not threaten their material interests, given further that such groups and leaders help secure their institutional survival and amelioration, there could be less inclination in the military to 'meddle in politics'. On the other hand, there would be a greater incentive to maintain or recover their professional character as military men.

Thus, even as the military could continue to exercise some influence in Philippine politics, such influence would probably be wielded within its constitutional limits. Eventually, the military itself could set up internal mechanisms which monitor and automatically penalize the active politicization of more ambitious elements.

The third scenario assumes that while it is possible to consolidate political control within the military in two years, the gains which pressure politics realizes in the same period could be maximized even further. Thus, in this scenario mass political organization leads to at least one or more viable national political opposition parties; constitutional political institution building accelerates such that functional, independent judicial, legislative and electoral bodies emerge; and political processes such as elections might be reasonably contemplated at least by the aboveground political opposition.

Economic conditions in the third scenario will have become much less critical, with the public generally becoming more confident that better times could soon come. This economic optimism will reinforce political perceptions regarding the public's ability to help determine desired political outcomes. As a consequence, there probably would be a decrease in strident political demands. The national mood could be more reconciliatory than in the second scenario. The president may then be allowed to resign as he anticipates a popular repudiation should he run for reelection in 1987.

The military's role in this scenario may be considered with greater optimism than in the second one. Although a military with internal political control fully consolidated retains the option to capture political power, the longer this option is put off the harder it becomes to consider it and, furthermore, to make it work successfully. After all, the most effective check on illegitimate military intrusion is operational civilian political institutions. These are precisely the instruments which in the second and third scenarios are activated, survive and increasingly become viable. It is even likely that a virtuous circle could start operating in the third scenario. As civilian political organizations and formal constitutional processes become stronger, the momentum for maintaining political control within the military would become harder to sustain. The more professionally inclined, senior military men will gain greater status and wield more influence in their institution. They could therefore more effectively check their politicized counterparts. In turn, this development would permit greater dynamism and assertiveness by the civilian institutions. Part of this civilian gain would eventually translate into more effective monitoring and control by civilian agencies over the military, a process which would not be greatly resented by the latter since it involves the collaboration of reputable professional military men.

Foreign dimensions of post-Marcos Philippine military scenarios

So far the discussions of alternative scenarios has limited itself to a purely national context, where the exercise of the military option has been considered as depending upon the interplay between Philippine civilian and military structures. However, perhaps more than any other Philippine institution (with possibly only the Catholic church to parallel its situation), the Philippine military is fairly susceptible to foreign influence, and specifically American influence. This tendency is due to historical and political factors.

Historically, the modern Philippine military was fashioned with a great deal of American participation. Soon after the establishment of the Philippine Commonwealth in 1935, a deliberate plan was undertaken to organize a military largely patterned after American experience and military doctrine. General Douglas MacArthur was in charge of this task and the Philippine military which fought with the Americans in the Second World War was largely the result of his efforts.

After the war, the various military agreements between the Philippines and the US involved the close co-operation of their respective militaries. The Philippine military depended primarily on the US for its hardware and ordnance, but even more critically on advanced military training for its senior military officers. (The success of this collaborative effort might be indicated by the fact that practically all of the higher echelon Filipino officers, from colonels to generals, have taken advanced training in the US.) The more junior officers, on the other hand, went through the various Philippine military academies or undertook reserve officers training courses where American military strategy and tactics and operational field manuals were staple orientation items. Both senior and junior officers have often participated in the joint military exercises of both countries.

The battle experience of Philippine military men also helped orient them towards the US. In addition to fighting the Japanese as allies of the Americans, they have joined the latter in campaigns against the communists in Korea and Vietnam. Furthermore, in their local struggle with the Hukbong Mapagpalaya ng Bayan (HMB), the fighting arm of the Partido Kommunista ng Pilipinas in the 1940s and 1950s, Filipino military men worked very closely with American counter-insurgency operatives, the most famous of which was Brigadier-General (retired) Edward Lansdale.

Despite an official programme to develop a self-reliance posture for the Philippine military(7) and strong official pronouncements regarding the need to assert and operationalize Philippine sovereignty in American military bases in the Philippines, Philippine authorities, both civilian and military, have shown little haste in severing Philippine linkages with the American military establishment. The official policy which underscores the US as the Philippines's most reliable ally has remained intact and no Philippine president has moved to dismantle American military installations in the country in the past thirty-seven years. Although it has become more and more difficult to sustain the cold war contention that external communism threatens the country, or for that matter that there is an external threat to Philippine national security be it communist or non-communist, the official policy which identifies the US as helping guarantee Philippine security against external threats has remained.

Whereas Philippine interests advanced by a Philippine-American military alliance might be debatable, American interests in sustaining the alliance with the

Philippines and maintaining an extensive military presence in the country are easier to understand. As part of a general policy of communist containment by primarily American forces, the American military bases in Clark and Subic were indispensable in the 1950s, 1960s, and even the 1970s. In the 1970s and 1980s the expansion of Soviet naval capabilities in the Pacific and the strategic importance of increased American operational capabilities in the Persian Gulf and the Indian Ocean have conspired to enhance the importance of Clark and Subic as American military bases. The fall of South Vietnam to the communists in 1975 and the subsequent access of the Soviets to military facilities in Danang and Cam Ranh Bay made it even more imperative for the Americans to maintain their bases in the Philippines.(8)

Furthermore, in a country where internal communism and radical nationalism appear to have made some headway in the past seven years, the military bases could also be appreciated beyond the primarily military or security sense. Sizeable American investments in the country, conservatively estimated to be at least $US 1.5 billion in 1982, might have to be protected against any threatening development, whether one inspired by radical nationalism or another spearheaded by leftist forces.

Finally, as part of a foreign policy of prestige, American interest in the Philippines could go beyond the military and economic dimensions. In the Philippines, the US has its oldest and historically most reliable Asian ally, at one time its touted 'showcase' for democracy in Asia. Given American foreign policy which recently appears to reflect a resurgence of hardliners and neo cold warriors in Washington, the loss of the Philippines even to domestic communists would be grossly unpalatable. South Vietnam was a bitter pill to swallow for cold warriors; the Philippines, should it go the way of South Vietnam, could choke the Reaganites.

For military, economic and even psychological reasons then, the US cannot but view current and potential Philippine developments with a great deal of interest. The long train of American civilian and military officials, especially in the last six months, attests to a rather heightened concern with the Philippines.

American interests and the Philippine military option

The above delineation of Philippine military linkages to the American military and current American interests in the Philippines already suggests the scenario modifications which could influence the exercise of the military option in Philippine politics. In consonance with this delineation, American active support of a decision for the military to take over could come if either radical nationalists or the radical left were to emerge as the most viable oppositionists in the Philippines after Marcos has left the scene.

The radical nationalists, with programmes calling for the urgent dismantling of the American bases, a significant delinkage of the Philippine economy from the American market, and strict regulation of foreign multinational activities in the Philippines, would probably incline American policy-makers to support even an outright military regime or one where the military ruled behind the facade of civilian technocrats. Such a regime modification would probably be cosmeticized by initial American pressures to have the Philippine authorities commit themselves publicly to implementing 'new society' programmes. A replay of 1972 Philippines would then be likely, this time without so much concern as to whether a civilian regime has remained inviolate or a truly martial regime has taken over.

Given the primacy of American security considerations in the Philippines, considerations which make radical nationalism even a secondary factor in its global power calculus, the resurgence of the radical left must be viewed as the greater incentive for American endorsement of a Philippine military take-over. A largely anti-communist Philippine military would inevitably be perceived by American policymakers as an indispensable ally in its global crusade to contain communism.

In this case, defusing the option towards military rule in the next three years demands, as in the second and third scenarios discussed earlier, the rapid build-up of civilian political institutions by Philippine opposition forces which would forgo, at least tactically, their radical orientations. Nationalist oppositionists would have to reach some kind of modus vivendi with American security if not economic interests. Even as nationalist economic demands might continue to press for greater Filipinization of the economy (whatever the specific operational forms such demands might take), prudence might dictate a modification of nationalist demands regarding the military bases. The maintenance of an unqualified demand to dismantle these facilities cannot but push American policymakers and opportunistic, politicized elements in the Philippine military into each other's arms.

As for the radical left, a highly developed sense of strategy and tactics might contribute to delaying the exercise of the military option for political control. Prudence too might incline the left to undertake more united front work, greater organizational efforts and finer-tuned guerrilla mobilizational activities. The radical left in 1983 appears to be wary enough of leftist adventurism which decimated the Philippine left in the 1950s and the early 1970s. Unless it loses this sense of history and its indicated strategy by blurring its own perception of the its current position as one of 'advanced stage of strategic defence', the radical left could help delay overt military take-over in the Philippines.

Without an untimely provocation of American support for a military regime, it is going to be much less likely for politicized military men either to attempt military rule, or if the attempt is somehow nevertheless made, for such rule to endure. Thus, in examining the dangers that contribute to military take-over, one might conclude by noting them to be any combination of intransigent nationalism, adventuristic leftism, opportunistic militarism, and cold-warrior hegemonism. This phraseology might sound sloganistic, but the realities they reflect are too serious to be ignored.

Filipinos, in trying to defuse the possibility of military rule at least within the next three years need to maintain a sense of sustained struggle in all sectors of Philippine society. Organization and mobilization, undertaken with an appropriate strategic sense, win campaigns for national liberation. Conscientiously pursued, such work could enable even the military to find its rightful place in a national struggle for a truly new society.

FOOTNOTES

1. As of 31 October 1983 over a thousand military men were detailed outside of the AFP to work with various civilian agencies and private functionaries. In the Ministry of National Defence 637 officers and enlisted men were part of this detail.

2. A recently circulated statement of the CPP Central Committee lists as one of the six urgent things to be done, to 'neutralize and win over the enemy's soldiers and para-military men', noting that the vast majority of those comprising the military and para-military 'come from the ranks of the people' (Ang Bayan 7 October 1983).

3. These estimates are from the International Institute of Strategic Studies, as cited by the Far Eastern Economic Review's Asia 1983 Yearbook, p.30. As of November 1983 there appears to be no more than a +10 per cent difference between the IISS figures and those that may be arrived at using figures from local Philippine sources.

4. In the early 1970s, the MNLF's military arm, the Bangsa Moro Army was estimated to have from 5,000 to 30,000 armed fighters. In May 1977 at the Eighth Islamic Foreign Minister's Conference, Nur Misuari, the head of the MNLF claimed to have about 50,000 men in the BMA. Lieutenant General Fidel Ramos, vice Chief-of-Staff and chief of the Philippine Constabulary, estimates the MNLF in 1977 to have had a peak membership of 21,200 armed men and in 1982 to have decreased to 14,000 members (Ramos 1982-83:108-109).

5. In the first quarter of 1984 about 300,000 workers are expected to be laid off, according to economist Bernardo Villegas of the Center for Research and Communication

(Business Day 13 December 1983).

6. Within the present military, only the distinction between
   politicized and non-politicized military men appears to
   be of crucial significance. The politicized are those
   who, particularly during the martial law period, by their
   vital access to top political leaders and sensitive
   information, developed an appreciation of political power
   and the various advantages its possession confers. Some
   of these politicized military men, upon gaining political
   influence may be tempted to use it for personal material
   gain; others, in the fashion of ideal type political
   men, may use it to gain yet more. The non-politicized
   are those who have largely remained professional military
   men, often discomfited by political or quasi-political
   functions the military has had to assume. They may also
   be referred to as the 'constitutionalists', to indicate
   their strong adherence to the principle of civilian
   supremacy over the military.

   The traditional distinctions within the military,
   e.g. the Ilocano v. non-Ilocano and integree v.
   non-integree, do not appear to be so important at
   present. Many analyses reflect public impressions that
   being Ilocano or being an integree (or both) gives one a
   special advantage within the military, with the
   implication that relatively disadvantaged non-Ilocanos
   and regular non-integree officers must be getting
   restless.

   No systematic study has been offered to substantiate
   this popular thesis. Yet there appears to be evidence to
   the contrary. If one assumes that generalship reflects
   or is a product of the operational biases within the
   military (and even among those who are not military men
   but control the military), some interesting findings
   emerge. The ethnic factor does not appear to be crucial.
   As of November 1983 there were almost as many Ilocanos
   (36) as Tagalogs (35) among the 104 active General/Flag
   Officers. The non-Ilocanos (68) are almost twice as many
   as the Ilocanos. In terms of operational commands, such
   as the regional unified commands, there is no Ilocano
   majority. It is only in the intelligence services that
   Ilocano generals appear to be preferred.

   The integree officers (lateral entries into the
   military whose backgrounds are in law, business, teaching
   and other civilian professions, and whose integration
   into the military was basically due to their having
   completed advanced reserve officer training courses while
   in college) do not appear to receive higher priority than
   non-integree regular officers (those with professional
   military backgrounds as graduates of military academies
   or who rose from the ranks within the military). Using
   the same data set of 104 Generals/Flag Officers, the
   great majority (61) are graduates of military academies.
   This professional military background appears to be

emphasized even among Ilocanos. Of the 36 Ilocano generals, 21 are military academy graduates.

Incidentally, if integree generalship is assumed to be an indicator of political promotions, being Ilocano does not appear to be a dominant consideration. Only 18 of 53 integree generals are Ilocanos. Again, if the same assumption of political inspiration were made regarding the presidential decision to extend one's service beyond one's compulsory retirement period, neither being Ilocano nor an integree may be considered the crucial factor. Of 26 extendee generals, 15 are non-Ilocanos and at least 13 are graduates of military academies. Finally, one might consider as politically inspired the recall of generals from retirement. Of four generals recalled from the retired list, three are graduates of the military academies and only one is an Ilocano, who incidentally is also a Philippine Military Academy graduate. It is therefore clear that as regards these three dimensions of analysis, neither being an Ilocano nor an integree helps.

The continuing appeal to analysts of these traditional categories in identifying possible bases of loyalty within the military is puzzling. It appears to be due primarily to a tendency among students of the military to resort to outdated, or current but largely impressionistic, data. It is probably time to lay these traditional categories to rest (assuming they worked at all at any time) and to explore others which permit greater insight into the dynamics of current military sociology.

7. The military's Self-Reliance Defense Posture Program (SRDPP) reports that, in 1982, the AFP was 'self sufficient in small [arms] and ammunition such as [the] M16 Assault Rifle, 5.56 mm Ammunition, 60 mm and 81 mm Mortar Tube and Ammunition'. Its export of 'tactical radio communication sets and One Quarter Ton Mini-Cruisers' earned the military almost $US 900,000. Encouraged by inquiries from other countries interested in the M16 assault rifle, mortar tube, mortar ammunition, cal. 5.56 mm ammunitions, rifle grenades, air force practice bomb, M16 magazines and 110 kg bomb, the SRDPP underscores 'the vast potential of these non-traditional export commodities'. See 'The AFP Self-Reliance Defense Posture Program', in Civil Relations Services, Armed Forces of the Philippines, A Year of Solid Achievement: AFP Annual Report '82, Quezon City, pp. 57-60.

8. For a very candid appraisal of the practically indispensable character of the military bases at Subic and Clark, see Cottrell 1982. Cottrell acknowledges, 'Nowhere in the world do we [Americans] have a more important basing facility than in the Philippines', and concludes that '...prudence would dictate no relocation of either Subic Bay or Clark Air Base'.

Chapter 7

MUSLIM AND TRIBAL FILIPINOS

R.J. May

The conflict between Moro nationalists and the Marcos
government, which has been dragging on for over a decade, has
posed a significant threat to the stability of the regime.
Confrontation with tribal communities, over a widening front,
has added to the pressures on the regime. The problems, let
alone any answers to the problems, of Muslim Filipinos and of
the various tribal communities are by no means identical;
there are, however, sufficient common elements to the
problems of all ethnic or regional minority groups that there
is some sense in considering them together.

This paper addresses two questions: (a) how have the
actions (or inactions) of the Marcos regime influenced the
situations of Muslim and tribal Filipinos over the past ten
years or so? (b) what are the prospects for a more equitable
and conciliatory approach to the problems under another,
post-Marcos regime (and, by implication, what threats might
these groups pose to the stability of a post-Marcos regime)?

THE MORO PROBLEM

The 'Moro problem', or as the late Peter Gowing
(1979:216) once expressed it, 'the Moros' "Christian
problem"', has its roots in the pre-colonial period. Before
the Spaniards came to the Philippines in the sixteenth
century there were extensive Islamic sultanates in Mindanao
and Sulu and Islam was in the process of spreading north to
Mindoro, Luzon and the Visayas; marital and political
alliances linked the Philippines with the wider dar al-Islam
in Southeast Asia and Jolo was the centre of a trading
network which extended north to China and west to Java.

For some four hundred years the Moros successfully
resisted Spanish colonial rule before eventually succumbing
to the military superiority, and the persistence, of the
American administration. With the loss of their
independence, Muslim Filipinos - and many tribal groups - saw
their homeland progressively integrated into the larger
Philippine society, under regimes dominated first by the
Americans and then by Christian Filipinos from the north.
From the beginning of the century migration to Mindanao was
actively encouraged, by land grants to individuals and

AREAS OF MUSLIM CONCENTRATION

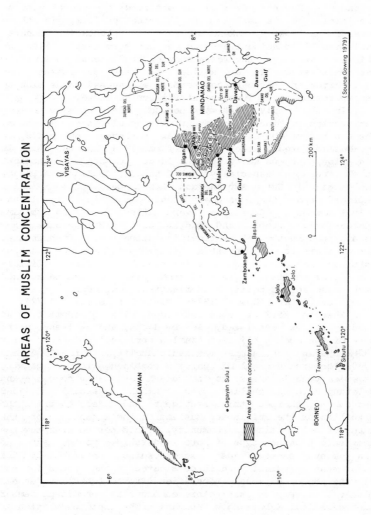

(Source Gowing 1979)

corporations and through a series of resettlement programmes. Between 1903 and 1939 migration added 1.4 million to the population of Mindanao, which at the end of the Spanish period had been estimated (though almost certainly underestimated) at 0.5 million. At the same time large amounts of foreign and (non-Muslim) domestic capital began to flow into Mindanao; 'Agriculture and commerce were expanded', Gowing (1979:36) has observed, ' - though most of the initiative, as well as most of the profits, in these enterprises were taken by American plantation owners, Christian Filipino settlers and Chinese merchants'. Even at this early stage the resentment of traditional communities was manifested in a series of anti-government and anti-Christian 'disturbances' and in widespread opposition to incorporation in an independent Philippine state.

In the early post-war period the already heavy inmigration to Mindanao substantially accelerated. Moreover, whereas before 1939 the bulk of new settlement took place in non-Muslim areas, the period from 1948 saw a shift in migration patterns which brought large numbers of settlers into areas - especially in Cotabato, Bukidnon, Davao, Zamboanga del Sur, Agusan and Lanao del Norte - which impinged upon the customary land ownership of Muslim and tribal groups. Conflicts over titles to land became increasingly common and Muslim and tribal groups, now handicapped by their historical isolation, were often cheated out of their land by Christian Filipinos and foreign business interests who were frequently assisted by corrupt officials and local elites. Alienated from their land and threatened with economic and political domination, some Moros resorted to violent action (Gowing 1979; Tan 1977; Stewart 1972).

Whereas earlier confrontations with government had tended to be localized, led by datus, and at least in the case of the much publicized 'Kamlon uprising' of the early 1950s having an almost messianic quality, in the 1950s and 1960s the ground-swell of unrest combined with a growing Islamic consciousness to produce a reasonably cohesive and militant Moro nationalism. The 'Jabidah massacre' of 1968 served to sharpen this sentiment and also to bring the situation of the Philippine Muslims to the attention of the international Islamic community. This period also saw the emergence of a new type of Moro leadership - young, educated (in many cases under scholarships provided by the government), radical - which culminated in the establishment of the Moro National Liberation Front (MNLF) under Nur Misuari, university instructor, commoner and prominent member of the radical Kabataang Makabayang. The rapid escalation of violence in the months leading up to the 1971 elections raised the death toll and caused extensive social and economic disruption among Muslim, tribal and Christian settler communities. One contemporary commentator described the situation: 'It is virtually a free-for-all. Muslims fighting Christians; government troops fighting Muslims; political private armies fighting Muslim or Christian farmers; private armies or hired goons fighting army men' (Glang 1972:7). It also served as a justification for the imposition of martial law in 1972.

The history of the recent unrest in the southern Philippines, and specifically of the conflict between the MNLF and the Marcos regime, has been well documented elsewhere (Gowing 1979; George 1980; Ahmad 1980; Noble 1976; May 1981); suffice it to say that after about fourteen years of bloody conflict, the war in the southern Philippines goes on and the Muslim population and the government seem no closer to reconciliation. In order to speculate sensibly on the future for Muslim Filipinos in a post-Marcos society, it is first necessary to understand how the present situation has developed, specifically: how has the government attempted to deal with the 'Moro problem' to date? and what is the current state of the Moro rebellion?

Policies towards Muslim Filipinos under the Marcos regime.

The responses of the Marcos regime to the problems posed by the 'disturbances' in the south have been at broadly four levels.

First, attributing the unrest to a sense of relative deprivation among Muslim Filipinos, the regime has made attempts to alleviate it through programmes of social and economic development combined with limited concessions to the religious and cultural demands of Moro nationalism. This line of approach, of course, pre-dates the Marcos administration. In 1957, following the report of a special committee of the Philippine Congress to investigate 'the Moro problem', a Commission on National Integration (CNI) was established to promote 'the economic, social, moral, and political advancement of the non-Christian Filipinos' as well as 'to render real, complete, and permanent' the integration of all 'national minorities'. The CNI, however, achieved little before being abolished in 1975 and in any case was never well received by Muslim Filipinos who took exception to the label 'national minority' and feared that the real objective of integration was the destruction of Philippine Muslim identity. Subsequently, in 1963 and 1971, a senate committee on national minorities reported on the deteriorating situation in the south; it identified inmigration and land-grabbing as the major sources of conflict but produced no real shift in policy, which remained integrationist and development oriented. Again, in 1973, as part of a package intended to win over dissident Muslims, Marcos announced a number of social and economic measures, including the establishment of the Muslim Amanah Bank, removal of restrictions on the historic barter trade with Borneo, creation of an Institute of Islamic Studies within the University of the Philippines, proclamation of Muslim holidays, and a number of specific projects. Commitment was

113

also made to the codification of Muslim laws (though this was not promulgated until 1977). A Presidential Task Force for Reconstruction and Development of the Southern Philippines (PTF-RAD) was set up to co-ordinate the efforts of the various agencies involved.

In 1975 the PTF-RAD was abolished, along with the earlier-established CNI, an earlier (but largely ineffective) Mindanao Development Authority and a Special Program for Assistance for the Rehabilitation of Evacuees (SPARE); in their place was created a Southern Philippines Development Authority (SPDA) which was charged with the responsibility 'to foster and accelerate the balanced growth of the southern Philippines ... for the national economic, social and political stability'. In 1979-80 the charter of the SPDA was revised to direct it to 'essentially development and economically viable ventures', while 'social development functions and non-corporate projects' were to be transferred to the appropriate agencies of government; at the same time, 'for closer administrative supervision' the SPDA was shifted from the Office of the President to the Ministry of Human Settlements (headed, of course, by Mrs Marcos). In 1980 the president also created a rehabilitation programme for MNLF 'and other allied groups/individuals now working/cooperating with all government development effort in southern Philippines', with a special fund of P25 million to be administered through the SPDA. Recent social development projects have included substantial assistance for madrasahs and mosques. The government has also established an Office (it was, briefly, a ministry) for Muslim Affairs, headed by Rear-Admiral Romulo Espaldon.

Secondly, playing on ideological and ethnic/regional differences within the Muslim population and on the insecurity of some non-Muslim Filipinos in the south, the Marcos regime has attempted to discredit the MNLF and to deny the strength of Moro nationalist sentiment. Thus in 1974, as the Islamic Conference of Foreign Ministers (ICFM) was attempting to bring the MNLF and the Philippine government together at the negotiating table, a consultative council of Muslim Filipino leaders was created under regime patronage and in June that year a conference at Marawi City, sponsored by the 'Federation of the Royal Houses of Mindanao and Sulu' (but in fact financed by the government), recorded a unanimous vote of confidence in President Marcos's leadership and presented a list of policy proposals which were broadly sympathetic with the government's attempts to deal with the situation through socio-economic reform. The following year, as negotiations in Jeddah between the Philippine government and the MNLF were in the process of foundering, Marcos orchestrated a series of peace talks in Zamboanga, at which selected Muslim leaders opposed the demands of the MNLF and rejected an agenda proposed by the ICFM. More generally, the regime has made strenuous efforts to enlist the support of conservative elements among Muslim leadership, to lure members of the MNLF out of the field with offers of amnesty and incentives ranging from cash grants, logging concessions and scholarships to military commissions, municipal office and seats in the regional assemblies, and to discredit the MNLF both by labelling it 'Maoist' and by holding it to blame for almost every act of violence and lawlessness occurring in the southern provinces. Also, although Marcos cannot claim all the credit, the divisions which have occurred in the overseas leadership of the movement since 1977 (see below) must be seen in this context.

Thirdly, under pressure from the international Islamic community the president has (within limits) negotiated with the MNLF over the settlement of Moro nationalist demands. In 1973, on the basis of representations from the MNLF supported by Libyan President Qaddafi, the ICFM discussed the situation of Muslim Filipinos. Following this discussion a fact-finding delegation was sent to the southern Philippines and its report was considered by the ICFM in 1974. A consequent resolution called on the Philippine government to put a stop to the violence against Muslim communities and to find a political and peaceful solution to the problem within the framework of the national sovereignty and territorial integrity of the Philippines. Fearful perhaps that the ICFM would accede to MNLF demands for an oil embargo against the Philippines if action were not taken, in early 1975 Marcos entered into negotiations with the MNLF, but the talks soon reached a deadlock, with the Philippine government accusing the MNLF of being manipulated by 'outside forces'. Attempts to revive negotiations made little immediate progress, despite the intermediation of the ICFM and of Qaddafi; however, they were resumed in Tripoli in December 1976 following a visit to Libya by Mrs Marcos. A ceasefire was negotiated and agreement reached on tentative provisions for a settlement. The provisions of this agreement, the 'Tripoli Agreement', included a Muslim-dominated autonomy in thirteen provinces of Mindanao, Sulu and Palawan, with separate legislature, administration, legal system, security forces, education, and financial and economic system, but with the right to participate in the central government. Further negotiations, scheduled for February 1977, were, however, abandoned, the MNLF rejecting the Philippine government's proposals for a referendum, the Philippine government accusing the MNLF of abandoning its earlier acceptance of regional autonomy and reverting to a secessionist position, and both sides accusing the other of ceasefire violations.

A subsequent exchange of telegrams between Marcos and Qaddafi produced an agreement to establish an autonomous region of thirteen provinces, to appoint a provisional government, and to organize a referendum to determine the administrative details. The MNLF, however, rejected an invitation to participate in the government and objected to the form and procedures of the proposed referendum; it was supported in this by the ICFM. Nevertheless the referendum was held, predictably producing a vote against the MNLF/ICFM-backed proposals for a single autonomous region and in favour of a more limited 'autonomy' along lines put forward earlier by Marcos. Autonomous regions have since been established in Regions IX (western Mindanao and Sulu) and XII (central Mindanao). With the MNLF, BMLO and Mindanao Alliance boycotting the elections for the regional assemblies in 1979, KBL candidates scored easy victories, the Commission on Elections reporting 'a general public apathy and apprehension over the credibility of the political exercise in the two regions'. The subsequent history of the assemblies (including further elections in 1982) has done little to restore credibility.

Since 1977, under continued pressure from the ICFM, the Philippines government has made what appear to be half-hearted efforts at reviving negotiations, but the preconditions set by Marcos (which have included action against perpetrators of ceasefire violations, and participation in any negotiations of all factions of the Moro movement) have been unacceptable to the MNLF. Nor has MNLF leader Misuari, for his part, displayed any willingness to compromise beyond the conditions he believes the government to have accepted in 1976; indeed in 1979 it was reported that Misuari had rejected the autonomist proposals of the Tripoli Agreement and had reverted to a hard-line demand for secession (a position which, however, the ICFM has subsequently refused to support). (Misuari's position is stated in Mahardika August 1980, and more recently in Arabia April 1984.) In 1980 talks scheduled in Kuala Lumpur and Jakarta aborted over the issue of preconditions and following a statement by a Philippines government official - later denied by the Foreign Affairs ministry - that the Tripoli Agreement was 'null and void'.

Meanwhile, in March 1982, on the eve of a visit by Marcos to Saudi Arabia, the speaker of the Region XII assembly and former MNLF Vice-Chairman, Abul Khayr Alonto, published a booklet, addressed to Marcos, which severely criticized the operation of the regional assemblies (Alonto 1982). Alonto called for the merger of the two regions and the granting of 'a meaningful and substantive autonomy' to a single assembly, in accordance with the Tripoli Agreement. The publication was suppressed by the government and Alonto was dropped from Marcos's Saudi Arabia entourage and from the KBL ticket for the 1982 regional assembly elections. Nevertheless on his return from talks with King Khalid Marcos announced that the executive council of the two regions would be merged and steps have since been taken to implement this (Dansalan Quarterly III(4) 1982).

Notwithstanding an invitation from Marcos, Misuari again boycotted the regional assembly elections, and attempts by the government to get Salamat to accept the chairmanship of the restructured regional executive council also failed. In mid 1982 it was reported, amidst a spate of coronations of new sultans, that the government was planning a role for traditional Muslim leadership in the new structure (ibid.).

Recently there have been further moves, principally from

Muslim leaders in the Philippines, to resume negotiations (see below), but whether these moves reflect initiatives from government sources and/or whether they are a function of the general 'succession-anticipation' atmosphere, is not yet clear.

Finally, and probably of greatest lasting impact, the Marcos regime has responded to Moro dissidence by military action. Already in the period before 1972 there was evidence of police and military participation in the violence against the Muslim population of Mindanao. Following the announcement of martial law there was a substantial military build-up in Mindanao and Sulu and an escalation of armed conflict. The attitude of the government towards a military 'solution' was perhaps well reflected by Defence Minister Enrile in 1984, when (as reported in Far Eastern Economic Review 5 July 1984) he told Southern Command Officers that, in contrast to the NPA insurgency, 'the Muslim rebellion was more or less a straight shooting war..."the problem was not ideological"'. In the course of this conflict, often what were seen by the government as military successes - as in Marawi City in 1972, Jolo in 1974 and Pata in 1981 - represented massive and sometimes indiscriminate overkills which alienated local populations, Christian and tribal as well as Muslim, and drove increasing numbers of young people into the ranks of the Bangsa Moro Army. Nevertheless the combined efforts of military action and amnesty programmes seem to have achieved a situation such that by 1981 it was possible for the Armed Forces of the Philippines (AFP) to announce a change in strategy: in future, it was said, AFP activities in the Muslim areas would be confined to small unit operations by soldiers trained in jungle fighting. (Also, in 1980 there were reports of a MNLF-AFP 'truce' to enable the AFP to shift troops from western Mindanao and Sulu to eastern Mindanao where NPA activity has been intensifying. Dansalan Quarterly IV(1) 1982.) Nevertheless, despite frequent statements (for example by General Ver in December 1982, cited in Dansalan Quarterly IV(2) 1983:117) that the MNLF no longer poses a threat to national security, there is still a substantial military presence in the Moro homeland, frequent clashes still occur, and despite a recommendation by Islamic Affairs Minister Espaldon in February 1982 that martial law be lifted in the south, it remains.

Some eleven years after the imposition of martial law, and sixteen years after the Jabidah massacre, then, how is one to assess the efforts of the Marcos regime to restore peace in the southern Philippines?

Perhaps it should be said first that the causes of unrest in the south are long-standing and complex and that the Philippines government is not alone in failing to solve problems of ethnic/regional separatism. That said, however, it is difficult to review the record with much enthusiasm.

With respect to socio-economic development, it is certainly true that in recent years Mindanao has been a high priority area for economic development, and that development has taken place. But except in such areas as the rehabilitation programme (and its predecessors) little of this development has been specifically for the benefit of the Muslim population (the charter of the SPDA says nothing about Muslim Filipinos) and indeed some of the larger development projects are seen by Muslims as likely to widen the gap between traditional Muslim communities and the inmigrant population, if not to have actually detrimental effects on the Muslim communities. The case most frequently cited by critics of the regime is the Agus River hydro-electric project, which will provide power to, amongst others, the Kawasaki sintering plant at Cagayan de Oro, a planned industrial park in Misamis Oriental, and other industries in Iligan, Cagayan de Oro and Davao (all predominantly Christian areas), but has affected the level of Lake Lanao, with serious consequences for the ecology of the lake and the welfare of the Muslim communities who inhabit its shores; this, and the methods used by the National Power Corporation to obtain the necessary land, help to account for the fact that NAPOCOR workers have been a frequent target of MNLF units. Similarly, continued inmigration to Mindanao is often seen as an indicator of the island's development, but most Muslims interpret it as a deliberate attempt to push the Muslim people on to the periphery of their own homeland. At a more abstract level, Moro spokesmen have argued that economic development does not provide the answers to the problems in the south, and particularly not the dependent, capitalist model of development employed by the Marcos regime (see, for example, Ahmad 1980). Such policy concessions as have been made to Muslim religious and cultural values have been welcome, but on perhaps the biggest issue, Shari'a law, Shari'a courts had still not been established in 1982 despite the government's undertaking on this question in 1973.

With respect to its attempts to discredit the MNLF and promote discord amongst Moro leadership, the Marcos government can probably claim to have had some success, at least in the short run. Through a combination of spontaneous centrifugation within the movement, and alternatively enlightened and devious policies on the part of the government, the Moro leadership now seems to be seriously divided (though undoubtedly less divided than is suggested by official propaganda and support for old society Muslim leaders of dubious standing). And, although many 'surrenderees' have returned to the hills (some more than once), the government's amnesty and rehabilitation programmes, combined with the effects of a long and essentially losing guerilla campaign and demoralizing disputes over leadership, have succeeded in attracting large numbers of MNLF mujahideen out of the field (in 1982 the government claimed 37,000). Divisions within the MNLF also have eased the pressures of external intervention.

In the longer run, however, attempts to promote divisions within the Muslim population may well prove to be counter-productive: on the one hand, attempts to manipulate divisions within the Moro nationalist movement cast doubt on the sincerity of the Marcos regime's commitment to meeting the more fundamental demands of Moro dissidents; secondly, to the extent that Muslim Filipinos themselves are divided, the prospects for peace in the south are diminished and the problems of accommodating the various demands of dissident Moro groups are increased.

On the question of negotiations with the MNLF the record perhaps speaks for itself. On the basis of this record it is difficult to accept that Marcos ever has had any real commitment to reaching a settlement with the MNLF, and the government can perhaps consider itself fortunate that the ICFM has stopped short of attempting to force the issue through an oil embargo. (Iran actually did announce that it would not supply oil to the Philippines but apparently did not put the threat into effect.) Nevertheless, the Tripoli Agreement probably still provides the starting point for a settlement, and the recent announcement, in response to local demands and pressure from Saudi Arabia, that steps will be taken to restructure regional assemblies show some evidence of willingness on the part of the government to make further accommodation. Though relations between Marcos and the Misuari faction, at least, are probably beyond repair, a post-Marcos regime if it were so inclined might well be able to take advantage of what earlier negotiations did achieve.

Finally, on the question of military action some evaluative comments have been made above. Most military sources appear to regard the military campaign against the MNLF as broadly successful (though obviously some commanders would like to have seen it waged differently at particular stages). Perhaps in narrowly militaristic terms they are right, but some military sources fail to recognize the extent to which military action, and indeed the military presence in itself, has tended (as in other parts of the Philippines) to increase confrontation, push radical Christians and Muslims closer together, and consolidate opposition to the regime. At the local level these problems have been compounded by hostilities between the military (AFP), the Philippines Constabulary and the Integrated National Police, and by low morale and poor discipline within sections of the AFP the effects of which include harrassment of local populations, the emergence of 'lost commands', and various commercial enterprises by military personnel including the sale of weapons to MNLF (and NPA?) units.

The state of the Moro movement

The other question which needs to be answered before projecting into the future concerns the present state of the Moro movement.

From the early 1970s the central committee of the MNLF operated from Libya, where its Suluano Chairman, Misuari, and other leading members of the movement had taken refuge under the patronage of President Qaddafi. In December 1977

Misuari's leadership was challenged by Hashim Salamat, a Cairo-based Maguindanaon who had served as Chairman of the Foreign Affairs Committee. Accusing Misuari of autocratic leadership, communist sympathies, and corruption, Salamat informed the ICFM that he had taken over the leadership of the MNLF, a claim which the ICFM, however, rejected. The same year saw the emergence of the Bangsa Moro Liberation Organisation (BMLO), a Jeddah-based group led by Sultan Haroun Al-Rashid Lucman and said to be 'supported by some "old society" Moro politicians and possibly having connections with certain private American commercial interests' (Gowing 1979:239). Also, in 1978, following a difference of opinion between Misuari and MNLF Vice-Chairman Abul Khayr Alonto, the latter surrendered to the government, subsequently becoming speaker of the Region XII assembly. The divisions in the Moro movement in 1977-78 roughly coincided with the abandonment of negotiations following on from the Tripoli Agreement and an apparent cooling off in relations between Qaddafi and Misuari. Misuari subsequently established MNLF offices also in Damascus, Jeddah and Tehran and appears to have shifted between these, receiving support from King Khalid of Saudi Arabia and from the Khomeini regime. Salamat meanwhile shifted to Pakistan, his support in the Philippines reportedly being greatly reduced by surrenders. (According to a report in Far Eastern Economic Review 26 April 1984 the Pakistani government has also received a request from Misuari to open a MNLF office in Islamabad.)

In 1980-81 Benigno Aquino visited Misuari on several occasions in Damascus and Jeddah, subquently announcing that he had accomplished a reconciliation between Misuari and Lucman (but not, more importantly, between Misuari and Salamat) and implying that he had laid grounds for a possible settlement with the MNLF on the basis of the Tripoli Agreement (Asiaweek 9 October 1981). However in March 1982 a further split occurred in the MNLF leadership, with Vice-Chairman Dimasankay Pundato, a Maranao, setting up a MNLF 'Reformist Group' (MNLF-RG) in Jeddah and entering into alliance with the BMLO and the Salamat faction (which has renamed its organization MILF - Moro Islamic Liberation Front)) in a 'Co-ordinating Council of the MNLF-BMLO' (CC-MNLF-BMLO). The split between Pundato and Misuari seems to have resulted from a dispute over the latter's reversion to a secessionist position (and the consequent failure of the moves for reconciliation initiated by Aquino). In June 1982 a 'Moro People's Congress', which claimed to represent the Moro masses and mujahideen, was convened in Sabah on the initiative of either the MNLF-RG or the CC-MNLF-BMLO; this congress confirmed the 'removal' of Misuari and elected Pundato as 'acting chairman' of the MNLF. At an ICFM meeting in Niger in August 1982 - which for the first time accepted the MNLF as a full member rather than as an observer - the ICFM was thus again presented with rival claims to leadership of the Moro movement. Again the ICFM decided in Misuari's favour. However it did not endorse his demand for secession; a conference resolution on the southern Philippines invited the Philippines government to reopen negotiations with the MNLF with a view to implementing the Tripoli Agreement 'in letter and spirit', and appealed to the MNLF to prepare to participate in the negotiations 'as a united front'.

In January 1983 the issue of leadership was once more muddied by the organization in Karachi, under the auspices of the World Muslim Congress (Motamar Al-Alam Al-Islami), of a 'Philippine Muslim Solidarity Conference'. Representatives of the four dissident factions were invited to meet with leaders of the 'Multi-sectoral Muslim Community' in the Philippines; this latter group, which quantitatively dominated the meeting, included 'old society' leaders Ahmed Domocao Alonto (Director-General of Ansar El-Islam) and Salipada Pendatun (a leading figure in the BMLO who had made a much publicized return to the Philippines in 1980 after seven years self-exile and subsequently founded the conservative Muslim Association of the Philippines), a number of surrenderees, including Abul Khayr Alonto, and some regional and local government officials. Lucman attended the conference as BMLO spokesman but both Misuari and Salamat stayed away, informing the conference of their continuing confidence in the ability of the Islamic Conference Organization to find a solution to the conflict. A 'Karachi Declaration' issued from the conference called for resumption of negotiations for a solution to the conflict on the basis of the Tripoli Agreement, and for the merger of the two regional assemblies. Subsequently the Secretary-General of the World Muslim Congress visited the Philippines, reportedly with a ten-point plan for the implementation of the Tripoli Agreement which is generally in accord with the proposals made by A.K. Alonto in 1982 (Dansalan Quarterly IV(3) 1983: 178-179); to date (mid-1984) no action has been taken.

In another recent development, in October 1983 a group of Muslim leaders (headed by former Senator Mamintal Tamano and including A.D. Alonto, A.K. Alonto and Pendatun) presented a manifesto in which they threatened that 'unless national reconciliation with justice for all is speedily effected, we may be constrained to reassert the historic identity of the Moro nation' and to take the 'necessary steps' to restore Bangsa Moro independence. The group also supported Cardinal Sin's call for national reconciliation (Philippines Sunday Express 9 October 1983; Malaya 10-12 October 1982). The same month a letter from the Salamat faction (MILF) urged the Secretary-General of the Organization of Islamic Conference, 'In the light of the violent restiveness in Manila...coupled with the seeming instability of the present administration of the Philippine government...to hold in abeyance any measure intended to implement the Tripoli Agreement...until such time that the political situation in the Philippines shall have finally crystallized'.

As opposed to this activity among the aspiring

121

leadership, the general picture in the field seems to be one of declining numbers, increasingly younger and less ideologically trained recruits, lack of co-ordination between regional commands, and an increasing incidence of kidnapping and banditry in the name of the MNLF but frequently by brigades with little or no formal relationship to the movement.

To summarize: it would appear that Misuari still has the predominant following in the field (he is alleged to have visited training camps in Sabah four times during 1982) and the most prominent status among the overseas Moro leadership. His leadership is, however, in dispute and if he persists with a hard-line demand for secession he seems likely to lose the support of both the international Islamic community (Qaddafi having already apparently withdrawn his sponsorship) and large parts of the Moro movement who are prepared to negotiate for a more realistic solution. More generally, the strength of the MNLF in the field appears to have waned and, perhaps reflecting the political climate nationally, there appears to be an increasing tendency for local Muslim politicians (notable among them A.K. Alonto) to be seeking a more decisive role in negotiations for a reasonable settlement of the conflict (and thus indirectly for a better stake in post-Marcos society).

Leadership struggles and attempts to count numbers in the field, however, are apt to draw attention away from the more fundamental question of what the Moro movement is about.

Though its ideology has never been very clearly spelt out, statements by MNLF spokesmen have emphasized two objectives of the movement: Moro autonomy and social reform within Muslim Filipino society. It is this latter objective, often expressed in Marxist phraseology, which led to the early falling out between the young intellectual leadership of the MNLF and traditional Muslim leaders (such as its early patron, Lucman), and which enabled Marcos to brand the MNLF 'Maoist'. One of the reasons given for the split between Misuari and Salamat in 1977 was Misuari's alleged communist sympathies and this may also have been relevant to Alonto's decision to quit his MNLF field command. Certainly the CPP/NPA has invited collaboration between the MNLF and the NPA (see, for example, Ang Bayan 31 October 1977) and the Ten Point Programme of the National Democratic Front (NDF) includes 'support for the national minorities, especially those in Mindanao and the Mountain Provinces, in their struggle for self-determination and democracy' (and its 1977 manifesto states that 'the right to self-determination includes the right to secede from a state of national oppression'); moreover, in recent years there has undeniably been limited but increasing collaboration between MNLF and NPA units in the field.

As against this, even the more radical elements of the MNLF have tended to distance themselves from the CPP/NDF, and collaboration between field units appears to have rested more on ad hoc arrangements between field commanders in the face of a common enemy than on any fundamental ideological sympathy. Many of the MNLF's supporters in the Philippines, as well as its patrons in the international Islamic community, see 'communism' as incompatible with the fundamental Islamic nature of the Moro nationalist movement. In a number of MNLF publications and in interviews (most recently in Arabia September 1982 and as reported in Far Eastern Economic Review 22 December 1983) Misuari has denied any formal ties with the CPP/NPA, accusing Marcos of using this as a bogey to gain more assistance from the US. (The 'dilemma of an Islamic revolution' is explored at greater length in Shoesmith 1983.)

Muslim Filipinos in post-Marcos society

Projecting into the future, I have little doubt that a post-Marcos regime of any description will face problems in the southern Philippines. The roots of Moro dissidence lie in a long history of separateness, a separateness defined in terms both of religion and of ethnicity, and in the effects of an irreversible process of demographic and economic change. Fear of assimilation and a desire for an autonomous Bangsa Moro are deeply felt across a wide spectrum of Muslim society, and the actions of the Marcos government appear to have strengthened rather than diminished these feelings. Shared opposition to the Marcos regime has created a common cause for Moro nationalists and other opposition forces - both on the extreme left, between the MNLF and the NPA, and further right, between the more conservative Muslim leadership and the traditional opposition(1) - but I believe that both the NDF and UNIDO are deluding themselves if they think that there is any deep empathy between Moro nationalism and the wider Filipino opposition to Marcos. Similarly, those who see a 'solution' to the Moro problem in terms of economic and social progress, and the eventual integration of Muslims into the larger Philippine society, fail to appreciate the fundamental religious-ethnic aspect of the Moro rebellion.

As with other elements of the post-Marcos situation analysed in earlier chapters, the prospects for Muslim Filipinos vary in different scenarios. If Marcos is succeeded by some form of elitist-military-technocratic regime, the prospects for significant change are probably slight, except in so far as one might expect any new government to take the opportunity of seeking to reach a settlement along the lines of the Tripoli Agreement, and except that in a potentially unstable political situation Moro nationalists would be able to exert greater leverage. Such an outcome, however, would almost certainly favour the more conservative traditional leaders of Muslim Filipino society and might well have the effect of delivering to the MNLF increasing numbers of disaffected young Muslims attracted by the movement's objective of social reform.

In the event of a succession scenario which yields

government to a coalition of above-ground opposition forces, such as envisaged in Diokno's 'transitional government' (see chapter 1), there is an explicit commitment to redressing 'the more immediate problems' of Muslim Filipinos, though how far this might go towards meeting demands for an autonomous Bangsa Moro remains unclear. Much would depend, obviously, on which of the several Moro factions were accepted as the spokesman for Muslim Filipinos (hence the recent manoeuvrings noted above). There is also an interesting smaller question concerning the future role of Moro nationalists in a broadly-based Minanao Alliance.

In the less likely scenarios of military dictatorship and of revolution one might expect a strengthened MNLF to throw in its lot with the NPA - partly as a strategy for survival and partly in the expectation of securing a more favourable settlement should a revolutionary government come to power. It might also extend its operations from the countryside to the cities, as has been threatened from time to time in recent years. Again, however, there would be uncertainty about the long-term compatibility of the two revolutionary movements.

But for any Philippine government, even one with the best intentions towards the Moro nationalist movement, there is the overriding problem that of the thirteen provinces in Mindanao-Sulu-Palawan with a significant Muslim population only five (Maguindanao, Lanao del Sur, Sulu, Basilan and Tawi Tawi) now have a Muslim majority. Given this demographic reality (and its economic, social and political correlates) the more extreme demands of the MNLF seem simply unrealistic (as the ICFM appears to have realized). Even in the case of a more limited Bangsa Moro autonomy, a post-Marcos government of any persuasion will have to balance the demands of Moro nationalists against the potential dangers of arousing a non-Muslim backlash in the south; if such a reaction does occur, the tensions of 1971 will be recreated all over again.

That said, it remains true that a first step to resolving the conflict in the south must be the negotiation of a settlement which concedes to a reasonable extent the legitimate demands of the MNLF for some degree of Islamic autonomy, under terms which also enable the Moro leadership overseas to return to the Philippines to participate in it. A second step would involve a commitment of resources to provide for reconstruction and rehabilitation in the south (there are, for example, an estimated 140,000 Muslim Filipino refugees in Sabah) and to help reduce the widening income gap between Muslim and Christian Filipinos.

Beyond that, even with a measure of autonomy the prospects for future generations of Muslim Filipinos are much the same as for any traditionally-oriented ethnic minority in a modernizing society: gradual integration and at least partial loss of cultural identity, or progressive marginalization.

The term 'tribal Filipino' describes some 3.5 million people, belonging to about fifty ethno-linguistic groups, who, in varying degrees, have maintained pre-colonial forms of economic and social organization. Most of these people are concentrated in northern Luzon and the interior of Mindanao, with smaller numbers in Mindoro and Palawan and several negrito groups spread throughout the archipelago.

In a number of important respects the situation of tribal Filipinos is similar to that of the Muslims. Like the Muslim Filipinos, tribal Filipinos resisted the incursions of the Spanish and American colonial regimes, either by force (as with the Kalinga and their neighbours) or by withdrawing into the hinterland (as for example with the Manobo, the Mangyan, and various negrito groups). As with the Muslim Filipinos, their disengagement from the larger Philippine society, and more specifically their dependence on shifting cultivation (kaingin) and on hunting and gathering, has left them, in the twentieth century, particularly vulnerable to the depredations of land-grabbers (private and corporate), logging operators, miners, and more recently large scale development projects. And as with the Muslim Filipinos, attempts to defend traditional homelands have often brought military intervention.

Encroachment on the lands of tribal Filipinos is not entirely a recent phenomenom. Among the Tiruray of Cotabato, for example, Schlegel (1979) has recorded how, early this century, the neighbouring Muslim Maguindanao as well as Christian inmigrants from Luzon and the Visayas penetrated the Tiruray homeland, cutting down the rainforest and replacing the Tiruray's shifting cultivation with plough agriculture. In the face of this, some Tiruray retreated further into the mountains, maintaining their traditional economy and culture, while others became caught up in the shift to plough agriculture and integrated into its market-oriented system, often as poorly-paid labourers in the employ of the new settlers. In 1971 this area became the scene of vicious fighting between Muslims, Christians and Tiruray - a conflict in which Tiruray frequently joined with Christian settlers against their long-time Muslim neighbours. In a similar fashion the T'boli of Cotabato, the Manobo of Bukidnon and numerous other tribal groups were pushed off their land by lowland settlers, frequently in collusion with corrupt officials and even educated tribal people, and eventually forced to earn their living by working as labourers for the inmigrant settlers. But while the process of marginalization of tribal communities may not be new, in recent years two things have tended to focus attention on the problem.

For one, the effects of the steady encroachment of lowland settlers on tribal Filipino lands have been greatly aggravated by the incursion of large-scale, regime-supported corporate enterprises and development projects.

Secondly, it would seem that relevant government agencies, far from protecting the interests of tribal Filipinos, have frequently provided means for their repression. Among the agencies most referred to in complaints by tribal people are the Bureau of Lands, the Bureau of Forestry and the Ministry of Local Government and Community Development (for example, see MSPC-MSCJD n.d.). Exceeding all these, however, has been the dubious role of PANAMIN.

PANAMIN was created in 1968 as a private foundation (Private Association for National Minorities) by Manuel Elizalde Jr, scion of the wealthy Elizalde family, who had been appointed in the previous year as presidential advisor on national minorities and in 1968 given cabinet status. Following the abolition in 1975 of the Commission on National Integration and the transfer of Muslim affairs to the SPDA (see above) PANAMIN was given formal responsibility for the non-Muslim national minorities. In its subsequent activities PANAMIN has been widely accused of, amongst other things, using its powers to facilitate access to tribal Filipino lands by selected loggers, miners and agribusinesses; forcibly relocating people from areas of MNLF and NPA activity ('hamletting') and employing tribal Filipino groups in counter-insurgency operations; and promoting dissension within tribal Filipino communities to serve its own ends. Elizalde's personal life-style, as it impinges on tribal people, has also been called into question.(2)

The case of the Kalinga resistance to the Chico River Basin Development Project (CRBDP) is probably the best known case of what is a widespread phenomenon. The CRBDP envisaged the construction of four dams and an associated irrigation project; it involves a total catchment area of 1,400 sq.km and impinges on the lands of some 100,000 Kalinga and Bontoc tribal people. Survey work for the project began in 1974 without any prior consultation with the sixteen tribal communities affected. Petitions against the CRBDP, including delegations to Malacanang, in 1974 were dismissed. In 1975 the communities affected joined in a peace pact to oppose dam construction. In the face of this resistance, plans for the construction of three of the dams were suspended, and PANAMIN officials were sent in to investigate the situation; subsequently, under the auspices of PANAMIN, a Kalinga Special Development Region was declared. The activities of PANAMIN officials, however, did little to reassure the people of the government's good intentions and in 1978 PANAMIN was withdrawn. From around 1976 the NPA became active in the region, finding willing recruits amongst the frustrated tribal people. The government's response to this growing unrest was - as in the Muslim south - to send in the troops: Civil Home Defence Force (CHDF) units (including, according to Rocamora 1979:20, a unit of tribal T'boli from Mindanao) and a PC battalion. The government also sought, with some success, to exploit divisions among the tribal people, to the extent of arming rival factions. There followed, between

1976 and 1979 a mass of arrests of tribal people and numerous reports of military abuses. Again as in the south, the effect of this was a further alienation of the indigenous people and an escalation of violence on both sides. The killing by PC soldiers in 1980 of Kalinga leader Macli-ing Dulag, an outspoken opponent of the CRBDP, is only the most publicized of a number of violent incidents since 1974, which also include the deaths of NAPOCOR and military personnel. But a statement by Deputy Minister of Defence Barbero, following the arrest of five soldiers involved in the shooting, is worth quoting (from Asiaweek 5 September 1980): 'You must remember these soldiers are lowlanders. Very few of them know the real culture of the place. You have language and culture problems'. As far as I am aware the decision to proceed with the fourth dam has not been revoked, and the violent confrontation continues.

Similar accounts of the invasion of tribal lands by lowland settlers, corporate plantations, loggers, cattle ranches and NAPOCOR, and of abuses by PANAMIN, the military and CHDF, and various fanatical gangs and 'lost commands' (some of them allegedly armed by the military) have been documented for a number of tribal groups. To the north of the Chico river basin, the land of the Isneg is threatened by the Apayao-Abulug River Hydroelectric Development Project, a project even larger than the CRBDP. Nearby in Abra the Tingguian people have since 1976 been unsuccessfully resisting the logging operations of the Cellophil Resources Corporation; the Cellophil concession, according to Claver (1983:20), covers an area of about 200,000 ha in the provinces of Ilocos Sur, Ilocos Norte, Kalinga-Apayao, Mountain Province and Abra, and affects four tribal groups: the Isneg, Bontoc, Kalinga and Tingguian. Further south, in Zambales and Bataan, the Aeta have for several years been resisting lowland settlers and plantations (having failed to gain the support of PANAMIN), as have the Mangyan in Oriental Mindoro. In Bukidnon, Mindanao, Manobo tribal people, having accommodated to increasing inmigrant settlement in the 1950s and 1960s, have in several instances found themselves forced off traditional lands by cattle ranchers and by corporations (notably the Philippine Packing Corporation, a local subsidiary of the Del Monte Corporation which has pineapple and banana plantations in Mindanao, and the Bukidnon Sugar Company (BUSCO)) frequently assisted by the Philippines Constabulary (PC). By the mid-1970s Bukidnon had become the centre of widespread and bitter conflict involving tribal Filipinos, lowland settlers, fanatical gangs, and the military (PC and CHDF units). Manobo houses and gardens were destroyed and a number of people killed. Since 1975 PANAMIN has been active in Manobo territory, introducing an amnesty programme and establishing PANAMIN reservations, but its activities have been widely condemned (see, for example, ICL Research Team 1979). To the east, in Agusan del Sur, Manobo people (and lowland settlers) have been threatened with loss of land to palm oil plantations in which the government's

National Development Company (NDC) is the majority partner in a joint venture, and there have been allegations that landholders have been intimidated by a local 'lost command' which has the covert support of the military (see, for example, _Far Eastern Economic Review_ 19 November 1982). In South Cotabato, the T'boli, having already lost agricultural land, forest and lake foreshore to inmigrant settlers, are now faced with competing logging operators (Habaluyas Enterprises Inc. and Sarmiento Logging) and the prospect of a hydro-electricity dam on Lake Sebu, which occupies a central place in the ecology of the T'boli (Mansmann 1982). There also PANAMIN has played an ambiguous role. Elsewhere in Mindanao, the Dibabawon of Davao del Norte have protested unsuccessfully against logging operations and commercial tree planting on traditional land by the Aguinaldo Development Corporation; the Ata of Davao City have attempted to resist logging operations and have come into conflict with PANAMIN; the Higa'onon of Misamis Oriental have complained of landgrabbing and of logging by Anakan Lumber Company; the Mamanwa of Surigao have been harassed for illegal panning for gold in the streams of their traditional land (the mining concession is held by the Andres Soriano Corporation, whose chairman, ironically, was an original member of the board of trustees of PANAMIN). And so on.

What is remarkable about this documentation is not so much that conflicts have occurred between the tribal groups, and lowland settlers and corporations but that government legislation and policy offer so little by way of protection for the land rights of traditional people; indeed it appears that the Bureau of Forestry has not only granted logging licences without prior consultation with tribal landholders, but has prevented _kaingin_ cultivation (as it has the power to do under PD 1159). Moreover, several of the large corporations operating in tribal areas - apart from government enterprises such as NDC and NAPOCOR - have links with the Marcos regime.

Given this background it is not surprising that in recent years the situation of tribal Filipinos has become politically salient, not only among tribal Filipinos (who at a National Consultation Of Minority Peoples in September 1983 formed a 'national peace pact') but among a variety of supporting organizations ranging from comparatively conservative church groups to the NDF; nor is it surprising that the NPA has been gaining strength in tribal areas of Luzon and Mindanao.

In terms of future scenarios, the position of tribal Filipinos is similar to that of Muslim Filipinos (both UNIDO and the NDF, for example, speak of them in the same breath) with the important exceptions, first, that there is no equivalent of the MNLF among the diverse tribal people, and, secondly, that apart perhaps from limited local self-government there is no autonomy/secession option. By providing a recruiting ground for the NPA and through sporadic local disturbances, however, tribal Filipinos do present a potential source of regime instability; moreover, continued inmigration to sparsely settled areas coupled with large-scale development projects (dams, plantations, etc.) will place further pressures on tribal groups and generate increasing opposition to the government. The demise of Marcos may affect the fortunes of some of the corporations active in tribal areas, and it may affect the status of PANAMIN(3). On the other hand an elitist-military-technocratic successor regime is unlikely to change the situation of tribal Filipinos significantly (except perhaps by increasing repression) and a more liberal regime can only meet the demands of tribal Filipinos at some cost to economic development, a cost which in the present economic climate no regime is likely to accept with enthusiasm. Perhaps the most that tribal Filipinos can hope for is that a more liberal regime will make effective recognition of traditional land rights and usage, will put an end to abuses of the military, 'lost commands' and so on, and will replace PANAMIN with a more credible agency.

FOOTNOTES

1. In an interview reported in _Arabia_ April 1984 Misuari was asked, 'If the Marcos regime falls tomorrow, do you hope to attain independence the next day?' Misuari replied 'I cannot be so sure of that' but went on to say, 'We are optimistic that the problem will be solved' and mentioned support for an independent Bangsa Moro state from the NDF and the PDSP.

2. The most comprehensive accounts of PANAMIN activities are in ICL Research Team 1979, MSPC-MSCJD n.d., _Southeast Asia Chronicle_ No. 67 1979, and various papers presented to the 11th Annual Seminar on Mindanao-Sulu Cultures, Central Mindanao University, Musuan, 1978. The other principal sources of information on tribal Filipinos are _Tribal Forum_ (published by the Episcopal Commission on Tribal Filipinos, Manila), _Sandugo_ (People's Action for Cultural Ties of the National Council of Churches in the Philippines, Quezon City), _Communications_ (MSPC, Davao City), and _Ichthys_ (Association of Major Religious Superiors of the Philippines, Manila). The issue of 'hamletting' has been documented in a publication of The Mindanao Documentation Committee for Refugees (n.d.).

3. In late 1983 it was reported that Elizalde had left the Philippines and, it was rumoured, had taken up residence in Spain.

Chapter 8

THE ECONOMY*

Hal Hill and Sisira Jayasuriya

Introduction

The recent performance of the Philippine economy has
been grim indeed. During 1982-83 the economy hardly grew at
all in per capita terms. Even before the recent political
turmoil there was bad news on almost every major economic
front: the balance of trade deficit widened; the interest
bill on the country's overseas debt ballooned; sales of
electricity for industrial use in Metro Manila declined, as a
result not of energy conservation measures but rather of
sluggish industrial growth; international prices of major
primary exports remained depressed; in the Middle East there
were indications that the burgeoning growth in manpower
exports and construction contracts - which had to some extent
cushioned the Philippine economy from the effects of rapidly
increasing real energy prices in the 1970s - was beginning to
falter.

1982-83 have of course been particularly severe. During
the 1970s the economy performed much better, and in fact grew
at unprecedented and internationally respectable rates. But
even though the record in the 1970s was reasonably good,
there is a widespread belief that it could have been
substantially better, and that it was accompanied by an
increasingly unacceptable equity performance. For example,
the influential International Labour Office report
characterized the record through to the early 1970s as one of
'narrow participation and unbalanced growth' (ILO 1974).
More recently, a group of Filipino academics concluded that
'Our economic growth has proved resilient in times of stress
... [but] the equity picture has been rather bleak' (PREPF
1980:180-181). The purpose of this chapter is to analyse
recent trends and future prospects for the economy in the
light of growth and equity criteria.

*Some of the issues examined in this paper were addressed in
Hill (1982). We are greatly indebted to Ted James and Peter
McCawley for helpful comments on an earlier draft and to
Param Silvepulle and Maree Tait for research assistance in
preparing this paper.

Recent macroeconomic trends

There are two major features of the macroeconomic performance since 1960. The first is moderate economic growth and structural change; the second is the continuing poor performance of the external sector, as evidenced by large and increasing balance of trade deficits.

In the years 1961-82 the Philippine economy grew at an average annual rate of about 5.5 per cent (Table 8.1). There was an acceleration in the growth rate for the period 1973-79 and this, combined with gradually declining population growth, resulted in per capita growth of around 3 per cent in the 1970s, as compared with about 2 per cent in the 1960s. Historically, this was an era of rapid growth for the Philippine economy - for example per capita GNP grew at a rate of only 0.2 per cent between 1902 and 1948 (Hooley 1968) - but comparisons between the colonial and post-colonial era are hardly valid.

Table 8.1

Annual growth rates by sector, 1961-1982
(per cent)

Sector	1961-65	1965-69	1969-73	1973-77	1977-82a
Agriculture	4.6	4.0	3.4	5.4	4.3
Industry	5.8	5.5	7.3	8.1	5.4
Mining	2.7	14.6	11.4	4.3	4.2
Manufacturing	4.8	6.6	7.5	5.0	4.7
Construction	10.8	-0.6	5.2	21.8	8.0
Utilities	3.0	5.3	7.9	11.2	8.3
Services	4.6	4.7	4.6	5.2	4.8
Net Domestic Product	4.8	4.6	4.9	6.1	4.5

Source : NEDA, Statistical Yearbook of the Philippines and Philippines Economic Indicators, various issues.
(a) The 1982 figures are preliminary and likely to have overestimates.

There have also been some important structural changes since 1961 (Table 8.1). Consistent with the general pattern of economic development, the share of agriculture has shown a steady downward trend, despite a quite good performance in the latter part of the 1970s. Manufacturing grew strongly in the late 1960s and early 1970s, but the limits to the import-substituting strategy pursued for most of the post-independence era resulted in sluggish growth for most of the 1970s. Construction and utilities, two sectors which benefited from the enlarged public sector in the 1970s, grew quite rapidly, the construction sector in particular benefiting from the hotel building boom in the mid-1970s.

The external sector has been a major preoccupation of policy-makers since independence. The Philippines has only twice recorded a surplus on its balance of trade over this period - in 1963 and 1973 - but in recent years the imbalance has become increasingly serious and in 1982 merchandise exports were only about two thirds of imports. There are two reasons why the external sector has performed poorly. One is inappropriate trade and industrialization policies, which are discussed below. The second, applicable since 1973, has been the marked deterioration in the country's terms of trade, which declined from a value of 100 in 1972 to just a little over 50 a decade later. This has contributed not only to poor economic performance but also to a slower rate of economic growth.

Problems in the external trade sector have not been without some positive consequences, however. For one thing, they have prompted increased commodity and country trade diversification. 'Non traditional' (principally manufactured) exports, which were negligible prior to the 1970s, have increased rapidly and now account for almost half the total. And the heavy dependence on the United States in the early post-independence era (at one stage accounting for almost 80 per cent of Philippine trade) has fallen substantially. A second positive consequence has been an increasingly flexible foreign exchange management policy. This was reflected, at least until August 1983, in an increasingly small disparity between official and black market exchange rates. Finally, some of the foreign exchange expended to finance the enormous increase in the cost of oil imports (which contributed to the terms of trade deterioration) has been recycled in the form of remittances from temporary emigrants working mainly in the Middle East.(1)

Agriculture

Agriculture continues to be of major significance in the Philippines, though its share in GDP has declined slightly during the past two decades. Agricultural production has grown at quite satisfactory rates: the average annual growth rate during the 1960s was 4.3 per cent, increasing to 4.9 per cent during the 1970s. In recent years, however, growth has been slowing down, reflecting the general downturn of the economy.

While some potentially cultivable land remains to be exploited in some of the 'outer' islands, land-extensive agriculture generally appears to have reached its limits. Output growth in recent years has come mostly from yield increases, particularly for rice, which occupies the largest cultivated area.

Historically the most important agricultural crops have been rice, maize, coconut and sugar-cane. While rice and maize are staple food crops grown mainly for domestic consumption, coconut and sugar cane products have also been major agricultural exports. The Philippines is the world's largest coconut producer and accounts for about 50 per cent of the world trade in coconut products. In recent years, bananas and pineapples have emerged as important export crops.

In terms of growth, the rice sector has shown the best performance. Production increased at a historically rapid rate in the 1970s from 5.3 million tonnes in 1970 to over 8 million tonnes in 1981. This was primarily due to the spread of new high-yielding varieties (HYVs) and increased use of chemical fertilizers. By 1980, over 75 per cent of the area was under HYVs and fertilizer use had doubled during the decade. The Philippines became a small net rice exporter after 1977, though imports of other cereal grains, particularly wheat, have increased (Onate 1982).

Until the mid 1970s, significant growth rates were recorded by the other major crops, too. Of these, maize production continued to increase throughout the decade. However, this came primarily from extension of cultivated area to marginal lands; unlike the situation in rice production, technical change was slow and yields remain very low.

Coconut production has declined in recent years after reaching historically high levels in the mid-1970s. Sugar, which expanded till the mid-1970s, has declined since then, particularly in response to external market factors. Technical change in both the coconut and sugar industries has been minimal. Expansion of the banana and pineapple plantations (with significant foreign investment) has taken place in the less densely populated outer islands, particularly Mindanao.

Forestry, a major traditional export earner, has declined in importance. Exports of logs have been curtailed to stimulate greater domestic processing but rapid (and often illegal) depletion of forests and greater domestic demand have reduced export potential.

The livestock industry remains primarily based on small, backyard producers, though the large scale commercial sector has been growing (with substantial foreign investment) quite rapidly in recent years (Escudero 1981).

The Philippines has an extensive coastline with numerous protected anchorages and extensive marine territorial waters. However, these are relatively under-exploited (Kintanar and Luna 1976). In addition, substantial fresh and brackish water fisheries exist. Exports of fresh shrimps, prawns and other crustaceans have grown rapidly during the 1970s, though some fish, primarily canned fish, are still imported.

Despite the quite impressive expansion in agricultural output, government policies generally have had the overall effect of depressing producer incentives. In contrast to the high levels of protection granted to industry '...price intervention policies have undervalued agricultural production during the last decade through lower product prices and higher input prices. Traditional as well as new agricultural exports have been penalized by negative protection through export taxes, export quotas, special levies on coconuts, and government trade monopoly' (David 1982:21).

The increased rice output came primarily from high yielding varieties grown in irrigated conditions with high levels of fertilizer and other modern inputs. The major government contributions to the rapid rice output increase were investments in irrigation and extension. By the end of the 1960s the Philippines had a considerable area under irrigation, whose productivity was enhanced greatly by the new rice technology during the 1970s. In the latter decade, while substantial investments in irrigation were made, the rate slowed down considerably. Between 1958/59 and 1967/68, 490,000 hectares were irrigated compared with 169,000 in the following ten years (Ongkingco et al. 1983). Extension services improved substantially in the last decade, greatly facilitating the diffusion of the new technology, which was primarily developed at the (externally funded) International Rice Research Institute.

Despite government claims that its initiatives, particularly the Masagana 99 programme which provided subsidized credit, were responsible for increased rice production, evidence shows that the effects of its overall price interventions were adverse. Subsidized credit reached only a minority of farmers even in the mid-1970s and has declined rapidly since. Domestic fertilizer prices have been above world prices since 1976 while large subsidy payments were paid to inefficient fertilizer manufacturers and importers (David and Balisacan 1981; Te and Herdt 1982). During the last decade real rice prices have declined; (barter) terms of trade for rice farmers fell by over 40 per cent. The floor price scheme of the government was ineffective in raising farm gate prices (Unnevehr 1982). The disincentive effects of most price policies could not be fully compensated by the subsidized irrigation and free extension facilities.

Until the mid-1970s the export crop sector grew satisfactorily. Despite domestic price interventions aimed at lowering consumer prices, access to the protected US market and generally favourable external market conditions enabled coconut and sugar industries to remain quite profitable. While preferential access to the US market was lost with the termination of the Laurel-Langley agreement in 1974, very high world commodity prices prevailed during 1973-75 for these crops. Since then the adverse effects of declining world prices and greater restrictions on market access (particularly for sugar) have been further aggravated by policies which generally reduced domestic prices of export crops below those which would have prevailed under the previous policy regime (David 1982). In both sugar and coconut, the government has intervened to establish regulatory bodies; these have been widely criticized as being mechanisms assisting politically influential groups to maintain control over the industries, often at the expense of small farmer-producers and farm labourers. In the coconut industry, for example, farmers have been compelled to pay a levy (deducted from the price paid for their copra by the millers), the benefits of which have largely accrued to a group of powerful individuals. In this manner, much of the proceeds of agricultural taxation have been lost to the public sector.

Employment levels in the agriculture sector have been affected by technical change, particularly in recent years. While some types of labour-saving technical change would probably have taken place even in the absence of policy-induced price distortions, some of the capital-cheapening policies have encouraged inappropriate mechanization and a switch to other labour-saving technologies. In recent years, labour absorption in the rice sector has shown signs of declining (Jayasuriya and Shand 1983); a similar trend has been reported in the presently very labour-intensive sugar industry (McCoy 1983; this volume).

Future prospects for rapid growth in rice production appear limited; irrigation investments are likely to decline due to financial constraints as well as the diminishing availability of easily irrigable land. However, the potential for substantial technical change in the maize industry appears to be large. More favourable pricing policies and better market prospects for the export crops are required if the agricultural sector is to regain high rates of growth. Even in the absence of much improved external conditions, however, removal of current producer incentives could have a substantial positive impact on rural incomes and agricultural output.

Manufacturing industry

The last thirty years of Philippine manufacturing provide a valuable case study in Third World industrialization strategies - and one that has been well documented (see in particular Baldwin 1975; Bautista, Power and Associates 1979; Power and Sicat 1971). For at least a decade the Philippines has appeared set to join the ranks of the newly-industrializing countries in the export of labour-intensive manufactures: it has a large and fairly sophisticated manufacturing sector, there is high-level awareness regarding the need for policy reforms, the financial and commercial sectors are well developed, and other countries in the region - the Asian NICs - are vacating the field of labour-intensive manufactures and moving into more skill- and capital-intensive activities. Yet the record to date has been disappointing. Although the Philippines would appear to have a comparative advantage in the field of labour-intensive manufactures, this sector's share of GDP has failed to rise appreciably. From the mid-1970s, in particular, its contribution to output and employment growth has been very poor. Its share of GDP has actually declined marginally. During the five years 1976-80 manufacturing employment grew at around 3.2 per cent annually, or at approximately the same rate as the workforce. In a labour surplus economy such as the Philippines this is a serious indictment indeed, especially given the limited scope for increased labour absorption in other sectors of the economy. Nor is the poor performance the result of the world recession, because the major downturn occurred in 1981-82.

What have been the reasons for this poor record of industrial growth? In many respects, the Philippine experience up to the late 1970s illustrates the problems of a prolonged period of import-substitution industrialization carried out under heavy protective barriers. After independence it was able to achieve rapid industrial growth because of the backlog in consumer demand following the Pacific War and because of import restrictions which hastened the establishment of domestic manufacturing capacity. But many of the industries were (and still are) not internationally competitive, and the general bias against export industries discouraged a more outward-looking industrial base. After the completion of the easy phase of import substitution, as manufacturing commenced the process of backward integration, the shortcomings of the strategy became apparent.

Protection varies markedly across industries, often penalizing labour-intensive activities in which the country could be expected to have a comparative advantage. A wide range of fiscal incentives has imparted a strong bias towards capital-intensity, contributing to the poor record of labour absorption. There are numerous examples where past policies have stifled the growth of potentially internationally competitive industries. In some instances protection of early stage activities has penalized downstream user industries - spinning and weaving is perhaps the best known of these, but there are others (steel may well become important in the 1980s). In the appliance and automotive industries, complex local sourcing requirements have inhibited the development of an efficient components goods industry (Hill 1981). And attempts to superimpose an export-oriented strategy on a basically inward-looking industrial base, through a variety of mechanisms (export processing zones, bonded warehouses, import duty rebates), while contributing to the growth of manufactured exports, have resulted in enormous administrative difficulties, often so complex that small and medium firms have been discouraged from attempting to export.

More recently the government has embarked on an ambitious three-pronged attempt to revive and rationalize the industrial structure, through a general liberalization of the trade regime, the development of several core industries, and the promotion of small and medium industry. The restructuring programme entails the unification and reduction of tariff rates and the promotion of industries considered likely to have good international market prospects. Funding has been provided through World Bank structural adjustment loans of $US 200 million (September 1980) and $US 300 million (March 1983). Tariffs, the second highest in ASEAN, are to be reduced to an average nominal rate of 28 per cent in 1985, and a range of non-tariff barriers (principally import licensing) are to be eliminated. To date, fourteen industries have been selected for rehabilitation, with emphasis on labour-intensive activities such as garments, food processing, footwear and furniture.

The success of the programme is vital to Philippine economic development. If manufacturing is to play a dynamic role, the basic choice is between emphasis on the export of labour-intensive manufactures and an attempt to foster greater backward integration into more capital-intensive industries. Neither alternative provides an easy solution to the current impasse, but there is little doubt that the former holds out the best prospects. Not surprisingly, the reforms have been subjected to much domestic criticism. There are problems also with their timing. There is little likelihood that the spectacular export-oriented success stories of the 1960s will be repeated in the current era of slower world economic growth, rising protectionism, and increasingly competitive export markets. For the reforms to be successful in the Philippines, a sustained government commitment to the liberalization and rehabilitation programmes will be necessary, coupled with policies to improve the country's inadequate industrial infrastructure and to remove the formidable bureaucratic obstacles to increased international trade.

The second element of the government's new industrial thrust is the decision to embark on a series of major industrial projects, largely in the field of heavy industry. The list of proposed projects - eleven to date - is extensive, and includes aluminium and copper smelters, a petrochemical complex, and an integrated steel mill. The government's stated objectives in promoting the projects is to develop an efficient industrial base for downstream user industries, which utilizes the country's natural resource base.

A few of the projects appear to be economically viable and proceeding on schedule. However, there are major doubts concerning the viability of the more capital- and energy-intensive projects. One problem is that, despite the government's claim that no project will proceed unless proven to be viable, insufficient information is publicly available to evaluate the projects. A careful evaluation of one of the projects - the copper smelter - concluded that it is at best little better than marginal (Emerson and Warr 1981). There is widespread belief that at least the petrochemicals, aluminium and steel projects are unlikely to be viable. The experience of more industrially advanced LDCs (for example, India) with heavy industry, particularly where technology and design changes are occurring rapidly, does not augur well for the success of the projects.

In late 1983 the government announced that all the projects are to be shelved in response to the deteriorating balance of payments situation. It is quite possible that at least some will be restored in more favourable circumstances, in which case the basic question of economic viability remains. If, as seems likely, not all the projects are internationally competitive, then downstream, export-oriented user industries will be penalized to the extent that they are required to source from domestic high-cost producers. Furthermore, the projects will impose further strains on the domestic banking sector, already stretched to the limit because of its extensive bail-out operations and the bad debts resulting from the disappearance of a prominent banker in 1981.

Poverty and income distribution

Perhaps more than on any other issue, critics have been vocal and united on the alleged failure of the government to eradicate poverty and improve the distribution of income and wealth. Philippine society was, of course, highly unequal during the colonial era, a pattern which changed little during the first quarter century after independence (ILO 1974:9). Unfortunately, it is difficult to obtain a reliable general picture of more recent trends in income distribution and poverty incidence.

There have been several informative micro-studies, but in an economy as heterogeneous as the Philippines it may be hazardous to generalize from them. We are thus left with the two main sources of information on trends in income distribution and poverty for the country as a whole, neither of which is entirely satisfactory. The first of these is the nation-wide Family Income and Expenditure Surveys (FIES), generally conducted at four- yearly intervals. The data in Table 8.2 have been computed from the five FIES for which results are available. Table 8.2 indicates, first, that there is considerable inequality - in 1971 the average income of the top 20 per cent was about 15 times greater than that of the bottom 20 per cent. Secondly, the Gini ratios suggest that the degree of inequality remained broadly constant from 1957 to 1975. Yet the incidence of poverty appears to have fallen sharply through to 1965, stabilized in the late 1960s and increased in the first half of the 1970s. The explanation for this apparent paradox is that the 1975 FIES was characterized by massive understatement (the 1975 FIES estimate of per capita income is only half the level of per capita personal income from the National Accounts of the same year), much more so than the previous surveys. Thus the suggested increase in poverty incidence may simply be a statistical artifact. Nevertheless, the understatement was particularly great among high income groups - even compared with the earlier FIES - so the possibility of increasing poverty in the early 1970s cannot be discounted. Whatever estimate is used, the incidence of poverty is disturbingly high for a country which has experienced thirty years of sustained economic growth.

The second piece of evidence relates to trends in real wages. Data collected by the Central Bank (for urban workers) and the Bureau of Agricultural Economics (for agricultural workers) suggest that wage-earners have actually become worse off since 1960. In the case of the former series there has been a steady deterioration since 1960 for both skilled and unskilled labourers, and a particularly sharp decline during the mid-1970s. This would appear to confirm the conclusion of the FIES that poverty has increased in the 1970s, to the extent that wage-earners are among the bottom 40 per cent of the population. Of course, the majority of the workforce is self-employed and the data say nothing about their position. But such a precipitous decline in earnings could hardly have led to an improvement in income distribution.

It has been argued that inferences about distribution cannot be drawn from the decline in real wages for two reasons: first, that workers transferring from self-employment to wage-employment could be better off even if real wages are declining; secondly, that non-wage allowances have increased significantly since 1970, and this has not been fully reflected in the wage data. Nevertheless, the first point neglects the sluggish growth of the 'modern' wage-employment sector referred to already, and the second that the majority of the industrial workforce is employed in small and medium firms where the payment of such allowances is not so widespread.

In contrast to the gloomy picture painted by the FIES and real wages data, most social indicators have recorded improvements since 1960. For example, per capita food supplies (that is, food production plus food imports less food exports and deductions for seed grain, storage losses, etc) have risen, reflecting the growth in agricultural output. The annual Food Balance Sheet series suggests that per capita calorie and protein supplies have been improving, and that both are more than 100 per cent of average requirements. Conversely, the 1978 First Philippine Food Consumption Survey, which NEDA believes is more accurate than the Food Balance Sheet data, found per capita calorie intake to be only 89 per cent adequate, and that 54 per cent of children aged 1-6 years were malnourished (80 per cent mildly so) (NEDA 1980:174). Unfortunately, there are no data on nutritional standards over time. But, clearly, increasing food supplies do not necessarily mean better nutrition for the poor.

To sum up, the evidence strongly suggests that the

Philippine record on equity has been poor. Moderate economic growth has not been accompanied by an improvement in the existing highly unequal distribution. Indeed, the poor may have become relatively more numerous. The present administration, hailed as a shift away from the disruptive bickering of the 'old politics' towards a new action-oriented and disciplined regime, has accelerated the rate of economic growth but has apparently done no better with regard to equity than its predecessors.

Table 8.2

Trends in poverty and inequality, 1957-1975

	1957	1961	1965	1971	1975
1. Income shares					
a.Per cent of family income received by:					
(i) lowest 20% of families	4.5	4.2	3.5	3.6	
(ii) top 20% of families	55.1	56.5	55.5	54.0	
b.Gini ratio(a)	0.48	0.50	0.51	0.49	0.49
2. Poverty incidence(b)					
Per cent of families below family poverty line according to:					
(i) World Bank	72.1	57.9	43.3	44.9	53.2
(ii) Tan and Holazo			41	44	52
(iii) Social Indicators Project			76	78	80

Sources: 1.a NEDA, Statistical Yearbook of the Philippines
              (1981)
          1.b   Tan and Holazo (1979)
          2(i)   World Bank (1980)
          2(ii)   Tan and Holazo (1979)
          2(iii) Mangahas and Barros (1979)

(a) This ratio ranges between 0 and 1, and indicates the degree of inequality in incomes or expenditure. The higher its value, the higher the inequality.

(b) The variations between the three sets of poverty estimates, even though they are derived from the same data set, reflect different definitions of poverty and the use of different sets of price indices.

Land reform

The chasm between large-landed elites and tenant farmers has long fuelled rural unrest in the Philippines; the peasant uprisings during the 1930s, the communist-led Huk insurrection in the post-war years, and the birth of the NPA in the late 1960s had their roots in the feudal and semi-feudal land tenure pattern in the countryside. In the search for political stability, successive Filipino governments prior to martial law, including the Marcos regime, proclaimed their commitment to land reform and passed legislation in congress, but in reality did little to implement any reforms.

When martial law was declared land reform was claimed to be a vital part of 'the revolution from the centre' to create the 'New Society' (Kerkvliet 1979). On the first anniversary of the proclamation of the Land Reform Decree (PD27), President Marcos stated: 'The land reform program is the only gauge for the success or failure of the New Society'. Indeed, martial law itself was justified on grounds that the legislative branch had obstructed Marcos's earlier attempts at rapid implementation of land reform legislation, despite substantial evidence that the opposite was the case (Kerkvliet 1979).

The record so far shows that the extent of implementation during the martial law years has been better than in previous periods. However, as Ledesma (1982) has documented in detail, the scope and effects of the programme leave out most landless rural poor. This is due to the limited coverage of crop lands and the complete exclusion of landless agricultural workers from the programme.

The decree in 1972 covered only rice and maize farmers whose landlords owned more than seven hectares. Operation Land Transfer (OLT) was initiated to distribute certificates of land transfer (CLT) to eligible tenant farmers, who became amortizing owners. Later, in 1974, Operation Leasehold (LHO) was launched to give fixed-leasehold status to share tenants of landowners who owned seven hectares or less. (Subsequently, presidential decrees have proclaimed the extension of the programme to cover share tenants on all crop lands, but this has never been implemented.) Landless workers have been completely excluded.

The limitation of land transfer to rice and maize farmers whose landowners owned more than seven hectares meant that 60 per cent of the tenant farmers could never obtain land ownership. However, they became eligible for fixed leasehold status. In terms of the total crop area of the country, these two groups covered only 20.6 per cent; they constitute only 13.7 per cent of the total agricultural labour force.

By 1979, 54 per cent of those under OLT were issued CLTs. At current rates only 42 per cent of the target group would receive such certificates by the year 2000. Since amortization payments start after the receipt of CLTs, the majority of these farms will not even be able to start making payments during their lifetimes, let alone own the land. Those who have started payments have run into financial problems; among respondents to a survey in 1977, 80 per cent had overdue payments (Montemayor and Escueta 1977).

Land reform proceeded faster in those areas in Luzon which were the centres of agrarian unrest. Rapid technological change in rice cultivation enables beneficiaries of land reform programmes to capture substantial benefits. However, in a 'progressive' village in Laguna where technical change had been rapid, careful analysis revealed that 'the inequality within the village has been aggravated by the land reform operations because larger tenants captured major benefits and no gain accrued to landless workers' (Hayami 1978:108-109). Indeed, Hayami (1979:7) later observed that there is a 'dramatic trend towards polarisation' in the village.

The link between tenure reform and productivity increases has not been convincingly demonstrated in empirical studies. However, land augmenting technical change (of the 'green revolution' type) raises more acutely the question of appropriate land valuation because the crucial issue of who ultimately controls the land remains unchanged. And Ledesma (1982:205) observes: '...tenure change by itself is no guarantee for increased production; but increased production before tenure change can be a formidable deterrent to the completion of land tenure reform'.

Thus, despite some achievements, the much vaunted land reform programme has had only limited success in eradicating the basic problem of rural landlessness and income inequalities, and there appear to be no grounds for optimism that the situation will change rapidly in the coming period.

Foreign investment, trade and debts

It is not possible to examine here these highly complex and controversial issues in any depth. Our basic argument concerning them is three-fold: first, that in purely economic terms, the importance of foreign investment and trade in the Philippine economy has been exaggerated by some writers; secondly, that the economy has probably been in some respects too open and in other respects not open enough in order to maximize national economic welfare; and, thirdly, that increased export orientation is quite consistent with the goal of improved equity provided suitable policy reforms are initiated.

First, the empirical evidence. Although the data are inadequate (Lindsey and Valencia 1981), there is little doubt that foreign investment increased sharply during the martial law years. Board of Investments, approvals suggest that real annual investment for the years 1973-80 was approximately double that of 1968-72. Nevertheless, in aggregate, the importance of this investment is still quite slight. For example, total net capital inflow into the Philippines averaged a little over $US 1 billion during the years 1977-81 (OECD annual), but more than half took the form of official capital inflows (that is from governments, the World Bank, etc.) and only about 16 per cent was private equity capital. Moreover, the stock of foreign investment, while totalling almost $US 2 billion in the late 1970s, was, as a proportion of GNP, well below that of other ASEAN countries except Thailand.

Similarly, the Philippines is not a particularly open economy in terms of international trade. The share of exports plus imports in its GNP is about 40 per cent, which is the lowest of the eight major East Asian developing countries - far below that of Singapore (about 400 per cent) and lower even than that of Thailand (about 50 per cent). It is only its foreign debt which is relatively large by regional standards. The Philippines is not in the big league of foreign borrowers, but its long-term overseas debt - estimated in late 1983 at $US 24 billion - is considerable. The debt service ratio (ratio of debt repayments to export earnings) is also high and increasing: according to World Bank estimates it reached 22 per cent in 1982, but this is a substantial underestimate. Much of the increased debt has occurred in the public sector (public sector debt as a proportion of GDP doubled in the decade 1970-80), and we will defer discussion of the debt issue until the next section.

The current regime has been criticized for adopting an excessively export-oriented strategy. However, this criticism ought to be directed towards particular aspects of the strategy, rather than the fundamental philosophy itself. There is mounting evidence from other countries in the region that a policy of labour-intensive export-oriented industrialization is likely to be conducive to improved income distribution, provided an appropriate mix of policies, including land reform, agricultural pricing and infrastructure investment, is instituted (on the Taiwan experience, see Kuo, Ranis and Fei 1981). The reason, essentially, is that promoting industries consistent with a country's comparative advantage - in the Philippine case, labour-intensive activities - is likely to generate employment growth and enhance the bargaining power of labour. The Philippine experience through to the late 1970s differs fundamentally from this scenario. In fact, one recent paper (Lal 1983) has argued - plausibly in our view - that the past inward-looking trade regime has contributed to the observed decline in real manufacturing wages, and therefore had an adverse effect on equity performance.

Administrative aspects of the trade regime have also had serious distribution implications. Ever since the introduction in 1946 of Republic Act 35 (which provided incentives for 'new and necessary' industries) all governments have been highly interventionist in the trade sector. This has extended, on the import side, to a highly differentiated tariff structure, import controls and quotas, and foreign exchange controls; and on the export side, to an assortment of levies and restrictions. Such a complex system inevitably creates enormous opportunities for political patronage and bureaucratic enrichment, which have of course been ubiquitous features of Philippine society in the post-independence era. The economic and political economy arguments for less intervention in the Philippine trade sector are persuasive.

This is not to deny that several aspects of current trade policies are of dubious value. For example, the export processing zones in their current form confer little benefit to the national economy, for at least two reasons. First, recent cost-benefit analysis has suggested that the returns to public sector investment in the zones are minimal, and that they in fact constitute a subsidy to the predominantly foreign-owned firms located there. Secondly, the zones by their nature attract foot-loose activities and generally make little contributon to technology transfer through linkages with the rest of the economy. Similarly, the operations of the fruit export industry, based mainly in Mindanao, have been widely criticized, and the benefits to the local economy do appear to be quite minimal. But in both cases the problem lies with the particular institutional arrangements rather than the export strategy itself.

The past trade regime has also affected the distribution of gains from foreign investment, probably to the benefit of the multinationals. It appears that much of the foreign investment in manufacturing has been import-substituting and domestic-market oriented in nature.(2) Many of these firms established behind protective trade barriers in the small, concentrated local market (see Lindsey 1977 for early estimates of seller concentration in the industrial sector), and the beneficiaries - to the extent that they were able to earn super-normal profits sheltered from foreign competition - were precisely these companies. In our view, the heavy domestic-market orientation of foreign investors has reduced the benefits accruing to the Philippines. But the cause has been the trade regime, rather than foreign investment per se.

The public sector

The Philippine public sector is quite small compared to many other developing countries at similar stages of development, but its share of GNP (currently almost 20 per cent) has increased substantially in the last decade. There are widely contrasting views on its performance over this period. On the one hand, it is argued that it now plays a dynamic role in Philippine development while at the same time its operations have been rationalized in several important respects. The contrasting view is that its expansion has ushered in a new period of patronage and cronyism unparalleled even by Philippine standards, and that much of the increased expenditure has gone to the military to finance mounting insurgency problems. Both these arguments contain an element of truth.

On the positive side, there has been a genuine attempt to rationalize and streamline government operations in several fields. Some of these have already been referred to. The chaotic system of industrial incentives existing prior to the 1970s is being reformed, and the intervention of the Central Bank, the Ministry of Trade and Industry, and the Board of Investments is becoming less cumbersome.

Another area in which important policy reforms are being effected is energy. Here the government is attempting a bold but basically sensible strategy of import substitution while at the same time adopting realistic domestic pricing policies. The Philippines is heavily dependent on imported oil - in 1980 it accounted for about 77 per cent of total energy (not just oil) consumption. A policy of energy diversification is sensible given the importance of oil in total imports and given the political vulnerability of the government to the use of the oil weapon by certain oil exporters. In adopting the programme, and unlike some other countries, the government has adopted a politically unpopular but economically sensible strategy of realistic petroleum and electricity pricing.

There have also been important changes in the composition of government expenditure. Increased militarization of the Philippines, especially in Mindanao and parts of the Visayas, has resulted in a larger proportion of the budget being allocated to defence - partly at the expense of education and welfare - as compared to the 1960s. Nevertheless, the proportionate increase has been quite modest, except for a sharp rise in the early years of martial law, and as a percentage of GNP, Philippine defence expenditure remains one of the lowest in the Asian region.

But the most important and contentious development in the last decade has been the increased government intervention in a wide range of economic activities, and the growing politicization of much business activity. The former is not necessarily undesirable, as the strong business-government links in Japan and South Korea have demonstrated. But in the Philippine case there are two interrelated and undesirable aspects of the intervention, which together account for much of the current foreign debt difficulties and which have important growth and equity implications.

The first is government bankrolling of dubious economic projects. There are numerous examples of these: hotel and tourism-related expenditure in the mid-1970s, some of the major industrial projects if they are reinstituted and, perhaps most important, the Kilusang Kabuhayan at Kaunlaran (KKK, or People's Livelihood Program), which was launched amid much fanfare in August 1981 by the wife of President Marcos. The government has committed P4 billion to the KKK, which will be used mostly as loans for small-scale 'people's' projects across a wide range of activities. A full evaluation of the programme is premature, and no doubt some of the funds are being allocated to projects which would have

145

received public sector loans in any case. But the evaluation and appraisal apparatus of the programme is suspect, and already problems of arrears and allegations of corruption have emerged.

A second undesirable aspect of the increased intervention is that much of it appears to be little more than the distribution of political largesse to powerful and well-connected individuals. This has occurred most notably in the foreign trade sector (for example, in coconuts, sugar, fertilizer and tobacco), and in the recent bail-out operations of the government, whereby the massive arrears of several large firms to the three government-owned banks were converted to public equity holdings.

The Philippines is not unique in experiencing domestic financial upheavals, of course, and the magnitude of the arrears problems pales into insignificance when compared to the Pertamina crisis in Indonesia in the mid-1970s. However, the public sector policies have contributed substantially to the current foreign debt problems. Borrowing on international capital markets is a sensible economic strategy providing, basically, that the return on investment projects exceeds the cost of borrowed funds. With the benefit of hindsight, it is easy to argue that the government has been less than prudent in its overseas borrowings. But it needs to be remembered that the Philippines, like many other debtor countries, has been seriously affected by the unusual coincidence of high real interest rates, contracting markets for its newly-established manufacturing export industries, and deteriorating terms of trade. A policy of increased foreign borrowing to maintain the growth momentum and to attempt to ride out the difficulties of a dramatic deterioration in the country's terms of trade is not without merit. Here also, however, the current problems have arisen primarily not because there is anything inherently undesirable in the borrowings but because of the uses to which some of the funds have been put.

Developments in perspective

A frequent defence of the faltering economic performance advanced by the government is that in recent years the economy has been subjected to unusually severe external shocks. The rapidly deteriorating terms of trade - primarily the result of rising real oil prices and declining sugar and coconut prices - has already been referred to. Increasing real interest rates have increased the debt service ratio substantially. Finally, rising protectionism in developed country markets has undoubtedly hampered the government's new emphasis on export-oriented industrialization. How significant have these developments been? The data for the period 1972-81 indicate that, despite the terms of trade deterioration, the international 'purchasing power' of exports has continued to rise in most years, and that it is now higher than a decade ago. In effect, what has happened

Table 8.3

Philippine development in regional perspective

Country/Region	GNP per capita 1981 $US	Av. annual growth in per capita GNP 1960-81 (%)	Life expectancy at birth 1981	Daily calorie supply per capita (as % of requirements) 1980	Adult literacy rate 1980 (%)	Primary school enrolment as % of age group 1980
1.ASEAN						
Philippines	790	2.8	63	116	75	110
Indonesia	530	4.1	54	110	62	98
Malaysia	1,840	4.3	65	121	60	92
Singapore	5,240	7.4	72	134	83	107
Thailand	770	4.6	63	104	86	96
2.Northeast Asia						
South Korea	1,700	6.9	66	128	93	107
Hong Kong	5,100	6.9	75	128	90	109
3.Low income countries	270	2.9	58	97	52	93
4.Middle income countries	1,500	3.8	60	110	65	100

Source : World Bank (1983)

is that the quantity increase has more than compensated for the price decrease (exports at current prices deflated by import prices).

The effect of the deterioration in the terms of trade may also be assessed by calculating a revised GNP which adjusts for the fact that a given physical quantity of exports can now effectively purchase fewer imports. The growth rate of such an adjusted real GNP is substantially less than that of actual real GNP after 1973. For this period the growth rate would have been 18 percentage points higher - 2.25 percentage points annually - in the absence of the decline.

How well has the Philippines performed compared to other developing countries? Table 8.3 provides information on a range of social and economic indicators for the seven developing countries of East Asia and for all low and middle income developing countries. Two main conclusions emerge from the data.

First, the Philippines has been by far the worst performer among non-socialist countries in East Asia. In the two decades 1960-80, its growth rate has been only a little over half that of the (unweighted) average for the region as a whole. The Philippine economy has been on a steady downward slide relative to neighbouring countries in the region for much of the post-independence era. Twenty years ago, its per capita income was second only to the city states of Hong Kong and Singapore, and similar to that of Malaysia. By the early 1990s, if current growth rates are maintained, it will be the poorest member of ASEAN.

Secondly, however, on the basis of official figures its performance appears better if compared with all developing countries and other indicators of development. For example, the economy grew faster than the average for all low income countries, and at a similar rate to middle income countries if the relatively advanced countries in this group are excluded. It has maintained relatively good achievements in social indicators, especially in relation to life expectancy and education, though declines in real expenditure on health and education have been noted in recent years. Moreover, compared to East Asian developing countries almost all countries have an inferior record. The performance of Hong Kong, Singapore, Korea and Taiwan - the so-called 'gang of four' - is virtually unparalleled, and it is unlikely that the experience of the city states in particular can be replicated by the populous low income countries (Cline 1982). In the case of at least two ASEAN countries, Indonesia and Malaysia, growth in the 1970s was fuelled by a strong resource sector.

A fairer comparison in the international context would be to evaluate the Philippine performance in the light of recent developments in Thailand, an economy with many similarities. They faced a similar deterioration in their terms of trade, are heavily dependent on imported oil to meet energy needs, have nearly equal populations and, despite growth in manufacturing exports in recent years, remain mainly primary goods exporters and are similarly endowed with many natural resources. Such a comparison shows that by almost any indicator, Thai economic performance has been superior to that of the Philippines. In 1960, its per capita income was about half that of the Philippines; in just two decades it has closed the gap. The Thai economy has registered faster growth rates in every major sector, the differences being particularly striking in the case of the industrial (and manufacturing) sector. It has also avoided the major currency instabilities and foreign debt problems facing the Philippines, while pursuing a more open exchange rate regime. Furthermore, it appears likely that the gains from growth, particularly in agriculture, have been distributed more widely in Thailand (Chapman 1984).

While it is difficult to evaluate the relative importance of various factors contributing to these differences, it is arguable that more prudent macroeconomic policies, greater consistency and continuity in development strategies, and the relatively less corruption of the crony-capitalism type have been important factors in the superior Thai performance.

Conclusion and prospects

Our main argument is that Philippine economic performance has been satisfactory with respect to growth (at least until 1981) but poor with respect to equity. During the 1970s there was a sustained economic expansion which, although less than the fast-growing economies of East Asia, was quite respectable in international terms, and occurred in spite of the generally unfavourable external circumstances after 1973. However, the equity picture is much bleaker. Philippine society was, of course, characterized by considerable inter-regional and inter-personal inequality during the colonial and early independence eras. However, there is no evidence to suggest that this has improved in the last decade; indeed the degree of inequality may have increased.

What are the prospects for the Philippine economy in the 1980s? The immediate problem is to resolve the critical shortage of foreign currency and to meet foreign debt repayment obligations. The problem of the short-term debt (estimated to be about $US8 billion) was serious but manageable before the post-Aquino assassination political instability. However, the current crisis has exacerbated the debt situation because of massive capital flight and the reluctance of lenders to 'roll over' short-term debts. In the process, and despite vehement domestic opposition from some quarters, the political leverage of the IMF has undoubtedly increased, both directly through the provision of standby credit, and indirectly because other institutions are reluctant to maintain lending unless the IMF continues to support the government.

The immediate options for the government - of any political persuasion - are therefore severely restricted. Nevertheless, the international banks, with considerable exposure in many developing countries, are equally reluctant to see a major default. Hence countries like the Philippines may be able to exercise some bargaining power on debt rescheduling and on the imposition of 'performance criteria' by the lending institutions.

In the present situation, it is clear that at least some steps will be taken to achieve a substantial reduction in domestic demand in line with the major thrust of IMF stabilization policies. In the short term, these steps (a tightening of credit, lower government expenditure and substantial devaluation of the currency) will result in slow or even negative growth. Credit has been particularly tight since 1981 following the disappearance of a prominent Filipino-Chinese businessman, and the bail-out operations which affected several large corporations. Business failures are therefore likely to be widespread, and the effects of these measures will be much more severe than the dislocation resulting from the first-round implementation of the tariff reform. The equity picture may become even bleaker, as the results of these measures are likely to have particularly adverse effects on wage-earners and farmers producing subsistence crops. Whether the political fabric, already seriously strained by recent developments, will be able to accommodate the tensions arising from economic deterioration is an open question.

In the medium to longer term, the two key variables are the world economy and domestic economic policies. If, as is generally expected, the world economy recovers during 1984 the Philippines can expect substantial growth in export volumes and prices. However, the debt situation will improve only marginally according to a recent study by Cline (1983), whose projections were completed before the current crisis. Even if the recovery does not occur, the fundamental choice between more open, export-oriented policies and an inward-looking import-substituting strategy remains. There is much scepticism in the Philippines of the virtues of the former, in part because the distribution of gains has in the past been particularly uneven. However, unless there is wholesale repudiation of foreign debts, any future government will have to maintain export growth in order to finance debt repayments and import requirements.

What are the economic implications if a radical nationalist government assumes power and embarks on a course of repudiation of the foreign debt and nationalization of foreign property in the Philippines? Much would depend on the particular policies adopted, but several responses are likely. First, the Philippines's foreign assets - which are quite small - would be confiscated. Secondly, the country would almost certainly be excluded from the western financial system - as the two countries which have repudiated their foreign debts in the past decade, Cuba and North Korea, have discovered. Even more important is the economy's dependence on trade. Most of its energy supplies are imported, and many local industries are highly import-intensive. A major disruption of trade and capital flows, much more severe than the dislocation in late 1983 and early 1984, would most likely have catastrophic effects on domestic production. It is possible that other governments (such as the Comecon group) would be prepared to finance the country's continuing energy imports, but in the case of machinery, parts and certain raw materials the substitution would be more difficult. In any case, the country's dependence on foreign suppliers and creditors would be far more severe and concentrated than at present. Nevertheless, a new government could regard this course of action more favourably than the current strategy.

Whatever course of action is adopted - an acceptance of the IMF and banks' austerity regime, repudiation and more inward- looking trade policies or a combination of elements of both of these - the immediate prospects for the economy are not bright.

FOOTNOTES

1. For example, the oil import bill in recent years has been around $US 2.5 billion, while remittances for 1982 were officially estimated to be over $US 700 million. (The inclusion of unofficial remittances could take the figure to close to $US 1 billion, or as much as 40 per cent of total oil imports.)

2. The evidence is most incomplete, but one indication is provided by United States Department of Commerce (1981) data relating to the sales destinations of US majority-owned foreign affiliates. For the Asia-Pacific region, local sales as a percentage of total sales for the year 1977 (the latest year for which data are available) for these firms was 39, as compared to the Philippine figure of 83.

Chapter 9

THE 'URBAN POOR'

Michael Pinches

A major post-war phenomenon in the Philippines has been
the migration of large numbers of people from the countryside
to Manila and the associated growth of a populace referred to
locally as the 'urban poor'. These are the people who make
up Manila's cheap labour force and who inhabit the city's
shanty towns and squatter settlements. According to current
estimates they represent up to one third of Metro Manila's
population of around eight million people. They form a major
element within the developing Philippine proletariat.

This paper examines the political character of the urban
poor in relation to Manila's upper classes and the Philippine
government. The first section deals with the socio-economic
make-up of the urban poor and argues that the urban poor are
best understood in terms of their dependence on wage labour.
The common distinction between 'workers' and the 'urban poor'
is rejected. The second section considers the social and
political attitudes of the urban poor and argues that whilst
their aspirations and the means by which they seek to fulfil
them are in some respects conservative, they remain
discontented and express deep hostility towards the rich, the
government and the owners of business. The third section
looks at the changing relations between the state and the
urban poor in the context of their places of residence in
Manila's squatter settlement. Finally, some speculative
discussion is offered on the urban poor in the post-Marcos
future. It is argued that new levels of political volatility
could be witnessed among the urban poor in the future and
that the focus of this could well move beyond the confines of
the anti-eviction campaigns which have in the past been at
the centre of organized protest.

The material presented in this paper is based primarily
on fieldwork carried out between 1979 and 1983 in one of
Manila's largest squatter settlements.

Urban poor or urban workers: conflicting perceptions

Among the middle and upper classes of Manila the urban
poor are variously looked upon with scorn, pity and fear.
These are the people the rich associate with crime, gang
warfare, prostitution, begging, scavenging and countless
other activities that are regarded as unsavoury or dangerous.

The most ubiquitous monuments to the unsightliness and danger attached to the poor are the high concrete walls that the rich construct around their own houses. The same thinking is also pervasive in government circles. One document, for instance, refers to Tondo, Manila's largest squatter colony, as 'a bed of crime, violence, filth and disease', (National Housing Authority n.d.) while Metro Manila governor Mrs Marcos, is well known for her attempts to 'beautify' Manila by driving poor people away from the city or by concealing them behind whitewashed fences.

Yet it is also within the ranks of the urban poor that the rich find much of their labour: their maids, their drivers, the workers who build their houses and their business premises, their factory employees and the purveyors of their commodities. Even when they do not make direct use of the labour of the urban poor they depend in numerous ways on city services which could not exist without such labour.

Despite this it is usual practice among government officials, intellectuals and activists to distinguish between 'workers' and the 'urban poor'. In part this distinction follows the separation between the spheres of production and consumption which have come with capitalist development. 'Workers' are considered at their places of labour and in terms of immediate industrial issues. The 'urban poor' are examined at home and in relation to their patterns of consumption, most notably in terms of their residential status as squatters. But this is not the only source of the distinction. Foremost in the middle and upper-class consciousness is an image of the urban poor as an underclass of people who are either unemployed or who eke out a marginal existence away from the centres of production, in what economists call the informal sector. Frequently they are viewed as an impediment to economic growth and a drain on scarce national resources. In short, the urban poor are regarded as a problem. Some advocate severe punitive remedies while others see them as a case for Christian charity or state welfare; in neither instance are they thought of seriously as workers.

This distinction between 'workers' and the 'urban poor' is fallacious and has done much to distort the way in which the people of Manila's slums and squatter settlements are understood. I would argue that Manila's shanty towns should be seen as labouring communities. In contrast to the perceptions of outsiders, this is also the way in which the people of these communities view themselves: certainly they regard themselves as poor, but they attribute this poverty to being lowly paid or to being out of a job. In the settlement in which I lived the principal difference most people saw between rich and poor was not simply between people with and without wealth, but between those who had capital and those who had only their bodily capacity to labour.

Clearly there are high levels of unemployment among the urban poor and many gain a livelihood from irregular, relatively unproductive occupations. Also, employment, occupation and income vary from one settlement to another. But evidence from my own and other studies shows a generally heavy reliance of shanty town communities on wage work (see National Housing Authority 1976; Tondo Foreshore Development Authority 1975; Hollnsteiner 1973; Decaesstecker 1978). Much of this wage work is casual and uncertain, yet a great many of the unemployed participate in wage employment at some time.

Even in the most demeaning jobs there is not only an upward economic linkage to modern industry but frequently also a capital-wage labour relation. In many cases this relation is not fully developed or is disguised as patronage or by what some call 'rent capitalism', but it is towards wage labour that the urban poor are most oriented, either directly or through others on whom they depend. In the case of small store operators, food vendors, tailors or water carriers who worked in the commumnity in which I lived, there existed a strong identification with those in wage labour employment on whose income they relied for custom. The unemployed depend on wage workers even more.

The crucial point here is that the urban poor generally live as communities closely tied through relations of mutual help, centred on kinship, regional identity and neighbour-hood. Strong tensions can exist between those with and without jobs, and some relatively prosperous families leave their communities in part to avoid the pressures which are placed on their incomes. But to a large extent these tensions and departures are minimized by the general instability of employment and by the low incomes that even those in regular employment receive, so that most people are anxious to maintain their networks of reciprocity.

The urban poor, however, are not totally reliant on wage labour. Many earn their living from self-employment or petty commodity production and there is significant variation between different shanty town communities in the types of occupations on which each depends. Similarly various forms of livelihood give rise to different kinds of labour consciousness. Nevertheless, in general wage work is the most important source of livelihood for the urban poor, the wage labour-capital relation is experienced in many forms of employment, and it is principally this which shapes the social consciousness of the urban poor. According to one man in the community in which I lived:

> The difference between rich and poor is great. For rich people it is their money that moves. The only capital for poor people is our labour. Poor people work hard to earn money. Rich people don't have to labour. They don't sweat like we do. That's the difference.

<u>Conservatism</u> <u>and</u> <u>resentment:</u> <u>urban</u> <u>poor</u> <u>attitudes</u> <u>to</u> <u>the</u>
<u>rich</u>

The collective resentment of the urban poor, born out of
their economic and political experiences as workers, has
posed problems for the Marcos regime. Any post-Marcos
government will have to contend with these feelings of buried
anger.

Two contrasting views are commonly expressed in relation
to the political character of the urban poor: one, that they
constitute a potentially violent, socially disruptive
stratum; the other, that they are essentially conservative,
having similar aspirations to those of the middle class. To
some extent my own findings support the latter view. Most
people who have migrated to Manila see themselves as having
improved their living standards and look to bettering
themselves through hard work and schooling. However the
conservatism and docility of the urban poor is usually
overstated; the common view ignores the widespread feelings
of hostility towards the rich and the comfortable, and to a
large extent begs the question of whether or not the people
are able to fulfill their aspirations. Despite early gains
that many rural migrants make, and the solace generated by
the school system, the longer people stay in Manila the more
they perceive their lives as a struggle against enormous
odds.

Sometimes people attribute their situation to bad luck
or to their own inadequacies, but more often they direct
their bitterness at the rich. The negative attitudes and
behaviour of the rich towards the poor are well known in
Manila's shanty towns. People often feel deeply humiliated
by them and this has promoted a strong sense of distrust and
disaffection. Being able to deceive and annoy the wealthy is
a matter of enjoyment. Whilst people in the community in
which I lived envied the upper classes, aspired in some
respects to their way of life, and individually sought out
their patronage, they also regarded them as selfish and
arrogant, and in many ways viewed their own community life as
superior to that of the rich. When I asked a group of men
what they thought about the people living in Forbes Park, one
of Manila's most plush residential suburbs, they simply
replied: 'These people are our enemy'.

However people do not just speak of the rich in general.
In discussing more immediate problems, hostility is directed
to employers and the government. People in my community
commonly complained about their low wages and about the ways
in which their employers abuse, coerce and unfairly deal with
them. Job dissatisfaction was most commonly expressed in
such actions as pilfering, absenteeism and minor sabotage of
property, but participation in open, organized protest was
minimal and most people had mixed attitudes to unionization
and strike action. There are several reasons for this, but
most important is the highly unstable nature of much wage
employment, due to the huge reserve of labour available among

the urban poor. For many, the greatest struggle is to find a stable job.

Nevertheless, sections of the urban poor have participated in strike action and illicit union activity, and in recent years this has increased. Indeed the first major strike under martial law, at the La Tondena Company in 1975, centred on the squatter settlement of Tondo and involved not only company workers living there but also a large number of their fellow urban poor from the settlement.

Complaints about work and employers inevitably turn to the government and the power it exerts in support of industry and against the interests of the common people. Most people, however, are reluctant to speak openly and critically about the government for they believe that the ultimate price of serious confrontation with the state is death. Repression and fear are a daily feature of life in Manila's shanty towns; most people in the settlements known to me had at some time experienced harassment at the hands of the military or other government agents. Government repression has inhibited active political opposition among the urban poor but it has also deepened the people's resentment towards those who rule over them.

The state and the urban poor: the nature and limits of squatter politics

Political interest in the urban poor has traditionally concentrated on the urban poor as squatters. This focus has drawn attention to the way in which the interests of the urban poor have been sacrificed to those of the rich: as squatters the urban poor are constantly liable to eviction as city land is required for infrastructural or industrial development, for middle and upper-class housing, and for tourism or urban beautification. But considering the urban poor as workers first and squatters second, analysis needs to go beyond this. Of central importance is the government's commitment to the promotion of capitalist economic growth in the Philippines. In this the state is faced with a number of contradictory demands: whilst it is called on to protect the landed property interests of the upper classes it is also engaged in fostering the development of a cheap and abundant labour supply for which the growth of squatter settlement is well suited; as it does this, the government is required to manage consequent worker unrest through political and bureaucratic containment. Simultaneously, the dynamics of capitalist expansion have drawn government into further promoting the growth of private property in urban real estate with the urban poor as newly-defined consumers in this market. It is in the light of these contradictions that we can best understand the changing pattern of politics in Manila's squatter settlements.

Prior to martial law, governments dealt with squatter settlements in an ad hoc manner based on neglect and expedience, the most important factors being the political power of different real estate interests and the opportunities presented to elected officials for political clientelism. Under the system of patronage politics which characterized government during this era, mayors, councillors and even congressmen could be easily swayed by the guarantee of a large block vote from squatters; since squatters in many areas were under constant threat of eviction, either by private landowners or city authorities, the easiest way in which politicians could gain votes in these areas was to promise land rights or to hold off ejection procedures.

As in many other spheres of public life it was also possible for squatters to win favour in the courts and in various government agencies through the payment of unofficial fees to the appropriate officers. Further, there was much irregularity in property law, large tracts of land around Manila were the subject of complicated title disputes, and eviction proceedings were typically long drawn-out affairs, so that once people took possession of land it was difficult legally to remove them. Even in cases where authorities or private owners had the political will to remove squatters, their efforts could be circumvented by vote-seeking or reformist politicians. A major consideration in the approach to squatter eviction was anticipated political unrest. In at least two cases in the late 1950s, involving Tatalon Estate and the Tondo foreshore, the issue of land rights for squatters was fought out between opposing alliances in congress; the outcome in each case was the passing of legislation for the expropriation of occupied land and its distribution to residents. Although such legislation was never implemented, in both settlements it gave squatters a claim to legitimate occupancy rights around which they have subsequently organized. In other cases, however, squatter settlements were demolished and their residents evicted, either by city or municipal authorities, or by private landowners.

Contrary to elite perceptions of social disorder in Manila's slums, there are high levels of involvement in various formal and informal mutual aid associations among the urban poor, and much collective effort has focused on gaining secure possession of the land the people inhabit. Under the circumstances of the pre martial law period this gave rise in many settlements to a particular kind of squatter politics which involved on the one hand the formation of mass-based squatter organizations and on the other the emergence of local power brokers who dealt with the politicians and the bureaucrats. In general, squatter organizations were strongest and most developed in settlements that were large and subject to greatest threat of eviction. Where several squatter communities existed in the same settlement it was common for them to form federations for the purpose of claiming land rights.

The main limitations of such organizations lay in their leadership and its incorporation into the patronage politics of the time. In some cases local leaders had no formal status outside of their communities; in others they were barrio captains or councillors. In either case their strength normally lay in having personal connections with lawyers, bureaucrats and politicians. Although they were often able to provide their followers with protection against eviction, some also enriched themselves at their followers' expense. Moreover their insertion into the vertical chains of political patronage made for the people's own political incorporation as dependents in a highly unequal system of participatory government. Sometimes the leaders lost their support and new leaders emerged, but the system itself remained unchanged.

With the rise of left nationalism in the late 1960s, a new form of politics started to take shape in some of Manila's shanty towns. Many people who had become frustrated with seemingly endless court hearings were inspired by the Patriotic Youth (Kabataang Makabayan) activists who came into their midst and advanced a more militant remedy to the land problem. The urban poor began to find expression for some of the deeper hostilities they felt towards those who ruled over them. On the eve of martial law, the urban poor in several squatter settlements had not only moved from a land rights strategy that focused on legal manoeuvres to one of more direct confrontation, but had also started to become more politicized in a wider sense and were active in various campaigns for change.

When martial law was declared in 1972 these settlements were subjected to immediate repression. On several occasions they were raided by the military and suspected dissidents, arbitrarily defined, were picked up. Organizations that had been operating in these areas were forced underground. For the first few years of martial law, active opposition among the urban poor was effectively stopped; but so too in several key settlements was the immediate threat of eviction lifted, partly in an attempt by the regime to win popular support and partly because a number of the elite families pressing for squatter clearance were those the Marcos regime was attempting to disinherit.

The main agency through which the regime sought to incorporate and control Manila's urban poor was the newly introduced barangay system of local government. Under this system elected barrio captains and councillors were replaced by appointed barangay officials who were no longer formally answerable to the people under them. In many cases this involved a change in political role rather than a change in personnel. Barangay councils were allocated substantially more local authority than their barrio predecessors, being made responsible, in particular, for the maintenance of what is euphemistically referred to as 'peace and order'. Where formerly many local leaders had gained their positions by championing the cause of land rights, they were now required to exercise the powers of martial law and to act as agents for the implementation of programmes superimposed from above.

New powers vested in the barangay councils have provided

them with opportunities for making money, and it is principally on this basis that their loyalty has been retained. In making them directly answerable to a centralized system of authority, the regime has also attempted to initiate them into the ideology of the New Society Movement (KBL) under the political patronage of the First Couple. Through the barangay officials the Marcoses have sought to cultivate patron connections with the mass of urban poor.

The government has further sought to bring the urban poor under state control through the establishment of a barangay youth movement (Kabataang Barangay), barangay ladies auxiliaries, and a number of barangay brigades, notably the barangay tanod brigade which is required to act as a community police force. Positions in all of these bodies are unpaid; membership has been sought through the dispensation of patronage benefits - the provision of uniforms, the right of special place in public ceremonies, occasional gifts of food and clothing, and, for some, outings to favourite leisure resorts. For members of the urban poor the main attraction of these groups lies in the material benefits and opportunities for gaining paid employment that they are assumed to offer. In general, membership comes from among the most destitute and insecure, though with the offer of more lucrative rewards the government has also been able to recruit into key position a few former activists of the pre martial law era.

In part the barangay system has been successful both in suppressing and incorporating political activity among the urban poor, and in some respects it has exposed a weakness which many believe this sector of society has for state co-optation. However, while barangay council officials have retained a certain legitimacy in the eyes of the people under them they are often regarded with suspicion, and in most instances popular support for their activities has been withdrawn. My own studies suggest that the inculcation of New Society values and of loyalty to the Marcoses among barangay officials has been shallow. Some, in fact, have been working covertly for opposition organizations while many others have been effectively pressured, through the social and moral ties they maintain with the people around them, to defend the latter's interests. The advantages that were expected to come with participation in the other barangay organizations have for most proven illusory. In the settlement in which I lived the Kabataang Barangay has all but been disbanded and in the local elections of 1982 many of its former key figures stood in opposition to KBL candidates; the co-operation that had existed between the barangay council and the National Housing Authority had deteriorated sharply, and one councillor who had been outspoken in his support of the New Society had by late 1982 resigned his position and was hoping to join his daughter in the United States, saying he believed the Philippines to be on the brink of civil war.

Despite the lull in squatter evictions in the early years of martial law and the efforts of the government to limit the growth of shanty towns, the number of squatters in Manila has continued to rise. Since 1975 the Marcos regime has launched several massive demolition campaigns. Many people have been moved to resettlement sites out of Manila but many others have been left homeless.

Squatters in several settlements have engaged in organized resistence to relocation, using tactics ranging from the filing of court injunctions and marches on the presidential palace to the use of human barricades. As in the pre martial law period the most successful have been those who obtained assistance from powerful outside groups, especially groups within the Catholic Church, assisted in some cases by intellectuals and lawyers.

The best known and most successful squatter organization since the declaration of martial law is ZOTO, a federation of many small groups which operated in a part of Tondo. At its peak ZOTO received support from the local clergy and from overseas. ZOTO's success prompted the formation of similar groups in other settlements and led to the establishment of a Manila-wide squatter organization, protected and co-ordinated through a network of church bodies.

The government has subjected these groups to continual harassment. Though not officially outlawed they have been branded as subversive or communist and many of their members have been detained and in some cases tortured. Several have disappeared; the squatters presume they are dead. Many members of such groups have now joined the underground opposition.

The political significance of organizations such as ZOTO is difficult to assess. Initially their campaigns were directed principally against demolitions and evictions; given the nature of the Marcos regime it was important that they be seen to operate within these limited goals. To a large extent this was also true of support from the church: it is argued on the left that the methods of community organizing adopted by the church in Manila's slums have discouraged the urban poor from participating in more radical campaigns for social change; in some cases where squatters have turned in this direction church supporters have backed off and in at least one squatter area priests were responsible for the setting up of a more moderate rival group.

In conjunction with its recent demolition activities the Marcos government has been engaged in two other programmes aimed at dealing with Manila's urban poor. One of these, carried out under the National Housing Authority with World Bank funding, involves the redevelopment of Manila's shanty towns. The other, Urban BLISS, is a project of the Ministry of Human Settlements and is supposed to provide more conventional low-cost flat accommodation. A high proportion of squatters who are ejected and sent to resettlement sites, return to squat elsewhere in the city. Indeed continued large-scale relocation of Manila's poor would remove from the city its main source of cheap labour. As an attempt to resolve this problem both of these projects aim at housing the urban poor within Metro Manila.

The alternate programmes of shanty town redevelopment and Urban BLISS are very different. Despite the publicity it has received and the large sums of money allocated to it, the accommodation provided by the projects of BLISS have no significant relevance to the urban poor: the housing provided is both insufficient and too expensive. In contrast, the programme of shanty town redevelopment could have a major impact on Manila's urban poor. It involves the subdivision of shanty town land and the sale to squatters of serviced lots on which to build their own houses. The logic of this policy is that it provides the urban poor with access to residential land that they can afford on existing wage levels, thereby avoiding the necessity for a redistribution of wealth; it provides for the extension of additional state controls over the urban poor; and, in allowing for the further development of private residential property, it serves to open up squatter settlements to the urban real estate market and to undermine existing communal relations.

The political consequences of the programme for the urban poor are not yet clear. In the settlements I am familiar with, bureaucratic rules governing eligibility have tended to turn people against each other. The rules have also been manipulated by local officials to threaten with exclusion those who are regarded as troublemakers. In my experience the majority of people listed as beneficiaries welcomed the prospect of being able to obtain a secure place to live but seriously doubted their capacity to meet the regular monthly payments required over twenty-five years. Already most people have failed to meet these payments, for however low such payments may appear to government planners, they represent a major burden to the urban poor. If people do not pay - and this appears likely under present economic conditions - the settlements may remain much the same as they were before, with similar patterns of communal life and collective response to evictions. On the other hand, the very fact of financial indebtedness could place the government in a position of advantage: instead of the large-scale opposition that mass demolitions arouse, the state may be able to deal with opposition on a household to household basis or else rely on private transactions to sort out those who cannot afford to stay.

Conclusion

Looking to the political role of the urban poor in the post-Marcos future, a number of important points can be drawn from this analysis. In their dependence on wage labour, in their social experiences with the elite and the government, and in their political attitudes and action, the urban poor of Manila form an integral part of the growing Philippine proletariat. They have the same grievances and the same hostility towards the Marcos government that they have towards the bourgeoisie at large. However, political repression and state incorporation have to a large extent prevented this opposition from being organized and actively expressed. State co-optation has been carried out with some success in squatter settlements, though it has been confined to a minority of people and even they cannot be regarded as a sure and lasting government ally, since in many cases the advantaged and the deprived maintain their social ties. Organized opposition among the urban poor, though limited, has emerged in squatter resistance to government campaigns of demolition and eviction; to some extent also it has provided a base for increased politicization and recruitment into the radical underground movement.

On a number of occasions the urban poor have demonstrated openly their opposition to the Marcos regime, as in the 'noise barrage' on the eve of the Interim Batasang Pambansa election in 1978 and in the current wave of street protests following the assassination of Benigno Aquino. What has been crucial in these campaigns is that they have offered the urban poor the protection and confidence of a broadly-based movement. Many people I know saw Aquino as an elite politician who would be unlikely to offer any major change in the circumstances under which they lived. But what he did offer, alive in 1978 and martyred in 1983, was a symbol behind which they could move together to express effectively their anger.

The current crisis in the Philipines centres on the combination of two factors: sharply deteriorating economic conditions and the crumbling authority of President Marcos. For the urban poor the added hardships yet increased freedoms this represents have opened the way for a new level of political action. My feelings are that the urban poor, provided with strong leadership either from the left or from a populist movement, perhaps organized along the lines described by Senator Diokno in chapter 1, could prove a major political force.

During the period of my fieldwork the radical movement in the Philippines had much implicit support among the urban poor. But the general view, at least until recently, has been that it is not yet a sufficiently powerful force to pose a real threat to the Marcos regime. Given this, most people have not been prepared to risk their lives or those of their families in actively joining the struggle, whose major organizational thrusts, in any case, have been in the countryside. Indeed the strategy of the left in recruiting cadres from the slums into the rural areas, though necessary in some respects, has tended to leave the urban poor without leadership and organization. Further, where left activists have been involved in organizing among the urban poor (according to the people I lived with) lack of support was also due in many instances to the display of the same class prejudices that the rich at large practise against the poor.

Additional problems arise in the promotion of a predominately nationalist, anti-imperialist ideology. Among some sections of the urban poor, as in the foreshore settlements of Tondo and Navotas where the people have experienced the immediate threat of foreign business in the development of port facilities and fishing industry, this ideology has found strong appeal; for most, however, the experience of exploitation and subjugation is such that the people identify their principal enemy as the local bourgeoisie.

The departure of President Marcos from political power will be welcomed by the urban poor and it will clearly have a profound impact on the conduct of Philippine politics and on the various elite elements currently contending for succession. The most likely short-term outcomes are a shift in the direction of liberal democracy or a shift towards a more repressive government. In either case the establishment of docility and compliance among the urban poor will be a major task. Whilst a more liberal political environmnet would be preferred, it is likely that for the urban poor very little will change, and that social unrest in Manila's shanty towns will continue. The urban poor are not as yet sufficiently organized or confident to carry out their own rebellion, but the manner and authority with which present and future opposition parties attempt to harness the class hostility that exists among them is crucial, for there is no doubt that they constitute, to twist the language that is often applied to their labour, a huge reserve army.

Chapter 10

RURAL PHILIPPINES: CENTRAL LUZON

Brian Fegan

The rural Philippines is not one but a congeries of regional societies with relatively autonomous histories influenced by the sociologies of their dominant crops and the way regional elites have extracted those for national world markets. The regions have been linked by the participation of those elites in national cultural and political as well as economic life since the nineteenth century. But since the 1960s, to an unprecedented degree, the villagers have been incorporated into national life as the market, roads, schools and officials of the increasingly powerful central state have penetrated to the remotest barrio. Problems of a population doubling every generation, pressure on land and rising landlessness, unemployment and underemployment, the effects of new technologies and new forms of organization of production, exposure to national and international markets not only for goods produced and consumed but now also for the inputs required to produce a crop and for their labour itself, have interacted with the distinct local histories to produce variants in people's responses. Today political events in Manila and decisions taken by meetings of remote international bankers affect the lives of villagers.

This paper looks at Central Luzon, the nation's premier rice-bowl, an area with a population of some 4.5 million that merges at its southern edge into the suburbs of Manila. It is here that the Huk revolt of 1946 - 1953 shook the first three presidents of an independent Philippines. It is here too that land reform, the green revolution, and extension of irrigation have combined with proximity to Manila to produce the most prosperous agricultural region in the country. The area also contains the US bases of Clark Field and Subic Bay with their service towns of Angeles and Olongapo. Its people are the best educated and most politically sophisticated villagers and townsmen in the Philippines. Central Luzon is therefore not typical of the rural Philippines but it has a strategic location and crucial product, rice.

The paper traces and projects into the future some underlying processes in the region in order to ask which of these might be affected by conceivable political outcomes in Manila, which will work themselves out whatever happens in the capital, and how both might feed back into what happens in Manila as the Marcos government and its successors try to deal with problems of state. Some underlying themes are, that it is unlikely that rural insurgency will resume in Central Luzon in the 1980s, because of factors that have demobilized the peasantry; that processes of incorporation of the villagers into the market and state may have created conditions for their mobilization as citizens and as producers and consumers; and that as citizens, Central Luzon's population is likely to respond much like urban Manila's lower middle and working class to the dilemmas of the succession, of economic policy, and of nationalism - that is they want on the one hand a strongman capable of restoring order and prosperity but on the other the restoration of democratic processes for selecting and above all removing governments; both prospects frighten as much as attract them.

It is as producers that the farmers of Central Luzon may prove volatile, for rice agriculture is now dependent on imported petroleum and petrochemicals whose supply may be cut. Prolonged political uncertainty in Manila and a further postponement of debt service, or the emergence of an economic nationalist and repudiationist regime, could leave the nation unable to fund essential petroleum imports. That would immobilize the hand tractors that replaced buffalo in the 1970s, take some marginal land out of cultivation and reduce multiple cropping, while lack of petroleum-derived fertilizer and crop protection chemicals would sharply cut yields. The subsequent shortfall in the national harvest would tempt farmers to withhold their grain in protest at government policy, to hoard for a price rise and for consumption. A Manila government would face a no-win choice. If to feed Manila it left price and supply to market forces then rice riots, strikes and urban unrest could follow. If it attempted to hold . down prices in the city then, given its financial problems and IMF policies against a subsidy to producers, it might have to seize their stocks, at the cost of rural unrest. Either response, following a period of paralysing uncertainty over control of the state, could invite military intervention.

Demobilization of the peasantry

The Huk rebellion of 1946-1953 arose from rural conditions that no longer prevail in Central Luzon though they have been recreated elsewhere, such as parts of the Cagayan valley and Mindanao. From around 1920 peasant unions proliferated in Central Luzon in protest at the way landlords were tightening the conditions of tenancy. At that time the land frontier was just passing in the region; most village households held tenant farms. As a result of virtual internal class homogeneity as tenants, villagers could unite against the town landlords. Rapid population increase, doubling at each generation, at first created the competition for farms that allowed landowners to increase rents. But that provoked unrest, culminating in the Huk rising. Thereafter continuing population increase produced a generation later a numerous and rapidly growing class of absolutely landless households in the villages. They had nothing to gain from confrontation with landowner or government over the conditions of tenure. Their interests were in conflict with the tenant farmers over access to houselots, dry season vegetable plots, but above all over access to the increasingly scarce farmwork and over the scale of pay to farm labour.

After the mid-1950s rural insurgency in Central Luzon declined as the villagers became increasingly divided internally on these lines. By 1971 over half the households in Central Luzon were landless, just when the land reform and the green revolution began to take effect.

The early effects of the green revolution were to increase the amount of landless labourer man-days that peasants hired to get a crop. This was because of more labour-intensive straight-row planting and weeding, and the coincidence of heavier crops to reap and thresh in a shorter period as double cropping and non-seasonal varieties spread. But in a second and third round of technological change, labour-displacing chemicals and machinery reversed this trend. The hand tractor replaced buffalo in the early 1970s. By the late 1970s improved chemical weedicides permitted direct-seeding the paddies, eliminating labour-intensive uprooting seedlings, transplanting and weeding, except in areas hard to drain. About 1979 the mini-thresher largely replaced hand-threshing for both wet and dry season harvest. This left to the landless labourers only one major task in the cultivation: reaping. In 1982 IRRI was about to release a small reaping machine designed to use as power source the handtractor many farmers already had.

The free sources of food - fish, frogs, snails, crabs - that poor villagers formerly got from the paddy fields and waterways were sharply reduced by the weedicides and insecticides farmers now use. Yet protest by the landless against the loss of work, cuts in pay rates, and loss of free resources has been muted. Some of the reason is that many men left the family in the village while they went to Manila or to town to find work. Those who stayed in the villages found it possible to raise small livestock, and to get bits of work here and there mostly from farmers or on the roads. Their children now move to Manila to seek work. More important, landless labourers are less visible than the more prosperous farmers who constitute the village leadership and its spokesmen.

The partially implemented land reform carried out under PD27 of President Marcos completed demobilization of the peasants on the tenancy issue. Although various writers have shown that the reform converted fewer tenants to amortizing owners than had been expected, most share tenants were able to shift from 50 per cent crop shares to 25 per cent of the average of the three harvests immediately preceding martial law. This was an immediate rent reduction, and a continuing windfall as harvest increases after that date, due to new seeds, fertilizers, improved irrigation and so on, did not raise the rent. Moreover, farmers were at first granted access to cheap institutional credit to replace high-interest landowner loans. Despite the indecision, delays and muddle in land reform implementation that allowed many owners to evade land transfer, tenant beneficiaries credit President Marcos personally with granting them what the Huk once fought for. The drawn out implementation served to remind tenant beneficiaries of the depth and persistence of landowner resistance and therefore of the importance of their benefactor Marcos remaining in power and motivated to complete the task. Tenant beneficiaries fear that return to pre martial law democracy could restore a landowner-dominated legislature and reverse the reform. Meantime, rumours circulate among them that the CPP and NPA would if they gained power follow the Chinese path, taking away the recently gained farms to redistribute them evenly among all villagers; or setting up co-operative or state farms.

The tenant beneficiaries of land reform today are the dominant class in the villages. They are able to divide and control the more numerous landless by allotting and threatening to withdraw permissions to occupy houselots, to use bamboo, firewood and drinking water from the tenant's lot, to fish in the paddies, to use a dry paddy to plant vegetables, and to take hay and grass from the fields to feed livestock. The farmers fear that democracy could reverse the land reform, that the left would take away their land. They are essentially conservative and cautious on the land issue. They look for a strongman regime that would secure their gains.

But the farmers have other problems occasioned by their greatly increased exposure to market forces. Up to the late 1960s farmers got a crop by using their buffalo and implements plus seed saved from the last crop or swapped with neighbours. They used cash only to pay for transplanting, and sold little of their crops. Today farmers must use money at every stage to produce a crop: to pay instalments on hand tractors and for parts, gasoline and oil; to buy fertilizer, insecticide, weedicide; to buy the latest seed variety; to pay lease rents, amortization instalments, land tax, irrigation fees and Samahan Nayon dues; to repay lending institutions and money-lenders. Though rent takes a smaller proportion of the increased crop, these other cash costs have increased so much that farmers are squeezed between rising input costs and the National Grain Authority (NGA) controlled price at which they are able to sell grain. The recent removal of petrol and fertilizer subsidies, on World Bank direction, should exacerbate the crunch.

Meanwhile, the early 1970s flood of cheap institutional credit, released and recovered on soft political criteria, has dried to a trickle and is released only to the lucky few with good credit records. These are also the best-off farmers. This has had two consequences. First, farmers were obliged to treat their farms as businesses, or lose them. They had to treat the labour of their landless neighbours as items in a balance sheet rather than as social expenditures, and turned therefore to mechanical and chemical techniques wherever these cut costs. Secondly, those cut off from cheap institutional credit had to turn to private money-lenders to get the cash without which agriculture today is unproductive. Private money-lenders, however, required as security the tenancy or farm purchase right. Though it is illegal to transfer these except to a sole heir, farm rights have been transacted by covert mortgage allowing a trend to re-accumulation of farms in the hands of rich villagers. Typically these kulaks control from two to six farms, worked with machines and hired labour making use of the most modern farm practices. The kulaks own and hire out hand tractors; they are first to obtain the latest seed varieties and thus able to multiply it for sale at a premium; they own or act as agents for mini-threshers; they buy fertilizer cheap in bulk for themselves and for resale on credit to neighbours, and buy the rice of their neighbours plus the rights to sell it at NGA floor price, for resale at a profit; they accept repayment of debts in discounted rice; they deal in commercial hog and chicken feeds and run small commercial piggeries. This new class of village entrepreneurs is able to obtain cheap institutional credit for relending at higher interst, and to take farm rights as security for the loan. Unlike the rural banks and town money-lenders, they are able to foreclose on farm rights of bad debtors through the collusion of the debtor and village officials. From my limited observations they are also KBL members and act as political brokers between villagers and the town and national government officials.

In summary, the situation in the villages is that the tenant beneficiaries of the land reform are essentially conservative. Their leadership consists of rich peasants, some of them KBL members, and village officials. They are grateful to President Marcos personally, but it is unclear whether this gratitude could be transferred to a successor. They fear both a resumption of electoral democracy that might allow former landowners to reverse the reform (much of which remains incomplete), and fear equally a leftist regime that could take their land. They hope for a strongman who would secure the land reform gains and maintain order. They are probably volatile only as producers, on the lines that we have seen among small farmers in the EEC countries, around the issues of input and product prices. Should petroleum imports be cut farmers would protest by reducing planting, withholding grain, and demonstrations. Any worsening of the squeeze between non-subsidized petroleum and fertilizer prices on one hand and an NGA-controlled price set low to avoid urban unrest could provoke such responses.

The landless gained nothing from land reform. Later

stages of the green revolution have been labour-displacing to a point at which the landless agricultural workers have little paid work left to them in the villages. They have turned to non-farm jobs in the towns and Manila, and to village sidelines. Their recent losses are muted since they are not the village leadership. Their conflict with the better-off farmers is, however, not likely to be mobilizable by the left within the 1980s; it is likely, rather, to cause intra-village disputes irrelevant to Manila outcomes. It is possible that they could respond as consumers to price rises, for they buy rice rather than sell and so far as they have cash incomes will respond like other poor consumers. It is conceivable that supply and price problems for petroleum and petrochemicals like weedicide could lead farmers back to labour-intensive techniques, absorbing some of their labour. Otherwise the landless will continue to migrate to Manila for work, presenting problems of employment, slum housing, and urban unrest relocated from country to city by the green revolution.

The rural towns: rise of the middle class

Central Luzon towns are no longer the residential quarters of the prosperous gentry landlords, receiving their tenants in the yard and following careers in the professions and politics as a civic duty. Today the grand houses in streets near the plaza are decaying or taken over as warehouses and business premises by entrepreneurs who have no illustrious family lineage but have risen by their own effort. Part of the income that absentee owners once drained from the towns to Manila, and which helped rebuild Manila in the late 1940s, now tends to stay in the town, reversing the stagnation that characterized all but the most centrally placed Central Luzon towns until the mid-1970s. The big landowners who shifted to Manila in the 1940s left professional managers or a poor relation to run their estates. The lands have now been distributed to tenants, so that the staff of overseers and managers has been disbanded; the manager has not even fixed rents to collect where the tenant beneficiaries pay through the Land Bank. With loss of economic control went the last vestiges of political control.

Today the dominant class in the towns is a commercial class of rice traders, truckers, inputs merchants, rural bankers, earthmoving contractors, garage proprietors, machine-shop owners, and small manufacturers. They are supplemented by professionals and semi-professionals like teachers, civil servants, and municipal officials. This middle class includes less wealthy branches of gentry families that have diversified into business.

A rump of fading gentry families failed to make the adjustment. They take little part in civic affairs. They are conservative, opposed to the Marcos regime as the thief of their ancestral lands. They vilify their former tenants as receivers of stolen property, ingrates who turned to bite the hand that had aided them in their troubles, cheats who refuse to pay even the absurdly low reform rents or price for land. The fading gentry are restorationists who want a return to the good old days but seem to have little following. The good old days they want to bring back are the discredited politics of the landed gentry that had become a myth, replaced by political machines and strongmen, even before it was overthrown in 1972.

It is the new class of entrepreneurs, and of medium landowners who diversified into new businesses, that is the dominant class in the towns. They man the Knights of Columbus, the Lions, the fiesta committees, and, some of them are KBL functionaries. The landowners among them did all they could to evade, delay and obstruct implementation of land reform but were forced to (if they had not already) set up diversified business enterprises. Many of them, once they had removed as much land as possible from land transfer and forced up the land transfer price or lease rents to a level they could accept, dropped opposition as unbusinesslike and got on with their enterprises. The new commercial class tends to be forward-looking rather than buried in nostalgia.

Many are allied to KBL officials for the business advantages it brings in access to contracts and influence that puts business opportunities in their way and spares them some unwelcome attention from officials. In the 1980 general elections the mayors and town councillors for the handful of Central Luzon towns for which I have figures were, aside from being all or overwhelmingly KBL, drawn from the new commercial class and rich peasants. Most of them were genuinely popular figures who would have emerged from the elections in strong positions even had the election rules and count not so favoured KBL. Many local observers commented that the local elections confirmed the domination of countryside over township that is the winners were either rich peasants or those popular with the peasants rather than the old gentry identified with the town. Moreover, the town officials then elected have democratic manners, are accessible and have more professional staffs than ever before.

Among these businessmen and professionals there was general approval of the 'development', and peace and order that brought them prosperity under Marcos. This was tempered by criticism of the waste and corruption of some figures in the regime, particularly those associated with Mrs Marcos, who was the focus of many stories about greedy officials. This bourgeois group welcomed the degree of democratic participation allowed in the 1980 local elections and the excitement of the political campaign. But they were afraid it might lead to or signal a weakening of the peace imposed by the central state on local politicians since 1972. No one wanted a return to the days when politicians were surrounded by armed bodyguards, whose off-duty arrogance and impunity was a source of terror in the towns. They seemed more ready to tolerate a regime that used arrest or violence against radical critics than one where private violence put respectable citizens at risk.

The town commercial and professional class are likely to take their political ideas and stances from Manila, where they were educated, have kin, and visit on business. It is unlikely that if Mrs Marcos and General Ver emerged from a power struggle they would be welcome, but it is also unlikely that this class would in the main protest or do anything other than try to protect their business interests. They would probably respond favourably to a strongman regime that looked capable of putting an end to disorder that is bad for business and threatens their safety. The minimum they want is a regime that can produce a climate of political and economic predictability, or better still, prosperity. Their hankerings for constitutional processes would be satisfied initially by the promise of restoration of elections 'once order is secure'. They would be apprehensive about disorder should power be abruptly transferred to a weak civilian regime, for weakness at the center would invite the reappearance of armed strongmen in the regions. Given that the prosperity of all rural business rests in the end on the fortunes of the dominant crop, this class would be apprehensive about the effects of a further squeeze between input prices and the producer price of rice. They could react by withdrawing their capital from lending to farmers and from handling inputs, rice, or credit. The effects would exaggerate and accelerate the squeeze on farmers and therefore farmers' response as producers.

Incorporation into the state: regime organization

Since September 1972 the central government has drawn the province, town and village governments under its control to an unprecedented degree, and has set up mass organizations that on paper look very strong. It is worth asking whether this degree of centralization will persist once President Marcos is no longer at the head of the state and whether the KBL, KB and other organizations have sufficient ideological commitment to a distinct vision of society to maintain their coherence and be able to transfer loyalty to a new head as legitimate successor.

The central government after 1972 swiftly reversed the tendency to local autonomy of provincial governors and town mayors. Some of these on the eve of martial law had control of independent revenues (from illegal logging, fishing, smuggling, road tolls, gambling and influence peddling), plus independent armed force, sufficient to ignore the central government and to pay only lip-service to much of national law. From the beginning of martial law the independent armed force of provincial politicians was broken up and the municipal police forces made subject for some time to the Philippines Constabulary. Meanwhile, the autonomy of governors and mayors was reduced by controlling more closely both their revenues and expenditures and subjecting these to central government scrutiny under the justification of efficiency and of directing local expenditure to fit national development plans. The installation of the regional tier of central government officials over the provinces, and the need for governors and mayors to get approval from regional development officers before undertaking major works expenditures, cut away some of the graft these officials collected from contractors. At the same time the central government's Ministry of Local Government and Community Development (MLGCD) and Ministry of Human Settlements (MHS) officers, posted in each town, gained new powers, budgets and control over local government and offered an alternative source of benefits that tied local influentials direct to the palace. 'Part of this centralization process was reversed from 1978 when the exigencies of getting the vote out for elections (1978 Interim Batasang Pambansa (IBP), 1980 local, 1981 presidential and 1982 village) required reversion to political pork-barrel expenditures sensitive to local conditions, rather than centrally planned developmentalist strategies. The creation of the KBL as a well-funded electoral machine, and its overwhelming success in installing its men in province, town and village office, gave a different sort of central control: political rather than bureaucratic. Meanwhile, between elections the MLGCD, MHS and regional officials of central government retain important funds and powers.

It is worth asking how ideologically committed to the New Society ideology are the overwhelmingly KBL officials elected since 1980 in province, town and village. In one view the KBL is a movement whose members are committed to Marcos's vision of the New Society. In another view the KBL is an electoral machine that is fed from the top with funds, selects candidates and conducts campaigns, but is little more than a coalition of candidates that has but a shadowy existence between elections. Given that many former opposition Liberal Party local politicians joined the KBL, after the IBP elections proved the futility of standing under any other banner, it seems reasonable to assume the latter view. In that case the local officials are best seen as pragmatists with little ideological commitment to KBL, inclined to look to their political survival. Hence when Marcos departs office it seems unlikely that the KBL elected officials will behave as cadres of a continuing party, or that they will automatically transfer allegiance to whoever claims legitimate succession to KBL leadership. On the other hand, if a coalition claiming succession to KBL leadership appears to have sufficient funds and prospects of producing an election result in their favour, elected officials would be foolish to switch.

The Philippines population is young: half is under twenty-five, and since President Marcos has been in power for eighteen years these people have known no other head of state. The inculcation of New Society values in the schools and the prolonged control of the media have reinforced a favourable image of the president. However it is doubtful whether this favourable image or legitimacy can be transferred from the unique individual to any other. If it could be transferred, it is hard to see to whom it might go. Mrs Marcos's picture is on school walls and in many houses, along with that of the president, but none of the other contenders for power has much public exposure. Against Mrs Marcos runs a popular stereotype of male versus female proclivities that regards her as concerned with money and family interests rather than the public good. This is reinforced by rumours of her demands for a share in any new venture. Imee Marcos, head of the Kabataang Barangay national youth organization, has no such drawback but is too young (and her divorcee husband a drawback) to be much in the running. Bongbong Marcos is dismissed as a playboy, whose rumoured escapades have been a trial to his parents.

The KKK and KB mass organizations headed by Imelda Marcos and Imee Marcos-Manutoc do not appear to have a large continuing membership between rallies when members are rounded up and given free transport and pocket money, or, in the case of KKK activities, when there are benefits to be gained. It does not seem likely, even if their organizational potential is greater than my assessment, that their members have a continuing ideological commitment or that the organizations could transfer headship successfully to a non-Marcos family leader.

Nevertheless, for those who want to prophesy the imminent overthrow of the last vestiges of the Marcos regime, it is as well to remember that these organizations exist. It is important that though the rules (but in few places the counting of votes) in the 1980 local elections made it difficult for non-KBL candidates to win, those elections were nevertheless a genuine contest and the winners for the most part genuinely popular candidates who would have had very good chances under open conditions. The KBL political machine selected very good candidates and they will be in office until 1986. In so far as they are attached to a developmentalist-authoritarian government as KBL loyalists, and are local influentials, they can help muster support for a group claiming succession at the centre and reciprocally could make it difficult for a group without that claim to win support. No other party has a nation-wide organization reaching from Manila to each village.

It is my impression, from the international press, that there is a mood in Manila that the end of one era is at hand and a new one about to open. I have been in the Philippines at another such time: during 1971-73 when the Constitutional Convention seemed to some to promise an entirely new beginning for the Filipino nation, and in the interim between the great floods of 1972 and declaration of martial law. At that time there was an undercurrent of chiliastic and apocalyptic irrationality to many conversations. People looked to the ending of one era and beginning of another with a mixture of hope and dread. There were rumours of signs and

portents; prophets foretold all sorts of destruction and
rebirth, the idiom fitting much of what Ileto has written
about in his book Pasyon and Revolution (1979). A recurring
theme was that a hero would appear in the East at the
suffering nation's darkest hour, to lead it to the Dawn of
Freedom. This myth has been able in the past to assimilate
Jose Rizal, Andres Bonifacio of the original KKK, General
Artemio Ricarte, Benigno Ramos of the Sakdal, Patricio
Dionisio of the Tanggulan, and General Douglas MacArthur.
Benigno Aquino's death transfigured him into that role. But
after that death, whatever the level of popular millenarian
sentiment, no successor has emerged as claimant to the role.
President Marcos has tried to attach some of its symbols to
himself and Mrs Marcos's KKK has adopted elements of the
initiation rituals of the original KKK of 1896. Filipino
friends tell me that letters and phone calls from kin speak
of prophecies of the ending of the Marcos era and beginning
of a shadowy new one. It would be ironic if this chiliastic
strand in folk-catholic Filipino consciousness should have
misled this gathering to thinking in apocalyptic terms. To
me, it seems that when President Marcos is no longer in
office, then, unless there is a stalemate or civil war over
the succession - and I regard these as unlikely - it is
probable that there will be another centralist,
developmentalist and authoritarian government in Manila.

There is the possibility, in my reading of the interests
of the various groups in Central Luzon town and village and
in this myth of the return, that should the succession bring
disorder there will be an attempt after the lapse of a few
years to bring back a state claiming succession from Marcos.
We are aware of how long the myth of Peron took to die in
Argentina. It is in the nature of strongman regimes to be
unpopular when they look weak but to gain a new lease of
legitimacy a few years after they have fallen, particularly
if their successors are unable to maintain order and produce
prosperity for the populace. I have indicated above that
both peasant beneficiaries of land reform and town
entrepreneurs prize order and stability above freedom. It
would be ironic if events should unfold in such a way that
power is rapidly transferred to a weak civilian government
only to create the possibility of what happened in France in
1848 and 1851, bringing to power a 'nephew' claiming
Napoleon's mantle.

Chapter 11

RURAL PHILIPPINES: TECHNOLOGICAL CHANGE IN THE SUGAR INDUSTRY

Alfred W. McCoy

During its two decades in power the Marcos regime has unleashed powerful forces of social change in the rural Philippines, forces far more lasting than the ephemera of Manila's palace politics. Through his political and economic policies President Ferdinand Marcos has set in motion a process of change that will, in a very few years, transform the structure of rural society. Although there are considerable variations among regions and industries, it appears that there are some common components of the regime's rural revolution: a massive injection of foreign development capital; the introduction of new labour saving technologies; and a major restructuring of primary industry marketing under the control of reliable political cronies, a process involving a centralization of power and profits.

Much has been written about social and technological changes in the rice industry; however export crops have experienced even more dramatic changes during the Marcos era. The coconut industry has undergone a major restructuring in marketing, research, and financial controls since 1975. The banana export industry has grown with an explosive speed over the past decade and now dominates large areas of eastern and central Mindanao. Responding to international and domestic pressures, the sugar industry introduced a revolutionary new technology in 1980 which will, within three to five years, produce a fundamental change in the structure of employment, particularly in the larger sugar plantations on Negros island.

After decades of abortive experimentation with new technologies, the Philippine sugar industry finally found a suitable form of mechanization in the early 1980s. It came from Queensland. Although never before exported, this innovative cane cultivation system proved ideally suited to the needs of the Philippine sugar industry. Now widely tested under experimental and commercial conditions in the Philippines, the Australian system has increased production significantly, slashed production costs, and will, when fully utilized, eliminate up to 90 per cent of the present labour requirement of the sugar industry. In a monocrop area like Negros, where sugar accounts directly for 25 per cent of all employment, and far more indirectly, such rapid technological change has the capacity for creating a major social crisis.

175

When the Australian cultivation system was first
introduced in 1979-80 few informed Filipino sugarmen expected
that it would spread beyond the very largest plantations.
Citing the constraints of cost and farmer resistance, most
were pessimistic about the technology's chances for
widespread acceptance. Events have proven them wrong.
Although Filipino sugar labour is notoriously cheap on an
hourly basis, it is costly and inefficient when measured on a
global scale of productivity. Even cheap human labour cannot
compete with an efficient machine in modern agribusiness. By
increasing production per hectare while simultaneously
reducing costs, the Australian farming system quickly
convinced even the most conservative planters of its cost
effectiveness. Once the demand for the new technology spread
to medium planters without the capital for costly imported
implements, Negros metal fabricators began imitating the
imported implements and within two years were producing
equipment comparable in quality for half the import price.
Once the price barrier was breached in 1982-83, the new
farming system spread to sugar districts across the
archipelago with remarkable speed.

Export agriculture

Diverse and disparate in its production, Philippine
export agriculture almost defies summary description. Among
the 12.1 million ha of land under cultivation in the
archipelago in 1980, there were five major crops with
significant areas: rice (3.5 million ha), corn (3.3 million
ha), coconuts (3.1 million ha), sugar (424,000 ha), and
bananas (317,000 ha) (NEDA 1982:252-256). The most extensive
of the export crops, coconuts are grown on 429,000 farms
scattered across the archipelago. Although there are large
plantations, 73 per cent of the coconut farms are under 5 ha
(Tiglao 1980:2-6). By contrast, until 1974 sugar production
was concentrated in just ten provinces in Central Luzon and
the Visayas. Although the recent construction of modern
sugar mills has spread production to new areas of Luzon and
Mindanao, sugar is still largely grown on farms over 50 ha.
Through its large labour force, 431,000 in 1976, and vast
capital requirements, sugar has been historically the most
profitable and powerful of the export industries. The newest
among the major commercial crops, export bananas are grown
largely on twenty major Mindanao plantations concentrated in
Davao province, with a total area of only 20,700 ha
(ICL Research Team, n.d.:1-6).

Since the declaration of martial law in 1972, the Marcos
administration appears to have adopted a common policy
towards the administration of export crops which contrasts
markedly with that towards the major food crops, rice and
corn. Produced by several million small farmers and marketed
for domestic consumers, food crops have been governed by
political imperatives: land reform, price controls, liberal
credit programmes and new technology for the small farmer.

In contrast to programme of social reform and political compromise in rice and corn, the Marcos regime has adopted a policy of bold entrepreneurial opportunism towards the export crops. Each of the major export crops - coconut, sugar and bananas - has been placed under the control of a reliable political crony. In coconut and sugar, crony control has brought the abolition of free market trading and the creation of quasi-governmental marketing boards which have expropriated significant shares of the farmer's profits. Centralization has been justified with a rhetoric of reform and modernization whose reality varies considerably within the various industries.

Among all major Philippine crops, sugar has experienced the greatest changes during the Marcos era. Even if martial law had never occurred, the Philippine sugar industry was at a turning point in its history in the early 1970s. After sixty years of access to the lucrative US domestic market, the sugar industry had grown into the most powerful, profitable and inefficient of Philippine primary industries. Sugar generally accounted for around 25 per cent of total exports and the industry's centralized structure allowed an easy translation of export profits into political power. With large farms, mills and workforce concentrated in relatively few provinces, the sugar industry aggregated its political influence into a 'sugar bloc' that was able to dictate its terms to a pre martial law congress and executive. By bartering US military base concessions for a liberal US sugar quota, the Philippine sugar industry was able to increase its exports to the US throughout the post-war decades. Strained to fill its increased quotas through the 1960s, the industry expanded production extensively by converting marginal lands to sugar instead of intensifying production on existing lands with improved technology. Between 1959 and 1972, sugar area doubled from 193,000 ha to 424,000 ha, while production per hectare dropped from 112 piculs of sugar to 68 (<u>Sugarland</u> (Bacolod) 11(4):25). In the process of becoming America's major foreign sugar supplier, the Philippines had become one of the world's least efficient producers.

Although the date of the transition had been known for decades, the sugar industry was utterly unprepared when the US quota expired in 1974. Filipino hopes for a new quota concession were crushed when the US decided, simultaneously with the end of the Philippine quota, to abandon its forty-year old quota system altogether and purchase its shortfall on the world market. Suddenly, the Philippine sugar industry was forced into a highly competitive world sugar market. With an American quota higher than any other nation before 1974, the Philippine industry was, in effect, a ward of the protected US market. The planters' lavish lifestyles, their paternalistic plantations and legions of field labourers were all manifestations of the industry's affluence and inefficiency. While sugar wages were scandalously low even by Philippine standards, the industry's manual methods had become too costly in comparison with Australia and Hawaii, both fully mechanized for over a decade. In 1973 it cost Australia's mechanized farms 2.5 cents to produce a pound of sugar which could then be sold on the world market for a price ranging from 1.97 cents in 1968 to 9.59 cents in 1973. It costs the Philippines 5.5 cents to produce the same pound of sugar - over twice the Australian cost and higher than the average world market price (<u>Sugar News</u> (Manila) February 1974:95).

President Marcos developed a twofold strategy to weather the crisis: first, he appointed his closest crony, Roberto S. Benedicto, as sugar industry 'czar'; secondly, he created a government marketing board, the Philippine Sugar Commission (Philsucom), to centralize control over sugar sales. Determined to break the power of the 'sugar bloc', a group generally opposed to him before martial law, Marcos began his centralization by establishing the Philippine Exchange (Philex), the genesis of Philsucom, in 1973 to take control of all sugar trading. By setting a mandatory purchase price far lower than the export price, Philex and its successor Philsucom were able to make vast profits for the central government and its allies. When world prices climbed to P678 per picul in 1974, Philex paid the planter only P134, enabling the government to earn an estimated P700-P1,000 million which would have otherwise gone to the planters (<u>Sugar News</u> September 1974:313, November 1974:409, February 1975:314). Thus, by 1976 Philippine planters were faced with circumstances that guaranteed them low prices for the foreseeable future: the loss of the US market, low world market prices, and government expropriation of any profits that might accrue from a rising world price. Unless the industry could develop a new technology that would either cut costs or raise productivity, it was faced with certain collapse.

Mechanization

Despite its centralization of marketing profits, Philsucom's control over the sugar industry's development remained weak and there was no coherent policy on mechanization. Although Philsucom's chairman, Benedicto, declared his support for mechanization, its progress was left almost entirely to market forces. Instead of attending to the crisis in cane cultivation, the regime used its capital and leadership to organize a massive expansion of sugar milling capacity. Ignoring pessimistic projections on the future of the world market, the government authorized a massive expansion of the capacity of the Philippine's thirty-five sugar mills by approving finance for seven new mills at a cost of $US40 million each (<u>Sugar News</u> December 1981:328-329). Sited in marginal sugar areas in Luzon, Negros and Mindanao, and faced with an uncertain market, the mills seemed certain to fail. Industry observers explain this seemingly irrational decision by suggesting that new mills were controlled by Marcos relatives or cronies and the major equipment supplier, Japan's Marubeni Corporation, was paying kickbacks of 12 per cent, or about $US6 million per mill, during the period when Benedicto was Ambassador to Japan (Shoesmith 1977).

Preoccupied with construction of the new mills, the government left resolution of the cultivation crisis to the planters. Among the three main traditional sugar areas, Negros Occidental has a long history of technological innovation. Most of Pampanga's sugar lands - 24,700 ha in 1971 - are worked by share tenants whose small-scale, family-farming operations are resistant to major change and insulated against labour cost increases. Although neighbouring Tarlac province has large administered haciendas, its total sugar area - only 11,300 ha in 1971 - is too small to create a sufficient pool of innovators. With large plantations and just under half the archipelago's sugar area (158,200 of 326,200 ha), Negros has both the scale and density of cane cultivation sufficient for innovation.

Since their establishment over a century ago, Negros's haciendas, operated as centrally administered agribusinesses, have been active in the search for improved production techniques. Negros planters are the only Filipino farmers with a long and consistent interest in tractor mechanization. At the century's turn, a small number of Negros plantations used large steam tractors for ploughing, but it was not until the 1920s that tractors became common on the island's sugar farms. By 1940 the La Carlota mill district in southern Negros had 61 tractors on 38 of its 97 haciendas. Most, however, were light tractors of the 15-40 horse-power range, so the same farms still required 1,580 water buffalo (Nesom and Waker 1912; Gordon 1940). The trend toward tractor use for ploughing continued after the war and accelerated markedly during the 1960s.

One of the key factors in the spread of tractor tillage during the 1960s was the consulting work done by American Factors Associates Ltd. (Amfacs) of Honolulu. Seeking to upgrade the industry's efficiency, the National Confederation of Sugarcane Planters (NFSP) retained Amfacs to devise improved production techniques and train hacienda managers in their use. After surveying the La Carlota district in February 1966, the Amfacs team reported that, with improved techniques, the 'yield potential of La Carlota can be as good as the Hawaiian irrigated and unirrigated areas'. Among its recommendations, Amfacs emphasized deep ploughing, beyond the current depth of 10 inches to 18-24 inches. Since this depth was well beyond the water buffalo's maximum of 10 inches, Amfacs' method required heavy tractors to break up hard pan and turn the subsoil. Through its extension work in the late 1960s Amfacs encouraged the use of heavy tractors in the 70-120 horse-power range. Although planters readily accepted experimental results that showed a 30 per cent production increase with deep ploughing, 70-80 horsepower tractors were very expensive and few farmers had sufficient finance for their purchase. There were several abortive experiments with tractor co-operatives in Negros during the late 1960s but they only succeeded in demonstrating that farm mechanization would not become a reality until each planter could finance purchase of his own tractor. In its time of crisis, the sugar industry would find its finance, ironically, in a World Bank rural credit programme aimed at benefiting small farmers and fishermen.

The World Bank

The World Bank, or more correctly the International Bank for Reconstruction and Development (IBRD), was largely responsible for the sudden proliferation of heavy tractors in the Philippine sugar districts during the 1970s. Through its four Rural Credit Programmes between 1964 and 1979, the IBRD provided $US 76 million on a matching grant basis, ostensibly for a wide range of rural development projects. Accepting the IBRD's 46.6 per cent share of the third loan as the ratio for all four, these investments 'mobilized' a total of $US 163 million for rural credit operations (IBRD 1979; Bello, O'Connor and Broad 1982). The bulk of the IBRD finance - some $US 56.5 million under the third and fourth loans - was released between 1974 and 1979, the period when the sugar industry was seeking a technological solution to its chronic inefficiency. Desperate for credit to finance mechanization, the sugar industry succeeded in subverting the purpose of the World Bank programme by appropriating over half its credit facility for tractor purchases by large planters.

After making relatively modest loans, totalling $US 17.5 million between 1965 and 1974, the IBRD decided to accelerate its rural credit programme by releasing a third loan of $US 22 million in 1974, with an anticipated disbursement period of three years. Providing the funds to the Central Bank for lending to rural banks, the World Bank had anticipated that the third loan would 'finance approximately 8,000 beneficiaries mainly small and medium sized farmers cultivating between two and ten hectares'. The World Bank had hoped that the loans would serve a range of rural projects such as livestock, fishing, dairying and industry. About 75 per cent of the first two loans had gone to purchase tractors and power tillers for sugar and rice farms; the Bank tried to avoid repetition of this experience by mandating a 64 per cent ceiling on mechanization loans and an 80 horse power limit on tractors. 'Reflecting the lessons learned under the first and second loans', reads the Bank's evaluation report, 'the project aimed at decreasing the share of farm mechanization, gradually shifting lending to other identified needs in the rural areas' (IBRD 1979:i-v).

Despite these restrictions, the Philippine sugar industry succeeded in transforming the World Bank's third rural credit programme into a tractor finance scheme for large plantations. In only eighteen months, half the projected disbursal period, the entire $US 47.2 million was

lent out and 63.9 per cent of the total went to finance 1,952
tractors. When the World Bank became aware that tractor
loans were rising far beyond the target 44 per cent of the
total credit programme it moved quickly to 'suspend...
financing of tractors for sugar-cane areas'. By the time the
suspension took effect, however, the demand for tractors had
been so high that the entire credit programme had already
exhausted its funds (ibid.:7-8). In its evaluation report
the World Bank tried to avoid admitting that its loan had
become a credit subsidy for the affluent sugar planters by
claiming that '62 per cent of these tractors went to Luzon
primarily for rice production' (ibid:10). In its commentary
on the World Bank evaluation, however, the Philippine Central
Bank pointed out that since 'big tractors destroy the hard
pan' in rice paddies, 'tractors financed in the Central Luzon
region were also largely for, sugar farms' (ibid.:39,45).

There was a number of factors which allowed the sugar
industry to transform a comprehensive rural credit programme
into a tractor subsidy scheme. Since rural banks, the
primary lending agencies, required land as collateral, large
sugar planters could outbid small farmers and fishermen for
credit. While the rate of return on a power tiller for rice
cultivation, the second largest loan category, was an
estimated 0.4 per cent, that for a heavy tractor (over 68
horse power) on a sugar plantation was 34 per cent
(ibid.:31,33). The World Bank's 80 horse power limit on
tractor size provided no restraint since 75-80 horse power is
an optimal size for a sugar cultivation. With inflation on
77 horse power tractors running at 80 per cent between 1973
and 1975, many farmers seized the opportunity of IBRD credit
to gain a hedge against inflation. Finally, 'strong
promotional efforts by dealers', combined with peak sugar
prices in 1974-75, encouraged rapid sales among sugar
planters (ibid.:45). Thus, over an eighteen month period in
1974-75 the sugar industry acquired a tractor capitalization
of P180.2 million, a sum that compares favourably with the
P724 million in total agricultural credit generated by all
Philippine development banks during the same period (ibid.:9;
NEDA 1982:601-603). Although tractor finance in the fourth
rural credit programme slipped to 48 per cent of all loans by
December 1978, total tractor capitalization for the four
credit programmes still amounted to between $US80 and 100
million, a vast capital by Philippine standards (IBRD
1979:45).

There are numerous indicators of the dramatic impact
that this massive infusion of capital had upon the sugar
industry. In its own evaluation report, the World Bank notes
the decline in the country's water buffalo population from
4.9 million in 1973 to 2.7 million in 1976 and attributes it
to rapid spread of tractors and power tillers in sugar and
rice farming. In 1982 a private equipment corporation
conducted a comprehensive survey of tractor population in the
Manapla district of northern Negros and discovered a
remarkably high level of mechanization. Among the district's

eighty-seven haciendas, with a total of 5,029 ha in cane, there were 113 working tractors, an average of one tractor per 44 ha. Among the district's eighty-seven farms, seventy-four (85 per cent) had tractors and implements for mechanized cultivation. In terms of cane area, 4,473 ha (89 per cent) of the district's 5,029 ha were serviced by tractors (Scorpion Equipment Marketing Corporation 1982).

Long-range statistics on individual haciendas shows a similar trend towards mechanization. In 1940 Hacienda Esperanza-Najalin in the La Carlota district in southern Negros Occidental had four light tractors (22-50 horse power) and 100 water buffalo. By 1980 it had twelve heavy tractors above 75 horse power and only twelve water buffalo, no longer used for cane work (Gordon 1940; Associacion de Agricultores de La Carlota y Ponteredra, 'Farm Survey' June, July 1981).

Despite its massive impact on the Philippine sugar industry, the World Bank apparently remained ignorant of the consequences of its credit programme. 'Since over 70 per cent of project funds were spent for purchase of tractors and power tillers', said the Bank of its third credit program', mechanized land preparation is...the main impact of this project. Tractors and power tillers in the Philippines are almost exclusively used for land preparation...' (IBRD 1979:15-16). Despite a marked paucity of appropriate data, the World Bank claimed that mechanization had not reduced labour demand. 'Although labour requirements for land preparation have been reduced substantially, increase of labour for harvest and other operations due to a higher land use have more than offset the labour reduced by mechanized land preparation...' The Bank did admit that 'under particular circumstances adverse social effects do occur', and ordered a study to accompany its fourth rural credit programme 1977, (ibid.:16) by which time any adversity would be irreversible. In its review of the World Bank evaluation report on the third credit programme, the Philippine Central Bank claimed that studies by the International Rice Research Institute had confirmed that labour lost in land preparation was recovered by increased demand for other forms of farmwork. There was, of course, one problem with these sanguine conclusions: they were based on detailed studies of rice cultivation, while 87 per cent of the mechanization credits were being used for sugar farming. The World Bank's ignorance of mechanization's impact upon the Philippines' 431,000 sugar workers was absolute.

Australian cane technology

Viewed from the vantage point of historical hindsight, the Philippine sugar industry's moves towards mechanization seem unplanned, even haphazard. The almost accidental infusion of World Bank funds for tractor finance had created a massive pool of mechanical horse power whose full and proper utilization was only dimly understood. As Amfacs had pointed out in the late 1960s, deep tractor ploughing would turn the subsoil, break up the hard pan and increase yields. The World Bank reported in 1979 that 'a substantial increase of 20 to 30 per cent [in yield] was observed for sugarcane as a result of deep tillage by mechanization' (ibid.:12). Since ploughing was a once-off operation with considerable flexibility in its timing, the large tractor pool created by 1976 could service the demand on a contract or custom basis for farms without tractors. Pressed by a slump in sugar prices, the pace of mechanization within the sugar industry slackened in the late 1970s.

Tractor ploughing had created the preconditions for a technological revolution in the Philippine sugar industry but was not a revolution by itself. Even within the existing cultivation system ploughing was but one of many labour intensive cultivation tasks - along with planting, fertilizing, weeding, irrigating, inter-row tilling, and harvesting. Unlike rice production, labour lost in one sugar operation is not recouped in another. Since much of the work in Negros haciendas was done by migratory workers (sacadas), resident labourers could be shifted from ploughing to weeding and harvesting work formerly done by migrants. Thus, the social impact of mechanized ploughing was relatively limited.

Even with mechanized ploughing, the Philippine sugar industry's cultivation techniques remained a model of inefficiency. In brief, its yields of sugar per hectare were too low and its costs of production too high. Vaguely, dimly aware that Hawaii and Australia were somehow, someway doing something different, Roberto Benedicto and Philsucom decided that the solution must lie in mechanized harvesting. With the co-operation of Massey Ferguson of Australia, Philsucom experimented with the MF-105 harvester in January 1979 on Benedicto's own plantation, Hacienda Carmenchita in Negros's La Carlota mill district. The study determined that under near-ideal field conditions the 'cost of cutting and loading cane [mechanically] is comparable with that of the manual method. The equivalent of 45 labourers to one mechanical harvester implies the great advantage of the machine as a labour saving device'. In short, it was not cost efficient to cut cane mechanically even under ideal field conditions. Moreover, there were serious drawbacks. Laid out for water buffalo ploughing a century ago, many Negros cane fields are small, irregular, rocky, poorly drained and ploughed with narrow furrows. In order to minimize down-time for repairs, the MF-105 requires level, rectangular fields with 400-500 metres furrows and turning headlands at each end. The cost of land formation is prohibitive when a MF-105 harvester can cut a ton of cane for P21.99 and manual crew can do the same job for P22.00 (Villanueva et al. n.d.). Until the fields can be land-formed for mechanized cultivation, mechanical harvesting will not be cost effective. Philsucom was putting the cart before the horse, or the harvester before the tractor. Planters showed little interest in mechanical harvesting and the Philsucom initiative was, over the short term at least, a failure.

Despite the Philsucom failure, conditions in the late 1970s were ideal for a major technological break-through. In earlier decades Hawaii and Australia had been forced to mechanize when labour supply declined and labour costs consequently rose to the point that investment of capital in the design and purchase of a new technology was warranted. In the Philippines the economic equation was more complex. Although labour was in surplus, President Marcos had courted organized labour's support for his martial law regime through a series of wage rises and cost of living allowances that doubled labour costs for field work between 1973 and 1980. Simultaneously, the depressed world market price and the government monopoly on marketing cut the planters' price from P160 per picul in 1974 to P79.50 in 1977-78, far below the actual production cost of P90. Pressed between rising labour costs and declining prices, sugar planters needed a new system of field cultivation to survive. Through its massive infusion of relatively cheap capital, the World Bank had created a sufficient pool of heavy tractors to power any new system of mechanized cultivation. In short, the sugar industry had both the means and the need for a new cultivation technology.

The solution was entirely a private sector initiative. As a late technological innovator, the Philippines had the cost advantage of being able to select among existing technologies for an appropriate solution to its dilemma. Within the Pacific Basin sugar industry, there are only two technological innovators: Hawaii and Australia. Although Hawaii had an established connection with the Philippine industry, as evidenced in the Amfacs consultancy, dating back to its transfer of milling technology in 1912, its cultivation technology was inappropriate. Heavily capital-ized, Hawaii had created a costly system of heavy hydraulic equipment drawn by expensive full-track Caterpillar-type tractors that was inappropriate for the Philippines. By contrast, Australia's equipment manufacturers had created a simple set of inexpensive, matched implements that were designed to be drawn by the 75-80 horse power tractors common to Philippine plantations. While the Hawaiian system required costly irrigation works for optimal productivity, the Australian encouraged deep rooting that enabled the cane to survive variable rainfall without irrigation.

In 1977 a Queensland implements manufacturer, Mick Hodge, came to the Philippines seeking someone to introduce his 'no touch' system of Australian cane farming. In 1979 Hodge signed a distribution agreement with Scorpion Marketing Corporation, a subsidiary of Gamboa Hermanos, a major plantation in the San Carlos district of Negros. With Hodge's assistance, Gamboa conducted a series of experiments that quickly established the viability of the Australian technology under Philippine conditions. By drawing a set of sixteen matched implements over a standard wide furrow with a tractor, the Hodge system reduced cultivation costs significantly and produced dramatic increases in productivity - more sugar for less money. The precision of mechanical cultivation cut labour costs, reduced fertilizer wastage, allowed additional harvests from the same cane plant, and eliminated the losses from sloppy field labour. The droves of planters who toured the Gamboa Hermanos plantations in 1980-81 were impressed. One Negros plantation administrator who visited in July 1980 described the new system as 'a giant step to progress':

> The Hodge system of farming...is a complete technological break-through on our central plain areas... Using mechanized farming such as Hodge system, I for one strongly believe that a 20% to 30% increase in both tons cane and piculs per hectare can easily be attained under normal conditions... Finally, I am fully convinced that using the system could practically reduce 50% to 60% of the manpower level in cultivation alone. And it can cut away the tremendous cost of production in terms of labour which is paid idleness (Fred G. Aplaon, 'Report on San Carlos Field Trip - The Hodge System of Farming', to: Jovencio, V. Pereche, field manager, Hdas. Esperanza-Najalin, 18 July 1980).

The initial results from the Hodge system at Gamboa Hermanos sparked a sudden drive towards mechanization in the Negros sugar industry that soon spread to the other districts. During the 1979/80 crop year, Gamboa achieved an average per hectare production of 215.45 piculs, which compared favourably with its peak over the previous ten years of 185.19 piculs (Gamboa Hermanos, 'Comparative Production of Fields Planted to Hodge System', n.d.). Less efficient producers were able to make even more impressive gains and all who used the new method achieved labour savings which approached 50 per cent. Impressed by the Gamboa field demonstrations, Negros planters began placing orders for imported equipment. By October 1981 Scorpion had sold seventy-seven Hodge sets which were already cultivating 5,710.64 ha (Scorpion Marketing Corporation, 'Summary of Areas Planted to Hodge', Bacolod City, n.d.; interview with Jose Ma. T. Ascalon, Office Manager, Scorpion Marketing, Bacolod City, 11 January 1982).

In August 1981 three delegations of Negros sugarmen, totalling about fifty, toured the Queensland cane districts and came home visibly impressed. The NFSP journal Sugarland editorialized: 'Because of mechanization, the [Australian] planters have been able to maximize their production and overall they were able to reduce the cost of production... In one plantation of more than 200 hectares, two brothers and one helper are the only ones working the farm' (Sugarland 18(3):2).

As the Hodge system spread and proved its capabilities

it gained some significant testimonials. During a television interview in Bacolod in 1980, Philsucom's Chairman, Benedicto, was asked about his agency's programme for meeting the rising cost of production:

> We have a program which we have announced time and again. The most important is mechanization. Mechanization is the solution to rising labour costs. I know because I have fully mechanized three of our farms and we found our cost has gone down... We start with the program of increasing the yield in the farms because that is where the sugar is made... We have of course the mechanization of the Hodge system which we will demonstrate soon in the pilot farms (Sugarland 17(5): 14-16).

The growing popularity of the Hodge method produced another boom in farm equipment sales. During 1981-82 Scorpion Marketing Corporation grew suddenly into a large firm with forty agricultural extension officers to train farmers in the use of the new equipment. Its salesmen covered the archipelago and its sales of Australian implements reached P15 million in 1980 (interview with Jose Maria Zabaleta, executive Vice-President, Gamboa Hermanos, Manila, 28 February 1983). After several years of slack sales, heavy tractors, required to pull the implements, were back in demand. In its 1979 evaluation report the World Bank noted that a large number of sugar farmers had begun defaulting on their tractor loans after the 1976 world price decline and the demand for new tractors had slackened (IBRD 1979:22). In 1981 tractor sales revived in the sugar districts of neighbouring Negros and Panay islands. During the first five months of 1981, 98 out of 232 tractors sold in the Philippines (42.2 per cent of the total) were sold on those two islands (G.A. Machineries Inc., 'Comparative Tractor Sales, All Competing Brands (National and Regional Market Shares), January-May 1981, Standard Tractors', 20 June 1981).

As the Hodge system won widespread acceptance in 1980-81, Philsucom officials remained pessimistic about its capacity to transform the sugar industry. The cost of imported tractors and implements, they argued, would limit its acceptance to large plantations with sufficient capital. Since tractors were, as we have seen, already widespread through the World Bank's financing, the only real barrier remained the high cost of Australian implements. To cover the expense of its training programme and extension agents, Scorpion Marketing was charging P145,000 for a basic set of six implements to perform the essentials of the Australian method. For the full set of sixteen implements the cost was an awesome P300,000. Scorpion's order books for the 1980-81 period show most sales in the P200,000-600,000 range, a cost that could only be borne by the largest haciendas (above 200 ha) (Scorpion Marketing Corporation, Customer Files, 'Hodge Sales', Makati, Manila).

While Scorpion's costly training and extension programme was necessary in 1980-81 when Filipino farmers did not understand the new method, they soon became an expendable luxury once the new technology began to spread into the cane districts. Sensing a threat from potential competitors, Scorpion urged Hodge to cut costs by local fabrication but he refused and left his market share open to penetration. Although other Australian manufacturers explored the Philippine market during this period, Filipino fabricators expropriated the technology and produced serviceable imitations for a fraction of the cost. By late 1981, less than two years after Gamboa first announced its experimental results, there were twenty local fabricators in Negros Occidental producing Australian-style equipment, some for less than half the import price.

Although most of the fabricators produced cheap imitations from inferior scrap steel for small planters in the 25-50 ha range, several, notably Baleda Corporation of Bacolod, were manufacturing equipment comparable in quality to the Australian originals with unique design features adapted for local conditions. Even though Baleda's implements contained up to 40 per cent Australian manufactured components, its cost for a basic set of five implements in 1982 was only P95,000, less than half the cost of the imported Hodge models (interview with Constancio M. Demerre, President, Baleda Corporation, Bacolod City, 17 February 1983). Once the price barrier was breached, the new technology spread from Negros to cane districts across the Visayas, Luzon and Mindanao. Negros fabricators began taking orders from as far away as the Cagayan valley of northern Luzon. Faced with strong competition, Scorpion's sales dropped from P15 million in 1980 to P8 million in 1982. As sales dropped, staff was trimmed and all but two of the forty extension officers were dismissed by the end of 1982 (Interview with Zabaleta, 20 February 1983).

While Scorpion had lost most of its market share by early 1982, Mick Hodge himself has retained his exclusive contract with Jose Cojuangco Jr for the mechanization of Hacienda Luisita and the Tarlac cane district of Central Luzon. With Hodge as his technical advisor, Cojuangco has led his district towards full mechanization and invested heavily in Australian cultivation equipment and Claas mechanical harvesters from West Germany. Cojuangco's vast Hacienda Luisita is approaching full mechanization and it is expected that the entire district will soon follow. If the transition continues, human hand will not touch cane or soil in Tarlac's sugar plantations by 1985/86. It will become the first fully mechanized mill district in the Philippines.

Labour displacement

Judging from the observable trends, it seems probable that Australian technology will save the Philippine sugar industry from an eventual bankruptcy by making it a viable world market competitor. Once the Australian method is fully assimilated, productivity per hectare will rise and costs of production will drop to international standards. Since labour accounts for some 40-50 per cent of production costs and is the only flexible input, these savings will involve a process of massive labour shedding. Philippine sugar plantations that now employ two to three hundred permanent, casual and migratory workers will within a few years, like their Australian models, require a workforce of less than twenty.

The social impact of such massive labour displacement will vary from region to region. In the new districts of Luzon and Mindanao the impact will not be serious since many of the plantations have compensated for initial labour shortages by early mechanization or employment of migratory workers. In Central Luzon the family economics of tenanted sugar farms in Pampanga has so far resisted mechanization. The workers of mechanized Tarlac have access to alternative employment in nearby Manila or the Bataan Export Processing Zone. The social disruption on Negros island could, however, be severe. Not only is it a monocrop island with little alternative employment, but its haciendas have fostered an attitute of dependence among their workers for over a century. Unlike the tenants of Pampanga, the Negros sugar workers are a rural proletariat without the savings, agricultural skills, or the entrepreneurial ability to create a new livelihood off the hacienda.

In 1976 a Ministry of Labor survey confirmed this worker dependence: 87.2 per cent of workers had free housing on the hacienda; 78 per cent borrowed money from the hacienda; 43.3 per cent were the children of sugar workers; and 40 per cent had no skills for alternative employment (Torres et al. 1977). Even without this exceptional dependence, loss of employment in the dominant industry of a monocrop province like Negros Occidental would present major problems. In 1975 the Negros Occidental sugar industry employed 134,000 workers, 25 per cent of the province's labour force, with dependents that comprised 45 per cent of the province's 1.8 million population (Sugar News July 1976:244). In a January 1982 internal memorandum the Ministry of Labor expressed concern over the potential impact of mechanization:

The overdependence attitude [of workers] that permeated has become a burden to the industry which at this point in time is no longer viable in sustaining the required rate of growth... One alternative that planters consider to achieve this is mechanization and this is where some social...imbalances shall emerge. From the general view of the sugar industry the imbalance would mean labour dislocations, more underemployment, and unemployment (Ministry of Labor 1982).

Taking a lead from its chairman, Philsucom has denied, without evidence for doing so, that mechanization will involve labour wastage. 'The idea of massive displacement of labour due to mechanization is a misconception', said Benedicto in a 1980 television interview. 'We have not displaced anyone in our farm. On the contrary, with full mechanization, they are earning more' (Sugarland 17(5):14-16). In defence of this novel proposition that a labour saving technology will not save labour Philsucom officials cite three main factors that will restrain its impact: (1) the vast majority of the sugar farms in Negros are under 50 ha, the minimum size for mechanization, so the spread of the new technology will be limited; (2) imported implements and tractors are beyond the reach of plantations below 100 ha; (3) to date no 'workers' have been 'fired' from mechanized plantations. Since this argument remains the official wisdom of Philsucom and other government agencies, and is the rationale for inaction, it bears examination.

Philsucom's main argument, that most farms are too small to finance mechanization, does not bear up under closer study. In the sugar industry, labour is applied on a per hectare basis not on a per farm basis; thus the critical question is not the number of farms above 50 ha but the percentage of total sugar land area held in blocks of 50 ha or larger. An examination of the data on farm sizes in three representative Negros mill districts shows the fallacy of Philsucom's logic. In the southern La Carlota district 77.7 per cent, in the central Hawaiian-Philippines district 63 per cent, and in northern Victorias district 54 per cent of the cane area was farmed in blocks larger than 50 ha in 1979/80.(1) Taking an average of the three districts' combined area as representative, 68 per cent of Negros Occidental's sugar land is in parcels of sufficient size to allow mechanization. Once mechanization advances further and becomes the industry standard for efficiency, small farms will be forced to combine with large mechanized plantations or switch to other, probably less labour intensive crops.

The second constraint, tractor availability and implement price, exists only in Philsucom's imagination. Despite its vast research resources, Philsucom had not, by early 1983, undertaken any systematic study of tractor population or implements' cost. The only systematic survey at a sufficient level of detail was done by Scorpion Marketing Corporation in 1982. Its results for the Manapla district, described above, showed a remarkably high level of tractor penetration, reaching 85 per cent of farms and 89 per cent of sugar area. Although the prices of imported Australian implements were prohibitive the local imitations were within reach of most farmers in the 25-50 ha range by early 1983.

The argument about lack of dismissals on mechanized farms is based on an overly literal impression of the character of the sugar industry's labour market. In fact, few if any 'permanent workers' have been fired. But permanent workers are the smallest among the four basic categories of employment on Negros sugar plantations - permanent workers, permanent casuals, casuals, and migratory workers. Preliminary observations indicate that mechanization is impacting on the Negros labour market with a reverse ripple effect. Instead of a direct blow upon the permanent plantation workers at the centre of the industry, labour shedding has started at the periphery with migrant workers and is rippling inward toward the plantation.

The case of Elizalde & Company's Hacienda Esperanza-Najalin, one of the first to mechanize, illustrates this pattern of labour displacement. Located in the La Carlota district of southern Negros Occidental, the plantation's 1,034 ha, of which 699 are prime sugar land, make it among the largest in the province. Of the 858 people resident on the hacienda on the eve of mechanization, 140 were workers, divided into three categories - permanent (78), priority casuals (17), and temporary casuals (45). The non-resident workforce consisted of fifty-five priority casuals from neighbouring barrios, several hundred more from the vicinity who did occasional work, 130-150 migratory cane cutters from Panay island, and teams of Cebuano migrants from the eastern side of the island who once did weeding and non-harvest labour.

By 1980/81 the farm had fully mechanized its ploughing with a fleet of twelve heavy tractors; it then added two sets of Hodge implements at a cost of P600,000. During the 1980/81 harvest the mechanized fields required only 30.43 man-days per hectare compared to 62.24 in manually cultivated fields, a 48.9 per cent reduction in labour demand. As mechanized cultivation spread to the whole plantation over the next two years, management discontinued recruitment of Cebuano migrants and non-resident casuals. Employment of migratory cane cutters was reduced and the work given to resident casuals to compensate for a marked reduction in traditional tasks rendered redundant by mechanization.

The invisible shock waves of labour displacement rippled inward, from Negros Oriental and Panay, to nearby barrios, to the plantations, leaving only the tiny minority of 78 permanent workers unaffected. There were no dismissals but there was a great deal of labour displacement. The labourers themselves claim that there has already been a marked drop in casual labour for temporary casuals, particularly women and children. One field supervisor stated frankly: 'Once the hacienda is fully mechanized, workers in this area will have only two choices - steal or starve. So they will steal. There is going to be trouble.' Experienced plantation managers now calculate that up to 90 per cent of the total labour in the Negros sugar industry will be lost when mechanization is fully implemented.

The impact of such massive wastage of employment on a monocrop island like Negros must, of course, remain speculative. There are, however, indicators that it might induce a major social crisis. With 45 per cent of Negros Occidental's population dependent upon sugar employment, any job loss in such a dominant industry would have adverse effects. The province's young and rapidly growing population complicates the situation further. Like the rest of the Philippines, Negros's population is young, with 55 per cent below the age of 19 at the 1975 census. While there were 275,000 in the 5-9 age bracket, there were only 33,000 in the 60-64, or pre-retirement stratum (National Census and Statistics Office 1975:11-12). So even to maintain its already miserable standard of living, chronic underemployment and low levels of nutrition, Negros needs massive job creation schemes, not an unprecedented labour displacement.

After generations of dependence upon the hacienda as a total life support system that provides free housing, electricity, education, health care and credit, much of the Negros proletariat is far less prepared for the shock of mechanization than the independent peasantry of Luzon. The Negros workers are, materially and culturally, the poorest of Filipino rural residents, with none of the assets of, say, a Pampanga sugar tenant - house, capital, water buffalo, managerial experience, farming skills, initiative and an adequate education. Negros plantation workers are, to a large extent, penniless, uneducated and incapable. Unfortunately, it is the least prepared who will suffer the greatest disruption from mechanization.

Political consequences

Although it is difficult to predict, it does not seem likely that Negros's impending immiseration will take on a radical or revolutionary political configuration. The province seems more likely to sink into a quiet misery punctuated by individual acts of violence than to produce some sort of protracted resistance. The planters have carefully manipulated the labour shedding in a way that leaves no visible target to inspire mass action. Workers are not fired; farm employment simply evaporates.

The situation in Negros seems to be evolving into a complex economic and social problem that will remain a liability for any future government, left or right. In the century past, the Negros sugar industry has used its export potential as political currency to win a de facto autonomy from the colonial or national state and secure its support in the suppression of any dissident labour. The external debt crisis that will dominate the Philippine economy for decades to come will increase, not reduce, the political leverage of the sugar industry. Given the need for foreign exchange to pay the debts and the vast capital invested in mills and plantations, no government, of any political persuasion, can afford to abandon sugar production in Negros. Although its social consequences may turn out to be brutal, mechanization was dictated by world market forces and has proceeded independently of any government authority - Philsucom, Benedicto or Marcos. No regime, not even a government of the left, can reverse the process. The sugar industry's choice remains one between mechanization or bankruptcy.

As in the century past, Negros planters constitute a strong political force that will support any regime which offers the basic political concessions they need for survival: suppression of workers; access to world sugar markets; a guarantee of land tenure; and sufficient operating capital. They will accommodate to any regime, from the far right to the democratic centre, that will offer these concessions. Although there is enormous resentment of the Marcos regime's expropriation of their sugar profits, they will quickly accept anyone, even Marcos's chosen successor, if that successor will reduce the burden.

Many Negros planters are preparing to jettison their dependent workers; the government has so far remained aloof. Planters are offering educational and cash grants to workers who agree to quit the hacienda. Some are shifting workers' residences from the central compound to a segregated block at the plantation boundary. The Marcos regime's coconut 'king' Eduardo Cojuangco has been the most ruthless in his approach. Since the mid-1970s he has purchased some 2,000 ha in Negros's La Carlota district, about 10 per cent of its total arable area, and required eviction of all resident workers as a condition of sale. New workers recruited for his estates are housed in a rental subdivision near the town centre and trucked to different farms daily to avoid any identification with a particular plantation. Despite its vast profits from sugar, the Marcos regime has denied the existence of the problem and refused any support, political or material, to the Negros proletariat. It is a policy likely to be continued by any successor regime.

In marked contrast to the planter's prospects, the sugar workers thus seem destined for a quiet, downward slide into a miasma of misery. Battling against invisible market forces that are robbing them of their social role and self-respect, the Negros proletariat, never a strong supporter of collective action, seems likely to atomize further in a desperate quest for survival. As Eric Wolff has taught us, revolutionary rural residents are historically independent owner-farmers with the confidence and capital to sustain a protracted resistance. Negros workers have neither. While the tenants of Central Luzon supported radical unions and revolutionary armed struggle for over a half century, the Negros proletariat mounted a single one-day millenial revolt in 1926. No matter how angry they might become, Negros plantation workers have only enough food and cash reserves for a one or two day protest. The New People's Army (NPA) has a strong liberated zone in the southern tablelands of Negros, but that is based largely on the support of peasant pioneers who rely on the NPA for order, justice and protection of property against bandits and land grabbers.

The Negros sugar lands have all the signs of a social disaster in the making. Locked on a monocrop island without the money or skills for a rapid transition to a new livelihood, the sugar workers face an uncertain future. Without the capital, land or government assistance to find an alternative to their traditional dependence, the Negros proletariat seems ready to receive the forces that have historically winnowed unwanted populations - migration, hunger, disease, or death.

FOOTNOTE

1. Data from Central Azucarera de La Carlota, 'Final Estimate for CY 1980-81 (Tons Cane)', 18 August 1980; Victorias Milling Company, '1981-82 Crop Estimate Including Left Over Cane of 1980-81', n.d.; Hawaiian-Philippines Company, Crop Survey Department, 'District Production Report No. 14 (Final) CY 1980-81', 13 May 1981.

Chapter 12

THE MEDIA

Amando Doronila

Introduction

Following the assassination of former Senator Benigno
Aquino there has emerged a powerful movement for the
emancipation of the Philippine information media from the
grip of President Ferdinand Marcos's authoritarian rule.
This movement is propelled by an ad hoc coalescence of
important social forces, including non-violent opposition
groups, students, the Roman Catholic church and the business
community; it has even found support from external sources
which have strategic and/or economic stakes in the resolution
of the current Philippine crisis. These groups agree that
the restoration of freedom of the press is crucial to the
return of constitutional democracy in the Philippines.
Indeed it has been seen as a major precondition for a
political accommodation and a peaceful transfer of power from
Marcos.

The Aquino assassination, as a catalyst of the crisis,
has had an immediate impact on the media landscape. It has
stimulated the growth of an independent press through which
the Filipino people's democratic impulses - submerged by
eleven years of autocratic rule - have found expression.
Developments have revealed the vulnerability of the control
of the media, in particular: the proliferation of small,
independent newspapers expressing protest despite possible
reprisals from the security forces of the regime; the
success of the opposition-initiated boycott of the controlled
newspapers, resulting in significant drop in street sales and
in the move by businesses to withdraw advertising support;
the loss of credibility of the controlled media, which has
reduced their usefulness as an instrument for regime
propaganda and has put pressure on their staff to steer
towards a more independent position or be totally
discredited.

The expansion of freedom of the press in recent months
has occurred not because Marcos has hastened political
liberalization but because one of his main instruments of
political control - the media - is cracking under the strain
of widespread civil unrest. The controlled and independent
sections of the press became polarized precisely over the
issue of the presentation of events flowing from the Aquino

194

assassination.   Filipinos in great numbers simply became fed up with the blatant one-sided portrayal of those   events   and turned   to   the   alternative   media   for information that they have been denied by the controlled media.

The media as a function of the political system

The   growing   revolt   within   the   media   against authoritarian   control   indicates   a temporary tendency which does not foreshadow a return to the free-wheeling   journalism of   pre-martial   law   days,   the   strengths and weaknesses of which require   more   careful   assessment   than   the   mindless regime   condemnation   of   the   press   as   'licentious'   and 'irresponsible'.   Neither does it give   us   a   guide   to   the state   of   the media in the post-Marcos period.   The question of whether the press will be more free   or   less   free   after Marcos   is   bound   up with the question of how the leadership changes - whether violently or   democratically.   Given   that Filipino   society,   in   anticipation   of   profound   political change, is now   in   a   state   of   flux,   there   is   universal recognition that the media will be a potent instrument in the hands of those contending for power in   the   transition   from Marcos.

It seems   useful,   therefore,   to   examine   the   present tendencies in the media in the light of historical traditions of the press, the structure of ownership and control   of   the media,   and   the   problems that may arise from changes in the control structures bearing in mind that media ownership under the   Marcos   regime   is   interlocked   with   capitalist transnational connections.   These structures will   determine the   issue   of freedom of the press much more decisively than the determination of Filipino journalists to   reassert   their freedom   in   the   classical   liberal   tradition or the formal guarantees   of   the   bill   of   rights   in   the   Philippine constitution.

The issue of freedom of the press has been well   put   by Salvador P. Lopez,   a   distinguished   Filipino journalist and former president of the University of the Philippines:

> My contention is that   so   long   as   we   have   the
> existing   political   system...we cannot have, by any
> stretch of the imagination, any semblance of a free
> press.   The reason is that the state of the art of
> communication of any country is a function of   the
> kind   of   political   system that is regnant in that
> country.   It cannot be otherwise, because the media
> are   merely   the   instrument   of the political system
> (quoted by Mila Astorga-Garcia in Business   Day   25
> February 1983).

The   historical   experience   bears   out   Lopez   (For   a   more detailed   history   of the press in the Philippines see Castro 1967; Lent 1971, 1978;   Ofreneo 1970.) The press   is   one   of the   oldest   institutions   in the Philippines.   The appearance of Tomas Pinpin's Succesos in 1637 precedes the first newspaper in America by fifty-three years. Between Pinpin's time and today, the press has experienced periods of censorship and restrictions alternating with spells of liberalism, depending upon the political tendencies of the governing order of the day.

During the second half of the nineteenth century, a period of reformist ferment, numerous political journals appeared, some of them attacking Spanish officials and friars. Journalism was put in the service of campaigning for reforms, or of the revolution. The polemical character of the press carried on through the war against the United States in 1898 and the ensuing campaign for national independence. Because of the parliamentary nature of the campaign for independence, Filipino nationalists relied heavily on political journalism to push their movement. After an early period of military censorship, the American colonial administration gradually relaxed restraints on the press, consistent with the general policy of building institutions that would support the development of liberal democracy in the Philippines. In such a milieu, a robust political press developed, only to experience again severe censorship in 1942-45 when the Japanese military occupied the Philippines. The restoration of democratic government in the Philippines after the defeat of Japan provided the environment in which freedom of the press was fairly uninhibited, although in many cases its exercise was abused.

Certain tendencies emerge from this brief history which are relevant to the present:

(1) the press has been largely polemical, and in promoting political causes has not been above using personal attacks;

(2) because of oscillation between censorship and liberalism, especially during the Spanish era, newspapers and journals have been short-lived;

(3) liberalism has been accompanied by a surge of new journals and by robust political debate in the press;

(4) censorship has not been a deterrant to the appearance of critical and protest journals;

(5) relaxation of censorship has been followed by the appearance of numerous small newspapers;

(6) the press has been Manila-centred, written mainly in the language of the colonizers (Spanish, then English), and circulated largely among the urban middle and upper classes; in other words it has been an elite-oriented press. From La Solidaridad onwards, its orientation has been reformist in the liberal democratic mould.

These tendencies have left an enduring legacy, and many

of the strands have reappeared in the contemporary media.

The newspapers in the service of the revolution fanned the flames of the rising against Spain and were in the vanguard of the nationalist movement that won independence for the Philippines. But the same press that helped liberate the nation from foreign rule has contributed to the entrenchment of political conservatism. The key to this is in the structure of press ownership.

The concept of private ownership of the press was introduced by the Americans as part of the liberal capitalist social order they sought to transplant in the Philippines. The Filipino oligarchy, composed of the landed gentry and wealthy entrepreneurs headed by Manuel Quezon, saw the need to publish a newspaper to offset the preponderance of anti-independence American newspapers, and in 1920 founded the Philippines Herald to serve as spokesman for the independence movement. This marked the beginning of a process of concentration of newspapers in the hands of wealthy families. The emergence of media giants, such as Vicente Madrigal's DMHM chain and the TVT chain of Alejandro Roces Snr, whipped up within the press intense competition and generated virulent, name-calling debates. This 'Press War' - a pattern that may recur in the post-Marcos period - offered Filipinos a diversity of points of view, but one which was limited to the agenda of public debate set by the conservative political and economic outlook of the newspapers. Lost in this plurality was the reporting of the social grievances of the peasantry, which were expressed in small publications and in social disturbances in Central Luzon. Immediately after the war several small independent newspapers were published - many of them recklessly courting libel suits - but it did not take long for wealthy interests to reassert domination and to gobble up the small papers.

The post-war concentration of the media follows a different pattern from that of pre-war days in that the interests behind the post-war media are more diversified and include an amalgamation of print and broadcasting facilities. The competing interests of the media owners have assured the plurality of views in the media, but only within the context of capitalist liberalism; the handouts written for politicians or public relations agencies, for example, have had easier access to the pages of the major newspapers than political statements from Ang Bayan, the underground organ of the Communist Party of the Philippines.

The concentration of media ownership, and the other economic interests with which the proprietors were linked, have been summarized, from 1969 data, by Rosenberg (1979:153). Of all of these, only the Roces family had publishing as its main economic interest, a fact which explains the independent position their flagship, Manila Times, had taken and the relatively high credibility of their newspapers.

Family ownership	Major newspapers	Major economic interest
Elizalde	Evening News Philippine Sun	Mining, insurance, import-export, iron and steel, paint and oils, rope, sugar, distillery
Lopez	Manila Chronicle	Meralco, sugar, finance, lubricating oil
Menzi	Manila Daily Bulletin	Mining, shipping, agriculture, lumber, school and office supplies & equipment
Roces	Manila Times, Taliba, Daily Mirror	Publishing
Soriano	Philippine Herald	San Miguel (food & beverages, containers, sand and glass, aluminium, plastic), mining, paper, oil development, copper products, insurance, finance

In addition to their newspapers, most of the media families owned radio-television stations: The Lopezes, ABS-CBN, the nation's largest network at the time with twenty radio and five TV stations; the Roces family, Associated Broadcasting with one TV and five radio stations; the Soriano family, the Radio Mindanao Network with eight radio stations and the Inter-Island Broadcasting Network with three television channels; the Elizalde family, Metropolitan Broadcasting with one television and eight radio stations (Lent 1978).

Media ownership may have given the proprietors a powerful weapon to defend their interests from official harassment and competition by business rivals, and a lever to promote the growth of their interests with the government. In this situation, journalists enjoyed considerable leeway so long as they did not advocate political and social doctrines that would bring down the system. The checks and balances worked well to the mutual benefit of the liberal bourgeois journalists and their capitalist employers.

Marcos, who was elected president for the first time in 1965, was caught in this period of consolidation of media concentration. Although he had wide media support for his campaign, it did not take long for him to reveal his intolerance of media criticism. He soon expressed antagonism to concentrations of media power independent of the government. Towards the end of the 1960s Marcos mounted a campaign to undermine the media as an institution and to drain away their powers. The campaign consisted of public condemnation of the media for their alleged 'irresponsibility' and 'sensationalism', public attacks on publishers whose newspapers were critical of the administration (the Chronicle and Times were the main targets), expansion of the facilities of government information services (the National Media Production Centre's budget was increased from P9.1 million in 1970/71 to P12 million in 1971/72), and the publication in 1970 of the Government Report, a weekly newspaper whose main task was to try to discredit the adversary press (Rosenberg 1979). In May 1972, just five months before the declaration of martial law, a Marcos crony, Roberto Benedicto, who had extensive interets in banking, shipping and the sugar industry, launched the Daily Express to promote the government's viewpoint in the face of a press becoming polarized along pro-Marcos and anti-Marcos lines. Said to be owned by Marcos himself (its editor is a relation of Mrs Marcos), the paper represented a direct intervention by the regime to compete with the private media, despite the fact that part of the media was either supportive or timid.

The media themselves were caught up in two antagonistic ideological tendencies involving the approaches of the media towards the issues of economic development and rising social unrest, the latter being manifested in the widespread student demonstrations of the early 1970s. One ideological stream, expressed by the term 'committed journalism' was voiced by socially-aware student activists coming from the University of the Philippines Institute of Mass Communication. My understanding is that it was a journalism of advocacy for social causes, in which events were to be interpreted from the perspective of their relationship to the distribution of power and wealth. From a practical point of view, it reported the protest movement from the students' side of the barricades. The other stream stressed 'developmental communication', which in plain words meant that the media must play a subordinate role to the government by serving as a vehicle to mobilize the people behind development programmes. This concept grew out of the technocratic, apolitical approach to promoting the 'Green Revolution', in which productivity took preference over equity. It represented an attempt to depoliticize the media, which had been accused by the Marcos administration of putting excessive emphasis on politics, crime and 'sensational news'. This concept, of course, gave ideological support to Marcos's efforts to destroy the power of the private media. In response to criticisms, the Press Foundation of Asia and the Philippine Press Institute adopted 'developmental communication' as a creed to instil in journalists the concept of the 'social responsibility' of the press and to improve their competence in writing about technological progress in agriculture. They thus became unwitting tools in Marcos's efforts to undercut the independence of the media.

The captive media

The concentration of the media in Manila played into the hands of Marcos when he declared martial law in 1972. It facilitated the closure of the multi-media networks and the arrest of journalists who had been critical of the administration. Through the exercise of arbitrary powers under martial law, Marcos was able to realign the media in accordance with the concept that their function was to serve as an instrument of political authority to mobilize public support for its policies, and to centralize control. But in taking such an action, he did not - and this point must be emphasized - overturn the concept of private ownership of the media. Like a true bureaucratic capitalist, Marcos did not seize the media and transfer control over them directly to the state; rather, he transferred the facilities and assets of his opponents in the media to private conglomerates in which his family had extensive private interests.

The official explanation for the restructuring of the media was that it was intended to purge them of 'subversives', to dismantle oligarchic control of it, and to transform them as an instrument for social change (Rosenberg 1979:172-175). Of the three objectives, that of dismantling oligarchic control is most vulnerable to critical examination. The permanent closure of the Lopez, Roces, Soriano and Elizalde media networks merely removed them from strategic positions in the media-communications sector and replaced them with a group of new oligarchs who are not only subservient to Marcos but also have more pervasive interlocking business interests than those they replaced.

According to a study by Sussman (1981), Marcos concentrated the print media into four major newspaper groups: the Express chain owned by Marcos through Benedicto and financed in part by the presidential contingency fund; the Bulletin group of Menzi; the Times Journal chain owned by Imelda Marcos's family; and the Focus-Evening Post-Orient Express combine of presidential assistant Juan Tuvera and his wife Kerima Polotan, Mrs Marcos's official biographer. In the broadcasting field, the Benedicto group 'was allowed to draw heavy Philippine National Bank loans to expand its Radio Philippines Network (R.P.N.) to all twelve regions of the country. Four of the five television stations and the most strategic radio stations which operate in the country are under the supervision of R.P.N. while a fifth is owned and operated by former presidential aide, Gualberto Duavit, together with the Filipino wife of the former American owner Robert Stewart' (ibid.:6). Space does not permit us to detail the many examples of media-communications concentration under the Marcos media-restructuring scheme; suffice it to say that after these changes had been implemented Marcos was confident enough to phase out censorship mechanisms imposed in the early days of martial law and to end the licensing of print and broadcasting media upon the lifting of martial law in 1981.

Layers of control

Several layers of control stand in the path of journalists audacious enough to test the veracity of Marcos's declaration that freedom of the press has been restored. The first consists of editors who screen journalists' copies and filter out stories which in their perception might offend the authorities. It is a widely known but unwritten rule in the Filipino media that the presidential family and the military are not to be criticized. The second layer consists of the proprietors themselves, who in several instances have sacked staff who have written offending articles. The third, and most feared, barrier is represented by the military which under security decrees carried over from martial law is empowered to detain journalists, for long periods, for offences in the open-ended category of subversion, sedition, rebellion, etc. The arrest of the editor and staff of the opposition tabloid WE Forum in December 1982, for publishing a series of articles on Marcos's war medals, is one instance among several of harassment and arrest of journalists who tried to take Marcos at his word, that freedom of the press had been restored.

The result of these controls is a suffocating stream of homogenized message packaged from the political centre. The insipidity of public debate in the media debases intellectual discourse, and this alone vitiates the policy goal of using the media as an instrument for social change. The effect of this was vividly demonstrated in the established media's handling of the Aquino assassination and the events following it. The controlled broadcasting media withheld for at least two hours the news that Aquino was murdered and when they did report they said merely that he was shot. The day after the assassination the three morning dailies had identical headlines - 'AQUINO SHOT DEAD' - but had no editorial comments on the murder. In a classic case of 'Afghanistanism' (a journalistic term for evasion), the major newspapers' editorial concerns were on the national railways mess, the employment situation, and the behaviour of the Democrats in the US congress! The second day after the assassination their editorials and opinion columns all chorused with the president in an appeal for calm (Malaya Crisostomo Ibarra III 29-31 August 1983).

This shameful response to a crisis was the last straw that broke the Filipino public's tolerance. It outraged them to the point where they enthusiastically followed calls for a media boycott. It drove them to the alternative media in search of news that the controlled media refused to print. The shift of public confidence to the alternative press is reflected in the increased circulation of such independent journals as Mr.&Ms., Malaya, and a number of small tabloids that have sprung seemingly from nowhere.

The alternative press

The current political stalemate - in which the regime has been so weakened by the deterioration of the economy and the political crisis of confidence that it has been unable to govern effectively, and the opposition groups have failed to muster enough strength to bring down Marcos - is a boon to the media. In particular, the regime's paralysis has allowed the alternative media to breach the restrictions on the press with relative impunity.

The explosive growth of protest journalism after the Aquino murder represents the rebellion by a segment of the Philippine press against the conspiracy between Marcos and media proprietors that has transformed the media into a propaganda machine. It heralds the reassertion of the little tradition of Filipino journalism - the dissident tradition that gives expression to the grievances of the Filipino people - and reveals the limits to which the media can be manipulated to promote bankrupt economic and political policies.

The proliferation of independent protest newspapers - otherwise called the 'Xerox Press' - represents an expansion of the activities of the alternative press that began with the martial law clampdown in 1972. With the established national media indirectly taken over by Marcos, the role of expressing popular grievances and points of view at variance with the regime's, fell on small newspapers and mimeographed newssheets, notable among them the defunct WE Forum, for several years the lone voice of opposition groups in Manila; Icthys, a mimeographed newsletter published by the Association of Major Religious Superiors, and the Communist Party's Ang Bayan.

In contrast to the established media, many of whose concerns were focussed on traffic problems, rubbish collection and the like, the alternative press has given emphasis to issues involving human rights violations and abuses by the military. It has also, in a more profound way, examined the issues of economic development from a left-wing perspective focusing on distributional aspects of developmental policies. It has examined the issues of widespread poverty and inequality in the context of transnational corporations' penetration of the Philippine economy, US-Philippines relations and Filipino dependency, the consequences of the regime's foreign investment and low-wages policies, and heavy foreign borrowings. The emphasis on these themes by the alternative press, which has addressed itself to the Filipino underclasses in the countryside, has contributed to the heightening of social awareness and the alienation of the rural population from the central government.

Journalism with this kind of social perspective has been given impetus, ironically by the curtailment of press freedom. The prospects of its influence spreading in the metropolitan area in the post-Marcos years cannot be discounted; there exist already in Manila latent conditions for such a journalistic approach to develop. One has only to point to the success of Business Day, an independent newspaper oriented mainly to economic affairs, in circumventing regime censorship through publication of analytical pieces departing from the orthodox and conservative perspective in the examination of economic policies. After the Aquino assassination, Business Day, together with Malaya (successor to WE Forum), stood out among the most credible sources of news about the protests which the major dailies pretended did not exist. It may well have established the potential to expand to the general news area in the post-Marcos years along the path taken by the London Economist or the Far Eastern Economic Review.

The withdrawal of the support of a significant segment of the Makati business community from the regime has been paralleled by the growing entente between business and the Catholic Church leadership in efforts to end the Marcos rule. Both Jaime Cardinal Sin, the Archbishop of Manila, and leaders of the Makati Business Club have demanded, among other things, the restoration of the freedom of the press as a precondition for a return to democracy. Each of these groups has different reasons for seeking an end to the regime: for the church, continued Marcos rule could deepen political polarization, possibly leading to social revolution and a communist take-over; for the businessmen, the crippling political instability under Marcos's ineffectual and corrupt rule has been disastrous to business growth and profits.

In recent months, businessmen's disenchantment with Marcos has taken more concrete forms, including threats to newspaper proprietors of withdrawal of advertising in retaliation for their lop-sided presentation of events (Malaya 29 September-2 October 1983), and the launching on 20 November 1983 of a church-business supported newspaper, Veritas. The birth of Veritas probably signals a bid by this alliance to stake a claim in newspaper publishing in the post-Marcos era. Such pressures have had a perceptible effect on the established media: faced with the reality that the Marcos rule has entered its twilight hours, that the boycott of their papers and the threatened withdrawal of advertising could be very damaging financially, and that it makes good business sense to buy political insurance in a transition period, the major newspapers have permitted a more even-handed presentation of news.

The clearly opportunistic response of the established media to the changing political climate poses a threat to the role of the alternative press: once the political system becomes more liberal and conditions for the press freedom less restrictive, a more balanced handling of the news by the major papers could rob the alternative press of the role that it is, now playing with admirable courage - that is to give the other side of the news. Two other factors may threaten the long-term viability of the alternative press. First, many of the tabloids that have proliferated to take advantage of the thirst for information have overplayed their hands by engaging in sensational and irresponsible journalism. The public is likely to react against such extremes, as it did against the other extremes of the established media. Secondly, there is the danger that many of the alternative press - not excluding Malaya and Mr.&Ms. - could be squeezing the emotional content of the Aquino assassination too hard. There is no question about the importance of the Aquino martyrdom as a symbol with which to mobilize broad protest against the regime. But the emphasis on emotional issues could distract public attention from the deeper issues of Filipino society - issues for which the Marcos regime is accountable and should be held responsible.

After Marcos, what?

If the assertiveness of the alternative press is a passing phenomenon, whose vitality is sustained by a crisis of confidence in the ruling political order, the more important question is, given the media structure built by Marcos, will the media be more free or less free after Marcos? Answers to this question depend upon alternative succession outcomes.

In the worst case situation of a military take-over, it is most unlikely that the controls on the media would be relaxed. Military regimes have never been known for being well-disposed towards the niceties of civil liberties. Because of its arbitrary inclinations and lack of political sophistication, the military would be likely to impose cruder forms of censorship than those of Marcos. In such an event, the alternative press would be driven underground to become a resistance press, part of which might join forces with the revolution.

Assuming the succession question were settled in accordance with the succession mechanism set up by Marcos, the factional infighting among more obvious contenders within the regime's inner circle and their allies in the military and the ruling Kilusang Bagong Lipunan (KBL) would be likely to split the established media. The demise of Marcos would dislocate the focus of loyalty and blur lines of allegiance. The positions of Benedicto and the Romualdez groups would bear watching. Should they take opposite positions in the succession struggle, they would not only split the KBL (Benedicto is Treasurer-General of the party) but also the media, resulting in a 'press war' among the media giants. Menzi's focus of loyalty is Marcos. Given occasional demonstrations that his media group is prepared to strike an independent course, the Bulletin might find the succession fight an opportunity to enhance its credibility and maintain circulation leadership by relaxing internal censorship and accommodating diverse political opinions. Many of the journalists in Menzi's group are ready to seize the first opportunity to assert their freedom. The Tuvera-Polotan combine is a puzzle. It has shown, on occasions, a willingness to publish what other media would not dare. But regardless of which configurations within the ruling circle a succession struggle might revolve around, the media would be likely to be divided - and this situation would favour some degree of freedom and diversity, though freedom by default rather than by design.

The third possibility is a political accommodation between opposition parties and the administration for a transition during which the opposition would be allowed to determine the rules of political competition. That such an accommodation could take place would be a signal for some of the established media to loosen the reins on their staff. The opposition parties could reasonably expect to be supported by the alternative press, especially the Roman Catholic Church media, which are now being supported financially by some members of the Makati business community. The most optimistic scenario for press freedom is thus a succession struggle fought in the political arena, without violent military intervention.

No-one can be bold enough to assert what form the succession struggle will take. There is, however, a constant in the equation, that presents a formidable problem to a more enduring relaxation of controls over the press: that is the extensive web of economic interests in which the media conglomerates are meshed. Sussman (1981) has argued that the process by which Marcos has encouraged international penetration of the economy was set in motion by the declaration of martial law and the take-over of the communication-information processes. He has detailed the penetration of transnational interests into the broader national communications system (telecommunications, satellite, radio, cables) in which Filipino entrepreneurs, many of them Marcos cronies or leading regime officials, are involved. The Filipino transnational partners include Benedicto, Defence Secretary Enrile, and Eduardo Cojuangco of the Philippine Long Distance Telephone Co. People like Benedicto and Enrile are known to have extensive interests outside the communications industry (Sussman 1981; Canoy 1981). Should the political opposition take power in a democratically elected government after Marcos, it would be faced with the problem of dismantling the structure of media concentration whose continued possession of media and economic power would pose a threat to a democratic government. The dilemma facing such a successor government would be that if it did not dismantle the media combines it would come under a rearguard guerila type of sabotage and obstruction from the media. But to dismantle the conglomerates might require measures more arbitrary than normal legislation. The danger of dismantling is that it could touch off reaction among the transnational partners interlocked with the domestic conglomerates in the communications-information industry. The continuation of interlocking interests could easily inhibit debate on the sensitive issues of national autonomy and sovereignty.

If we have under Marcos an alliance between private conglomerates and public authority to curtail the freedom of the press - which in the last analysis is the freedom of the people to be heard through the facilities of the media - we may have to face after Marcos another struggle to free the media from the control of the leviathans of economic concentrations.

Chapter 13

FOREIGN POLICY

Robyn Lim

The most likely outcome of a power struggle in the Philippines following the death or permanent incapacitation of the president is a more 'respectable' regime in which the technocrats have more power than they have enjoyed under Marcos, although it is impossible to predict who the president might be. Such an outcome is the most favourable to the US and would be strongly supported by the American intelligence, military and diplomatic community in the Philippines. There would be no threat to the US bases in such a situation. A pre-emptive US-backed <u>coup</u> to prevent General Ver and Mrs Marcos coming to power is not to be ruled out, although it is not as favourable to US political interests as the first scenario. Again, there would be no threat to the bases.

A more interesting (for our purposes) outcome would be a strong left-led insurgency. Since the US bases are the most visible component of 'American imperialism' in the Philippines, left-dominated political forces could not ignore the continued massive US military presence in the islands. In order to attempt to predict the likely responses of the US, ASEAN, and other Asian powers, it is proposed to examine five main issues:

(1) the 1975-83 debate about the importance of the Philippines to US strategy in Southeast Asia and the Indian Ocean;

(2) the nature of the US-Philippine security relationship;

(3) ambiguities in that relationship;

(4) the 'fall-back' position;

(5) the ASEAN response to a Philippine political crisis.

The debate about the importance of the Philippines in US strategy, 1975-83

The debate about the utility to the US of the bases in the Philippines has taken place in the broader context of the search for a US strategic doctrine for Asia to replace the 'containment of China' of the 1950s and 1960s. US policy since 1975 has been 'unsure and piecemeal, with policies seemingly patched together in response to domestic political concerns, pressure from allies, and presidential predispositions' (Weinstein 1982:117). Scalapino (1980) has identified three 'strategic alternatives' in US thinking on Asia since 1975: the 'minimalist'; the 'united front strategy'; and the 'equilibrium' strategy.

The 'minimalist' thesis argues that the primary threat to the US comes from the Soviet Union. Asia is not seen as an area of primary strategic concern to the US, and American economic and political relations with various Asian states would be enhanced if the US moved out of the region strategically.(1) In the period immediately following the end of the second Indochina war the 'minimalist' thesis had its echo in ASEAN, which had long been committed to the view that foreign bases in the region were temporary in nature. The heart of ASEAN'S ZOPFAN (Zone of Peace, Freedom and Neutrality) concept was that the great powers should desist from fighting their proxy wars in Southeast Asia. Assuming that Vietnam remained equidistant from Peking and Moscow, the achievement of a 'solid agreement' on neutralization of Southeast Asia was likely to make the utility of the US bases in the Philippines 'diminish to the point of making their abandonment not only politically expedient but also militarily and economically sound' (Zasloff and Brown 1978:167).

The uncertainties surrounding future US strategic thinking about the region prompted President Marcos to intensify his struggle to wean Philippine foreign policy from an almost exclusive focus on the relationship with the US. The American withdrawal from the bases in Thailand, in which both 'push' and 'pull' factors were evident, seemed to have lessons for the Philippines, although exactly what lessons were far from clear. In the view of those Filipinos who subscribed to the 'Recto view', the US bases in the Philippines were a liability since they would automatically be magnets for a Soviet attack in time of war.

In his efforts to widen the scope of his foreign policy, Marcos normalized Philippine relations with China and the USSR in 1975 and 1976 respectively. He attempted to reach a settlement on the Moro National Liberation Front (MNLF) rebellion in the south, which had implications for the Philippines' ability to import oil from Arab states. Relations with a unified Vietnam were normalized in 1976; under the terms of this normalization, both parties agreed 'not to allow any foreign country to use one's territory as a base for direct or indirect aggression and intervention against the other country or against other countries in the region',(2) an agreement which caused some consternation in the US (Cottrell and Hanks 1980).

Marcos also drove a hard bargain with the US on the question of the renegotiation of the bases agreement. During a brief visit to the Philippines in December 1975, President Ford agreed that demands that the negotiations be conducted in clear recognition of Philippine sovereignty. Secretary of State Kissinger had offered $US 1 billion over five years in economic and military aid as compensation for an agreement on the bases. Marcos, however, continued to question publicly the utility of the bases to the Philippines. Kissinger's warning of 23 June 1975 should presumably be read in this context.(3) Despite his bluff, Marcos had nowhere to go. He relied heavily on the US to supply weapons and training to suppress the insurgencies, both Muslim and Marxist, for which his own repressive and corrupt government was largely responsible. As one observer noted, 'in Manila and Bangkok particularly, the naive hope appears to remain that by getting rid of U.S. bases one can get rid of insurgency' (Far Eastern Economic Review 16 May 1975).

Negotiations on the bases agreement were broken off in December 1976. The Carter administration came to office with an expressed concern for human rights issues and pledged to withdraw American ground forces from South Korea within four years. Both policies had clear implications for the Philippines. Early in 1977 the new assistant Secretary of State for East Asia and the Pacific, Richard Holbrooke, asked US ambassadors in the region for their comments on the negotiations on the Philippine bases. A report by ambassador to Malaysia, Francis T. Underhill, former political coun-sellor at the American Embassy in Manila, was leaked to the press. Whether this was a deliberate ploy is unclear. The report urged the Carter administration to withdraw completely from Clark and Subic on the following grounds:

> Southeast Asia no longer has critical military and political importance to the US despite the US economic presence in the region;

> Countries belonging to ASEAN aren't willing to support the American military commitment in the Philippines;

> The bases are at best of limited usefulness because in many cases they could not be effectively used without the approval of the Philippine government and the US Congress;

> The effort and cost associated with maintaining the bases is not necessarily commensurate with their potential military benefit;

> The presence of the bases has caused problems for

the Philippines in dealing with Third World nations and with its Communist neighbors and is a source of irritation within the Philippines;

The bases are not necessarily an effective deterrent to Soviet and Chinese moves in the region (_Asian Wall Street Journal_ 20 March 1977).

This is the clearest expression, albeit in a 'leaked' document, of a position held in some sections of the State Department which corresponds with Scalapino's 'minimalist' view.

In 1978 the 'minimalist' position was seriously undermined by important strategic shifts in Asia. These included the signing of a treaty between Vietnam and the USSR in November 1978, which gave the USSR access to bases at Cam Ranh Bay and Danang; the signing of a treaty between Japan and China in August 1978, which provoked the USSR into moving troops into the southern Kuriles (four islands of which are claimed by Japan) thus aiding American efforts to persuade Japan to spend more on defence; and, in January 1979, the normalization of US relations with China, but not Vietnam. As a result of these shifts, the USSR and Vietnam found themselves opposed by a strategic alliance of the US, China, Japan and the ASEAN states.

The increasing tension in Indochina, and its great power ramifications, effectively sank the ZOPFAN concept. In May 1978 there were disclosures that Singapore was permitting the US to use the military airfield at Tengah for reconnaissance flights over the Indian Ocean. The tacit acquiescence of Jakarta and Kuala Lumpur could be assumed (_Congressional Research Service_ 1979:150).

Marcos apparently came under pressure from ASEAN and Japanese leaders to accept terms on the bases negotiations which were financially less favourable that he could have received previously. In June 1977 Teodoro Valencia, a Filipino columnist closely connected with the Marcos family, wrote that other ASEAN governments were pressing Marcos to accept a compromise on the bases (_ibid_.; see also _Far Eastern Economic Review_ 17 June 1977). Prime Minister Fukuda during an official visit to Manila in September 1977 stated that he thought there should be no change in the US presence in the region, a clear if indirect reference to the US bases in the Philippines (_Far Eastern Economic Review_ 2 September 1977). In the last days of 1978 the Philippines and the US signed the renegotiation of the agreement, under whose terms the US retained in essence the _status quo ante_.

The 'strategic shift' in Southeast Asia in 1977-78 was followed by the Iran and Afghanistan crises of 1979-80. A decision was made in mid-1979 to sustain a permanent US naval presence in the Indian Ocean. In order to move ships and aircraft into the Persian Gulf the US relied heavily on the forward basing facilities in the Western Pacific, particularly in the Philippines. As a result of these developments, the 'minimalist' thesis has been substantially undermined. US strategic thinking in Asia now focuses on two alternative theories, which Scalapino had labelled the 'united front strategy' and the 'equilibrium strategy'. The former sees the USSR as a threat not only in Europe but also in Asia. It accepts the 'minimalist' thesis that in the past US commitments were too heavy, unilateral, and partially misdirected, but envisages the reduction of US commitments via a 'strategic alliance' of Japan and the PRC. The 'equilibrium strategists' accept most of these arguments, but part company with the 'united front strategists' on the issue of the wisdom of a de facto alliance with China. Whether the 'united front' strategy wins over the 'equilibrium' strategy in internal US debates need not concern us here, since both strategies asssume that the US bases in the Philippines are central to the US position in Asia.

The fundamental reason for the importance of the Philippine bases to the US is the strategically located position of the Subic Bay Naval Complex and Clark Air Base. The complex includes the Naval Station (Port Olongapo), the Cubi Point Naval Air Station, and the Naval Magazine at Camayan Point. It is a crucial component of the Seventh Fleet, based at Yokosuka in Japan. Subic has important natural assets, including a large well-protected harbour with a depth in excess of fourteen meters. It can dry-dock all major combatants except aircraft carriers. Cubi Point is the central and most important naval aviation support facility in the western Pacific. Subic also houses a significant proportion of the Seventh Fleet's pre-positioned wartime oil reserves.

Capable of supporting, servicing, and repairing over 800 combat aircraft at a time, Clark Air Base is the headquarters of the 13th Air Force (Cottrell and Hanks 1980:8-12). Major training operations are also performed at Clark. The proximity of Clark and Subic enhance their utility. In the US world-wide satellite communications system, the Philippine bases play a crucial role; the NAVCOMMSTA facility at San Miguel is part of the US Naval Ocean Surveillance Informartion System.

Soviet access to Cam Ranh Bay and Danang, 1,300 km west of Subic, makes the Philippine bases even more important to the United States. In 1979, the USSR established a permanent naval presence in Cam Ranh Bay which has grown to approximately fifteen warships including submarines and auxiliaries. Long-range naval aviation Bear-D (reconnaissance) and F (anti-submarine warfare) aircraft maintain a nearly continuous deployment to Cam Ranh.

The Nature of the US-Philippine Security Relationship

American security commitments to the Philippines consist of three major agreements - the Military Bases Agreement of 1947 as amended; the Military Assistance Agreement of 1947; and the Mutual Defence Treaty of 1952. There are also

American obligations under the Manila Treaty of 1954 and a number of 'executive agreements' between Philippine and American presidents.

After the Second World War Philippine leaders were almost completely dependent on American assistance to restore their shattered economy; 'utterly defenceless, this was no time for them to insist on neutrality as a national policy or to resist the re-establishment of American bases on Philippine soil' (Taylor 1964:113). Under the terms of the Military Bases Agreement of 1947 the US government secured a ninety-nine year agreement providing for use of twenty-three army, navy or air force bases in the Philippines. The US gained the right to use the bases as determined by military necessity. The Military Assistance Agreement of 1947 stipulated that the United States would provide a Joint Military Advisory Group (JUSMAG) and military assistance in the training of troops and the loan of weapons and equipment. The Philippine government agreed to purchase the bulk of its military equipment in the US and to secure American approval of purchases made elsewhere.

Fearing a repetition of its 'abandonment' by the US in the face of the Japanese onslaught in the Pacific War, the Philippines pressed for a binding guarantee that the US would come to its defence in time of war. It was not until the Korean War that the US agreed to the 1952 Mutual Defence Treaty. Article IV states:

> Each Party recognizes that an armed attack in the Pacific Area on either of the Parties would be dangerous to its own peace and safety and declares that it would act to meet the common danger in accordance with its constitutional processes.

In Article V, an armed attack includes the metropolitan territories of the parties, as well as 'the island territories under its jurisdiction in the Pacific, or on its armed forces, public vessels or aircraft in the Pacific' (ibid.:147). In 1954, the Philippines signed the Manila Treaty which established SEATO, although it was disappointed that the language of the SEATO treaty was weaker than that of NATO.

Ambiguities in the Philippine-US security relationship

Given the time which has elapsed since the ratification of the Mutual Defence Treaty in 1952, it is not surprising that ambiguities have arisen in the defence relationship between two unequal allies. These have been essentially four:

1. Would the US automatically respond to an attack on the Philippines which did not involve the US bases?

2. Is the US committed to support Philippines' claims to Sabah and the Spratlys?

3. Does the US have the right to unhampered use of the bases, especially involving operations in the Middle East?

4. Is the US committed to sending combat troops to aid a Philippine government threatened by domestic insurgency?

The answer to the first question is still not clear-cut.(4) The answer to the second is 'no'.(5) The crucial questions for our purposes are the third and fourth.

The original US-Philippine security agreements did not deal with the question of prior consultations for the use of the Philippines bases in various contingencies. In 1959 growing nationalism in the Philippines resulted in an agreement between the American ambassador to the Philippines, Bohlen, and Foreign Secretary Serrano. Among other things the agreement required that 'prior consultations' be held before the direct use of US bases for military operations, except those conducted under the Mutual Security Treaty and the Manila Treaty. During the Vietnam war both governments agreed that the US and the Philippine involvement in Indochina was based on the SEATO Treaty, so the question of 'prior consultation' did not arise. All the major American facilities in the Philippines were used to support operations in Indochina. Nevertheless, the US did not carry out bombing missions in Indochina directly from Clark, using Guam and U-Tapao in Thailand instead. The ostensible reason was air traffic problems, but fear of political repercussions in American-Philippine relations was also a factor.

The 1979 amendments to the Military Bases Agreement made some significant changes. The acreages retained as US facilities at Clark and Subic were reduced substantially and Philippine sovereignty over the bases was acknowledged in a number of ways. All military bases became Philippine bases with Philipppine base commanders and the Philippine government assumed responsiblity for the security of the bases, including perimeter security (perimeter security has long been a thorny issue in relation to shootings of Filipino civilians by US servicemen). A thorough review of the basing arrangements is to be held every five years.

Within the bases, however, there are areas that are designated for the unrestricted use of US military forces. These correspond roughly with the core areas of Clark and Subic. The most significant line in the amendment is that: 'The United States shall be assured unhampered military operations involving its Forces in the Philippines'.

The first five year review was completed in June 1983 after a short negotiating period. According to the new Assistant Secretary of State for East Asia and Pacific Affairs, Paul Wolfowitz, the US achieved its key objectives: '...the continuation of unhampered use of the US facilities, consistent with the respect due to Philippines sovereignty'.(6)

One interpretation of the 'prior consultations' issue is that:

> The Bohlen-Serrano Agreement remains intact and no restrictions have been placed on logistical operations from Clark or Subic. Today controversy over US rights in the Philippines focuses more on the jurisdictional control the United States enjoys over official duty cases than on missions originating at its facilities (Cottrell and Hanks 1980:29).

There is some logic to this view. On many occasions in recent years Seventh Fleet carriers based at Subic have been sent to the Indian Ocean. In February 1980 US marines and vessels were deployed from Subic into the Arabian Sea. Consultations between the Philippine and US governments were reported at the time (New York Times 19 February 1980). Yet in certain contingencies the 'prior consultations' question could lead to a Philippine veto (or attempted veto?) on the use of Philippine bases for US operations in the Middle East. The Philippines imports some 90 percent of its oil from Saudi Arabia and is vulnerable to an Arab oil embargo. In the past, radical sections of the MNLF, supported by Libya, have called for an oil embargo against the Philippines to force a settlement in the south. Saudi Arabia imposed a brief boycott in late 1980, as did Iran.

If the Philippine bases are as important for US operational capability in the Persian Gulf as the US military asserts, 'the prior consultation' issue presumably gives Marcos considerable leverage. A 1979 congressional study concluded that it was 'reasonably certain' that the Philippines would not favour the use of Clark to support Israel in the event of another Middle East war. In such a contingency, the Philippine government 'might exercise a veto under the Bohlen-Serrano agreement' (Congressional Research Service 1979:157). The US Defence Secretary, Caspar Weinberger, said in April 1982 that Philippine leaders raised no objections to use of the bases for support of the Indian Ocean Fleet (New York Times 3 April 1982). Yet during his state visit to the US in September 1982 (his first since 1966), Marcos reminded his hosts that Philippine-based US forces do not have carte blanche to operate in the Middle East but are restricted to hostilities 'necessarily relevant to the safety and security of the Philippines and Southeast Asia' (Far Eastern Economic Review 24 September 1982).

This may also have been a hint that there could be contingencies in Southeast Asia, as well as the Middle East, in which the Philippines might wish to veto US operations out of the bases. In 1976, as has been noted, the Philippines normalized its relations with Vietnam on terms which called for each party to agree 'not to allow any foreign country to use one's territory as a base for direct or indirect aggression and intervention against the other country or against other countries in the region'. The Philippines has been anxious not to antagonize Vietnam, which in turn has drawn a distinction between US military bases which are a product of old agreements (Philippines) and those which were specifically built to bomb Indochina (Thailand). When the 1979 amendments to the bases agreements were finally negotiated, Marcos reiterated that the Philippine-US security relationship was defensive in character and 'not meant for aggressive operations anywhere in Southeast Asia' (New York Times 8 January 1979). The ambiguity in the American position, namely that the bases are under Philippine sovereignty but that the US retains the right to unhampered use of the US facilities, apparently continues. Press reports of the 1983 renegotiations stated that the US promised to 'consult' more often about how it intends to use the bases, but embassy officials declined to say what would happen if the two governments disagreed (Asian Wall Street Journal 1 June 1983).

Marcos has made a number of statements recently about 'Philippines security'. Shortly before he left for his visit to the US in 1982 he renewed earlier hints that the 'usefulness' of the bases to Philippine security should be re-examined (Gordon 1982:8; New York Times 7 September 1982). Referring to the events of the Pacific War, he said he wanted a clear idea of US intentions (Asian Wall Street Journal 1 June 1983). The 1983 Military Bases Agreement review also apparently included a revision of contingency plans for the American response in case the Philippines is attacked.

One of the issues canvassed in the 1969 Symington hearings was the question of an attack on the Philippines which did not involve an attack on the US bases. Relations between the Philippines and Malaysia had been very poor in the 1968-69 period, and a Malaysian attack in the south in response to provocations such as the 'Corregidor incident' was the contingency presumably at issue (Symington Hearings:18). In present circumstances it is difficult to envisage an attack on the Philippines coming from any quarter other than Moscow, in which case the US bases would be the targets. The gathering economic and political crisis in the Philippines is what Marcos has in mind when he refers to 'Philippine security'. The central question is whether the US would respond with its own forces to defeat an insurgency in the Philippines. It seems apparent that Marcos is using the ambiguity of the 'prior consultation' clause as leverage to obtain an American commitment to intervention in the Philippines, if necessary using US forces.

This has been a long-standing issue. The US aided the Philippines massively during the Huk revolt of the early 1950s, but did not need to use combat troops. After 1969 the logic of the Nixon Doctrine and the slogan 'let Asians fight Asians' dominated the Ford and Carter administrations. In

1974 Ambassador Sullivan made it clear to Marcos that any future military co-operation between the two countries would not involve the commitment of US ground forces (<u>Far Eastern Economic Review</u> 20 May 1974). Filipino sensitivities resulted in the statement in a <u>joint communique</u> of President Ford and Marcos, of 7 December 1975, that 'President Marcos explained his efforts to attain military self-reliance and his policy not to allow the introduction of foreign troops into the Philippines for its defence except as a last resort'. While Ford's 'Pacific Doctrine' promised a continued American stake in the security and stability of Southeast Asia, it was clear that the use of US ground forces was precluded.

Annex III of the 1979 amendments states that 'the United States Commanders may participate in security activities within the base but outside the United States Facility and off the base in accordance with mutually agreed procedures. The Base Commanders and the United States Commanders shall contribute security forces to carry out the agreed security plan'. Some observers have seen this as a 'tripwire' provision, placed in the agreement at Marcos's insistence, to provide an excuse for U.S. intervention if a threat to the bases eventuated (Wurfel n.d.:26). This interpretation was specifically denied by US officials during congressional hearings on the bases amendment. Holbrooke was asked whether he could give an assurance that US forces would 'not be used in conjunction with the Marcos regime for internal security purposes'. He replied:

> The phrases you quote are really our protection to make absolutely sure that there is no misunderstanding about joint use and the Philippine protection so that they can demonstrate to their people that the United States cannot operate outside their designated facilities without their permission which seems to me to be a reasonable attribute of sovereignty (Foreign Assistance and Related Programs Appropriations, Fiscal Year, 1980, Part I. House Appropriations Committee, 22 March 1979, p.408).

If the US decided to intervene with its own forces in the Philippines, it needs no 'tripwire' provision. A 'threat' to the safety of US citizens would suffice. Vance's letter to Romulo of 6 January 1979 also makes it clear that 'in the context of the Mutual Defence Treaty, we would define "aggression" as external armed attack'. It seems that the quoted provision of Annex III is there as a result of US rather than Philippine insistence.

Southeast Asia has not been a crucial area for any administration since Nixon's. Reagan's priorities have been the central nuclear balance, Western Europe, the Middle East, Central America, and Northeast Asia. His administration has resorted to the use of force, but what Reagan is prepared do in Grenada, or perhaps even in Nicaragua, is not necessarily an indication of what he would be prepared to try in the Philippines.

A 'quick fix' could not be guaranteed. Despite the importance of the bases in the Philippines, US direct involvement in another Southeast Asian guerrilla war would be hard to sell at home.

> The lasting legacy of Vietnam is not (although in most circumstances it should be) a greater national squeamishness about using force. Rather, it is a greater skepticism about the ability of outsiders, even those willing to employ a large-scale military intervention, to control the politics of Third World states over the long haul (Maynes and Ulman, 1980: 10)

Even after an apparently successful intervention to remove a leftist government, what level of political cost would the US tolerate in order to maintain its position in the Philippines? Given the large number of Filipinos who work on the bases, and the proximity of Clark and Subic to areas of population density, urban terrorism could be a major problem. In such circumstances, debate about the US 'fall-back' position could be expected to intensify.

The 'fall-back' position

Guam is often mentioned as a possible alternative for Clark and Subic. It offers the political advantage of being a US 'incorporated territory'. It is the headquarters of the 43rd Strategic Wing of the 3rd Air Division of the Strategic Air Command. Anderson Air Force Base is the only B-52 base outside the continental United States. Guam's major disadvantage is that it is too far east. Based at Guam, a US naval force would take three days longer to reach the Arabian Gulf than one based at Subic (Feeney 1982). Extra response time to the Malacca Straits would also be three days. Considerably smaller than Subic, Apra cannot accomodate carriers. Labour costs would be high.

American political control over Tinian and Saipan, just to the north of Guam, is similar to that in Guam. In a 1975 plebiscite the population of the Northern Marianas opted for 'commonwealth' status after the US strategic trusteeship is terminated. This will ensure a continuation of US sovereignty. The islanders will have full US citizenship and defence and foreign affairs matters will remain in American hands. The agreement with the US also ensures that no adversary of the US or its allies will have access to the islands for military purposes (Dorrance 1983).

The US maintains the option to lease land for basing facilities. At present there are no major naval or air bases in the Marianas, but a US state department official has recently stated that 'any further reactivation of the World War II airfields on Tinian would complement bases on nearby Guam and could be of critical importance should the US lose access to major facilities elsewhere in the Western Pacific' (ibid.). The attraction of the Northern Marianas for the US navy is considerably less. The harbour at Saipan is even smaller than Apra and does not have dry-dock facilities. Saipan also suffers from the same response time/labour cost disabilities as Guam.

Micronesia is another possible alternative to Subic. Malakal Harbour and Babelthuap Harbour in Belau are large enough in size and depth to accommodate aircraft carriers. In February 1983 a plebiscite in the Republic of Belau resulted in a choice of 'free association' with the US. Later in the year the Federated States of Micronesia (FSM) and the Marshall Islands conducted plebiscites which produced similar results. Unlike the Northern Marianas's 'commonwealth' status, the three new Micronesian states (Belau, the FSM and the Marshalls) will be sovereign states 'in a political relationship with the U.S. that has no precise precedent either in international practise or in U.S. constitutional law and will provide to the Micronesian governments authority and responsibility for their internal and foreign affairs' (ibid.). The defence and security provisions of the Compact of Free Association with the three states provides that the US has the right and obligation to defend the islands, and to disapprove any action by any government. The US also has the right to prevent any third nation gaining access to bases in Micronesia. These arrangements, which will terminate the US trusteeship, must eventually be approved by the UN Security Council, on which the USSR has a veto. This possible political impediment is probably not as significant as the geographical liability of being too far east.

The geographically best positioned alternative to Subic is Singapore. Its location provides the shortest response time to points both in the South China Sea and in the Indian Ocean. Singapore has an excellent harbour, although it is not large enough to provide a turning radius for a carrier, and well-developed facilities. There would, however, be difficulties in operating US carriers in such a crowded environment. The fact that Singapore provides repair facilities for Soviet merchant ships would be a problem. It is also very doubtful whether Singapore, despite its endorsement of a US naval presence in the region, would be prepared to offer permanent facilities to the US navy. The cost of labour would be a significant additional problem in Singapore.

In short, none of the possible alternative sites is remotely as convenient as Subic, although Clark would not be such a serious problem to relocate. The US could be presumed to tolerate a high level of political costs in the Philippines in the current strategic environment. One factor in US thinking would be the ASEAN response to a political crisis in the Philippines.

ASEAN response to a Philippine political crisis

The Philippines was the least enthusiastic member of
ASEAN when the organization was established in 1967. Its
economic and cultural ties with the other five are still
tenuous. The other members have long been concerned about
the recent poor economic performance of the Philippines and
the possibility of a crisis following Marcos's demise. It is
unlikely, however, that they fear the spillover effect of a
Philippine insurgency in any crude 'domino theory' sense.
There would be no immediate military threat such as that
Vietnam has appeared to pose to Thailand.

Yet a serious insurgency in the Philippines would
puncture ASEAN's carefully constructed image of stability and
progress. Foreign investors might well be alarmed. A
Philippine crisis would be potentially more worrying for
ASEAN than the Indochina crises have been. It is also
possible, although unlikely, that if the AFP's attention were
diverted from the south, pressures for the establishment of a
Muslim state might intensify.

From the time of ASEAN's inception there has been talk
of a greater degree of military co-operation among its
members. There is a range of bilateral and trilateral
military co-operation arrangements, some more successful than
others. Marcos himself has blown hot and cold on the
question of greater military co-operation within ASEAN, but
has in general kept a low profile on Indochina. The
Philippines is not directly threatened by Vietnam, which has
only a small navy. It was not affected as drastically as
Thailand or Malaysia by the Indochinese refugee crisis of
1978-79. Although there is a dispute with Vietnam over the
Spratlys, Marcos has avoided a clash on this issue. Marcos
has also resisted entanglement in Thailand's problems with
Vietnam. As has been indicated, soon after the end of the
second Indochina war the Philippines managed to forge
surprisingly good relations with Vietnam. In 1980 the
Philippines tacitly accepted the 'Kuantan principle', the
central thrust of which was that Malaysia and Indochina
rejected China's policy of trying to 'bleed Vietnam white'.

One reason for resisting pressures towards
'militarization' of ASEAN is the fact that the ASEAN states
know they are no match for Vietnam. There has been a steady
upward movement in ASEAN defence spending. From 1971 to
1980, the defence expenditures of the ASEAN states have
increased by the following percentages (Asian Wall Street
Journal 22-23 April 1983): Philippines 379; Malaysia 293;
Thailand 61; Singapore 53; Indonesia 50.

Yet the ASEAN states do not spend heavily on defence, as the
figures of Table 13.1 show.

Table 13.1 Defence spending as percentage of GNP

	1975	1981
Philippines	2.6	2.2
Malaysia	4.0	8.3
Thailand	3.7	3.5
Singapore	5.3	5.7
Indonesia	3.8.	3.3

Source: The Military Balance 1982-83:125

Vietnam's expenditure is unknown but is estimated at over 10 per cent of GNP. Although its navy is still small, Vietnam has a formidable capacity to project power beyond its frontiers. The ASEAN states have very little capacity to project such power. Even Indonesia, with the largest army in non-communist Southeast Asia, 'would be hard-pressed to supply even a token force of one battalion to a threatened ASEAN member and has little to spare in the way of ammunition or equipment' (Far Eastern Economic Review 24 October 1983). The 1975 invasion of East Timor revealed serious deficiences in Indonesian military and intelligence capabilities. Within ASEAN, also, the co-ordination of weapons systems, training, and logistical arrangements has a long way to go.

Building a capacity to meet a perceived external threat would detract from developmental needs at home, needs which must be met if real 'regional resilience' based on national resilience is to be attained. The military thrust in ASEAN, in the short term at least, will continue to be the strengthening of capabilities to deal with subversion and infiltration. Pressures towards making ASEAN a military 'pact' will probably also be resisted.

In present circumstances, any notion of ASEAN countries participating in military operations in a member state is far-fetched. Such action would set dangerous precedents. Fear of Indonesian expansionism is not entirely dormant, particularly in Singapore. Its pro-Western orientation notwithstanding, the Jakarta leadership itself can be expected to be very cautious indeed about intervention in the Philippines; Indonesia has experienced both the US and China aiding anti-government movements in Indonesia at different times and is deeply opposed to foreign interference in the domestic affairs of regional states.

Yet in the current situation in the region, any threat to the US bases in the Philippines is a threat to ASEAN. It would also be regarded with alarm in Tokyo and Beijing. Much depends on the behaviour of the USSR and Vietnam. Whatever Vietnam's intentions, the Vietnamese have no capacity for directly influencing events in the Philippines without the active support of Moscow. Moscow has increased its naval presence in the region significantly. Via access to the base at Danang, Russian aircraft are only two hours flying time from the Straits of Malacca, and have greatly improved surveillance capacity in the South China Sea. The Soviets have shown their willingness to probe Western 'soft spots' but they have a great problem in translating military power into political influence. They do not have historical ties in Southeast Asia or economic capacity to compete effectively with the West in an area in which, despite the reduction in force levels since the Vietnam war, the US has clear military dominance. Soviet operations in Asia have been opportunistic, but always low-risk. A major Soviet objective, shared by Indonesia and Malaysia, would be to ensure that China was not a beneficiary of political upheaval in the Philippines. Given China's small (although growing) naval capacity, and the fact that the Philippine communist movement is no longer pro-Beijing, that outcome seems unlikely.

To date the US response to events following the murder of Aquino has been cautious. Reagan's cancellation of his late 1983 proposed visit to the Philippines was prompted not only by safety considerations but by the desire to avoid openly endorsing the Marcos regime. Bush's effulgent praise of Marcos in 1981 is not likely to be repeated. There have been whiffs of the US 'doing a Diem' in the Philippines, a possibility that Marcos has long feared. Carter's 'abandonment' of Somoza and the Shah, however, make it impossible for Reagan to ditch an obviously ailing Marcos. With no obvious successor in sight, the Philippines presents grave problems for the US. Marcos's regime has been corrupt, inefficient and repressive, although perhaps not unduly so by the standards of other Third World states. It has left behind very serious economic problems. Yet Marcos has been a highly astute politician whose passing will leave a vacuum. Given the semi-colonial nature of the Philippine-American relationship, it will be difficult for the US to influence the course of events without foundering on the rock of Philippine nationalism. One of Washington's assets, however, is the fact that Philippine nationalism, unlike its Vietnamese counterpart, does not have a strong xenophobic content. There is still a widespread admiration for America in the Philippines. The Philippines is also very vulnerable (much more so than post-1976 Vietnam was) to American economic sanctions should a left-dominated regime attempt to come to power. The US military is the largest employer in the country after the Philippine government.

The tragedy of the current Philippine situation is that the international and regional environment strongly militates against the coming to power of any meaningfully distributive regime. Given the fact that the distribution of income in the Philippines is among the worst in the world, a regime with a serious commitment to equity is likely to be strongly leftist. Any credible politician must support the left, and thus oppose the retention of US bases. The only 'old' politician with a reputation for integrity is Senator Diokno, who advocates such a policy. Yet the 'strategic alliance' of the US, China and Japan is highly likely to prevent the coming to power of a leftist regime.

A further dilemma is that a US withdrawal from the bases, if it occurred, might well have consequences unwelcome to the Philippine left. Indonesia has accepted the necessity of a US military presence in the region to balance growing Soviet power. But Indonesia aspires to a much more prominent regional role in the longer term (Weatherbee 1980). The withdrawal of the US from the Philippines could further destabilize the region and increase the level of Sino-Soviet rivalry. An intensified Indonesian drive to exclude extra-regional powers might well be a consequence.

A more immediate possibility could be even less welcome to the Philippine left. A US withdrawal from the bases might produce an expanded Japanese naval presence. With its advanced technological base and the formidable capabilities of its people, Japan could become a major military power within five years. Even the Philippine left would probably prefer 'US imperialism', the devil it knows, to the prospect of renewed 'Japanese militarism'.

FOOTNOTES

1. See Ravenal (1978), Harrison (1978), Pringle (1980), Scalapino (1980), Stanley (1982). The most unequivocal 'minimalist' view was expressed by Ravenal. Ravenal called for complete and unconditional American withdrawal from Korea; the dismantling of the remaining US bases in Japan, Korea, Taiwan and the Philippines; the end of military assistance to Asian countries; and retrenchment to a mid-Pacific posture, with American forces based on US territory (ibid.:11).

2. Within four months of the US defeat in Vietnam, a Filipino diplomat apparently signed an agreement with Vietnam which went even further, and stated explicitly that 'the Philippine side will not allow the United States to use Philippine territory against the peoples of Vietnam and other Indochinese countries'. This was never officially acknowledged, and the diplomat was retired (Far Eastern Economic Review 16 July 1976, 21 January 1977).

3. Kissinger said: 'No country should imagine that it is doing a favour by remaining in alliance with us...No ally can pressure us by a threat of termination; we will not accept that its security is more important to us than it is to itself. We assume that our friends regard their ties to us as serving their own national purposes, not as

privileges to be granted or withdrawn as a means of pressure. Where this is not the mutual perception, then clearly it is time for change' (Buss 1977:118).

4. This question was extensively canvassed during Congressional Hearings in the US in 1969. See Hearings before the Sub-committee on United States Security Arrangements and Commitments Abroad of the Committee on Foreign Relations United States Senate, 91st Congress, 1st Session (hereafter cited as the Symington Hearings). See also Pringle (1980).

5. A letter from Secretary of State Cyrus Vance to Romulo dated 6 January 1979 reconfirmed US defence commitments to the Philippines. It also clarified the limits of US responsibilities and made it clear that the US does not support the Philippine claim to Sabah or to the Spratlys. See Philippines: Military Bases in the Philippines, Agreement amending the agreement of March 14, U.S. Government Printing Office, Washington D.C., 1979, pp.25-26.

6. The review resulted in some new arrangements, the most important of which is the establishment of a joint committee, similar to those the US has with Japan and South Korea, to facilitate implementation of the MBA. Other points include procedures to give the Philippine base commander access to the US facilities, and procedures for the submission of information on US force levels and their equipment and weapons systems (Statement of Paul Wolfowitz to House Foreign Affairs Sub-committee, US Information Agency Wireless File 16 June 1983).

Under the terms of the first interim bases agreement (1978-84) the US promised $US 500 million on top of other aid for the period, making the offer worth close to $US 1 billion. There were, however, strings attached. The Carter administration promised to exert its 'best effort' to produce the $US 500 million, making it dependent on annual Congressional approval and thus potentially vulnerable to cuts on human rights grounds. Half of the $US 500 million was in the form of foreign military sales credits, which were loans which had to be repaid. By 1983 the Philippines had used only a third of those credits because of the 16 per cent interest rate charged was high. $US 50 million was set aside for military assistance, and $US 200 million for security supporting assistance (Asian Wall Street Journal 24 March 1983).

The 1983 review provides that President Reagan will make his 'best efforts' to provide $US 900 million in security assistance during the five fiscal years beginning 1 October 1984. More than half is to be provided in economic support funds, some to improve conditions in areas adjacent to the bases and most to support national economic priorities. $US 120 million was designated for the military assistance programme and $US 300 million for foreign military sales credit guarantees. The administration pledged to request Congress for FMS credit having a ten year grace period and repayment over twenty years.

REFERENCES

Abueva, J.V., 1979. 'Ideology and practice in the "New Society"', in D.A. Rosenberg ed., _Marcos and Martial Law in the Philippines_. Ithaca: Cornell University Press, pp. 32-84.

Ahmad, Aijas, 1980. 'Class and colony in Mindanao', New York, Mimeograph.

Alonto, Abul Khayr, 1982. 'Autonomy by the people'. A position paper submitted to the Office of the President of the New Republic of the Philippines.

April 6 Liberation Movement (A6LM), Central Committee, 1981. 'The Philippine Struggle', Filipino Information Service, San Francisco, Mimeograph.

Baldwin, R.E., 1975. _Foreign Trade Regimes and Economic Development: The Philippines_. New York: Columbia University Press for the National Bureau of Economic Research.

Bautista, R.M. and John H. Power and Associates, 1979. _Industrial Promotion Policies in the Philippines_. Makati: Philippine Institute for Development Studies.

Bello, W., O'Connor, D. and Broad, R., 1982. 'Technocrats versus cronies', in W. Bello, D. Kinley and E. Elinson, eds., _Development Debacle: The World Bank in the Philippines_. San Francisco: Institute for Food and Development Policy, pp. 183-196.

Buss, C.A., 1977. _The United States and the Philippines: Background for Policy_. Washington and Stanford: American Enterprise Institute for Public Research and Hoover Institution on War, Revolution and Peace.

Canoy, R.R., 1981. _The Counterfeit Revolution: Martial Law in the Philippines_. Manila: Philippine Editions.

Castro, J.L., 1967. 'The press', in G.D. Feliciano and C. Icban, Jnr., eds., _Philippine Mass Media in Perspective_. Quezon City: Capital Publishing House.

Chapman, E.C., 1984. 'Thailand's recent economic growth and its continuing dependence on foreign agricultural trade', in _Economic Development in East and Southeast Asia: Implications for Australian Agriculture in the 1980s_. Canberra: Australian Government Publishing Service, pp. 203-217.

Christians for National Liberation (CNL), n.d. (?1981). 'Program of the Christians for National Liberation'.

Claver, Bishop F., n.d. 'Conversations with Marxists'. Unpublished manuscript.

Claver, Bishop F., 1976. 'Reflection'. 41st Eucharist

Congress. Philadelphia.

Claver, W.F., 1983. 'The role of the Igorot professional and lawyer in the cordillera', _Sandugo_, (1st Quarter):20-23.

Cline, W.R., 1982. 'Can the East Asian model of development be generalized?', _World Development_, 10(2):81-90.

Cline, W.R., 1983. 'International debt and the stability of the world economy', Institute of International Economics, Washington. Mimeograph.

Congressional Research Service, Library of Congress, 1979. 'United States foreign policy objectives and overseas military installations'. Prepared for the Committee on Foreign Relations, United States Senate, by the Foreign Affairs and National Defense Division.

Communist Party of the Philippines (CPP), n.d. 'Nature of the church sector, orientation of our political work and tasks of comrades with the sector'. Third draft.

Cottrell, A., 1982. 'The U.S.-Philippine security relationship'. Paper presented to joint seminar on United States-Philippine relations, Washington.

Cottrell, A.J. and Hanks, R.J., 1980. _The Military Utility of the U.S. Facilities in the Philippines._ Washington: Georgetown University, Centre for Strategic and International Studies, Significant Issues series.

David, C.C., 1982. 'Impact of price intervention policies on agricultural incentives in the Philippines'. Paper presented to the Second Pacific Food Trade Workshop at Jakarta, 22-23 August 1982.

David, C.C. and Balisacan, A.M., 1981. 'An analysis of fertiliser policies in the Philippines'. Paper presented at the workshop on the re-direction of fertiliser research, Tropical Palace, Metro Manila, 26-28 October, 1981.

Decaesstecker, D.D., 1978. _Impoverished Urban Filipino Families._ Manila: University Santo Tomas Press

Del Carmen, R.V., 1979. 'Constitutionality and judicial politics', in D.A. Rosenberg, ed., _Marcos and Martial Law in the Philippines._ Ithaca: Cornell University Press, pp. 85-112.

Dorrance, J., 1983. 'Coping with the Soviet Pacific threat', _Pacific Defence Reporter_, X(1):10-29.

Emerson, C. and Warr, P.G., 1981. 'Economic evaluation of mineral processing projects: a case study of copper smelting in the Philippines', _Philippine Economic Journal_, 40(2):175-197.

Escudero, III, S.H., 1981. 'The livestock based food processing industry: an overview' in _Food Map of the Philippines._ Manila: Development Academy of the Philippines, Productivity and Development Centre, pp. 47-49.

226

Feeney, W.R., 1982. 'The Pacific basing system and U.S. security', in W.T. Tow and W.R. Feeney, eds., U.S. Foreign Policy and Asian Pacific Security: a Transregional Approach. Boulder: Westview.

George, T.J.S., 1980. Revolt in Mindanao. Kuala Lumpur: Oxford University Press.

Glang, A.C., 1972. 'Why the shooting won't stop', Solidarity, VII(4):6-8.

Gordon, A., 1940. 'Ninth annual report'. Central Azucarbra de la Carlota: Department of Agriculture and Experiments.

Gordon, B.K., 1982. 'The United States and Asia in 1982: year of tenterhooks', Asian Survey, XXIII(1):1-10.

Gowing, P.G., 1979. Muslim Filipinos - Heritage and Horizon. Quezon City: New Day Publishers.

Harrison, S.S., 1978. The Widening Gulf: Asian Nationalism and American Policy. New York: Free Press.

Hayami, Y., 1978. Anatomy of a Peasant Country. Los Banos: The International Rice Research Institute.

Hayami, Y., 1979. 'Economic consequences of new rice technology: a view from the barrio'. Paper presented at the International Rice Research Conference, Los Banos, Philippines, 16-20 April, 1979.

Hernandez, C.G., 1979. 'The extent of civilian control of the military in the Philippines: 1946-1976', unpublished doctoral dissertation, State University of New York at Buffalo.

Hernandez, C.G., 1983. 'Institution building in the Philippines: the dominant party system and the mix in civilian-military controls - evolutionary potentials for the late 20th century'. Paper presented to workshop on development stability and security in the Pacific-Asian region, Manila.

Hill, H., 1981. 'Subcontracting and interfirm linkages in Philippine manufacturing', Philippine Economic Journal, 20(1):58-79.

Hill, H., 1982. 'The Philippine economy under Marcos: a balance sheet', Australian Outlook, 36(3):32-39.

Hollnsteiner, M.R., 1973. 'Socioeconomic themes and variations in a low-income urban neighborhood', Philippine Economic Journal, 12(23):345-403.

Hooley, R.W., 1968. 'Long-term growth in the Philippine economy, 1902-61', Philippine Economic Journal, 7(1):1-24.

ICL Research Team, n.d. The Human Cost of Bananas. Manila.

ICL Research Team, 1979. A Report on Tribal Minorities in Mindanao. Manila: Regal Printing.

Ileto, R., 1979. Pasyon and Revolution. Popular movements in the Philippines, 1840-1910. Quezon City: Ateneo de Manila University Press.

Ileto, R., 1980. 'Tagalog poetry and image of the past during the war against Spain', in A. Reid and D. Marr, Perceptions of the Past in Southeast Asia. Singapore: Heinemann, pp. 379-400.

Ileto, R., 1982. 'Rizal and the underside of Philippine history', in D. Wyatt and A. Woodside, eds., Moral Order and the Question of Change: Essays in Southeast Asian Thought. Yale University, Southeast Asia Studies, monograph, pp. 274-337.

International Bank for Reconstruction and Development (IBRD), Operations Evaluation Department, 1979. 'Project performance audit report: Philippines Third Rural Credit Project (Loan 1010-PH)'.

International Labour Office (ILO), 1974. Sharing in Development: A Programme of Employment, Equity and Growth for the Philippines, Geneva.

Jayasuriya, S.K. and Shand, R.T., 1983. 'Technical change and labour absorption in Asian agriculture: an assessment', Canberra, Australian National University, Development Studies Centre, Occasional Paper No. 35.

Kerkvliet, B.J., 1979. 'Land reform: emancipation or counterinsurgency?' in D.A. Rosenberg, ed., Marcos and Martial Law in the Philippines. Ithaca: Cornell University Press, pp. 113-144.

Kintanar, Jr., A. and Luna, Jr., T.W., 1976. 'Natural resources of the Philippines' in J. Encarnacion et al., Philippine Economic Problems in Perspective. Quezon City: University of the Philippines, Diliman, Institute of Economic Development and Research, School of Economics,pp. 3-50.

Kintanar, G.C., 1979. 'Contemporary religious radicalism in the Philippines', Quarterly National Security Review, National Defense College of the Philippines. (An extract of this article appears in IDOC International Bulletin,1980(8-10).)

Kuo, S.W.Y., Ranis, G. and Fei,J.C.H., 1981. The Taiwan Success Story: Rapid Growth with Improved Distribution in the Republic of China, 1952-79. Boulder: Westview.

Lal, D, 1983. 'Real Wages and Exchange Rates in the Philippines, 1956-78', Washington, World Bank Staff Working Papers No. 604.

Ledesma, A.J., 1982. Landless Workers and Rice Farmers: Peasant Subclasses Under Agrarian Reform in Two Philippine Villages. Los Banos: The International Rice Research Institute.

Lent, J.A., 1971. 'The Philippines', in J.A. Lent, ed., The Asian Newspapers' Reluctant Revolution. Ames, Iowa: State University Press, pp.

Lent, J.A., 1978. 'The Philippines', in J.A. Lent, ed., Broadcasting in Asia and the Pacific. Philadelphia: Temple University Press, pp. 176-188.

Lindsey, C.W., 1977. 'Market concentration in Philippine manufacturing, 1970', Philippine Economic Journal, 16(3):289-312.

Lindsey, C.W. and Valencia E.M., 1981. 'Foreign direct investment in the Philippines: a review of the literature', Philippine Institute for Development Studies, Working Paper No. 81-11.

Macapagal, D., 1976. Democracy in the Philippines. Downsview, Canada: R.J. Cusipag.

Makati Business Club, 1982. 'Issues and prescriptions 1982'. Working Document, Plenary Conference, 28 August.

Mangahas, M. and Barros, B., 1979. 'The distribution of income and wealth: a survey of Philippine research', University of the Philippines, School of Economics, Discussion Paper No. 7916.

Mansmann, R., 1982. 'The case for T'boli rights to their ancestral territory', Dansalan Quarterly, III(4): 204-216. (An abbreviated version of this paper appears in Communications, 1981 (37):33-34,45-46.)

Marcos, F.E., 1977. The Democratic Revolution in the Philippines. Manila.

Marcos, F.E., 1978. An Introduction to the Politics of Transition. Manila.

Marx, K., 1977. The Eighteenth Brumaire of Louis Bonaparte. Moscow: Progress Publishers.

May, R.J., 1981. 'The Philippines', in M. Ayoob, ed., The Politics of Islamic Reassertion. London: Croom Helm, pp. 211-232.

Maynard, H.W., 1976. 'A comparison of military elite role perceptions in Indonesia and the Philippines', unpublished doctoral dissertation, American University.

Maynes, C.W. and Ulman, R.H., 1980. 'Ten years of foreign policy', Foreign Policy, 40.

McCoy, A.W., 1983. 'The "Extreme Unction": the Philippine sugar industry' in Political Economy of Philippine Commodities. Quezon City: University of the Philippine, Diliman, Third World Studies Program, pp. 135-179.

Mindanao-Sub Pastoral Conference (MSPC) and Mindanao Sulu Conference on Justice and Development (MSCJD), n.d. (.?1978). Worldview, V.

Ministry of Labor, Rural Workers Office, 1982. Strategic policies for RPB-MOLE livelihood program for sugar workers.

Miranda, F.B., 1983. 'Demonstrations and rallies in the Philippines: the first two months after Aquino's assassination'. Unpublished manuscript.

Miranda, F.B., ed., in press, Policy Directions for the 1980s.

Montemayor, J., Escueta, E., 1977. A Sociological Study on the Economic and Non-Economic Burdens of the Recipients of the Certificate of Land Transfer. Los Banos: University of the Philippines, Agrarian Reform Institute.

Muego, B.N., 1975. 'The "New Society" of the Philippines', unpublished doctoral dissertation, Southern Illinois University.

Nagkakaisang Partido Demokratiko-Sosyalista ng Pilipinas (NPDSP) 1979. 'Political line of Nagkakaisang Partido Demokratiko-Sosyalista ng Pilipinas'. Typescript.

National Census and Statistics Office, 1975. 1975 Integrated

Census of the Population and its Economic Activities: Population Negros Occidental, Manila: National Economic and Development Authority.

National Democratic Front (NDF) Secretariat, 1983. 'National/ political issues, II'. Manila.

National Economic and Development Authority (NEDA), 1980. 'Philippine Development Report', Manila: NEDA.

National Economic and Development Authority (NEDA), 1982. 'Philippine Statistical Yearbook', Manila: NEDA.

National Housing Authority, n.d. 'A background on the Tondo Foreshore and Dagat-Dagatan project', Mimeograph.

National Housing Authority, 1976. 'A census survey study: Tatalon Estate of Quezon City'.

Nemenzo, F., 1982. 'Rectification process in the Philippine communist movement'. Paper presented to Institute of Southeast Asian Studies seminar-workshop on armed communism in Southeast Asia, Singapore, 17-19 November 1982. Published 1984 in Lim Joo-Jock and S. Vani, eds., Armed Communist Movements in Southeast Asia. Hampshire, England: Gower Publishing Co. Ltd., for Institute of Southeast Asian Studies, pp. 71-105.

Nemenzo, F., 1983. 'The Philippines: current crisis', Arena, 65:36-51.

Nesom, G.E. and Walker, H.S., 1912. Manual de la Industria Azucarera de las Islas Filipinas. Manila: Bureau of Printing.

Niehaus, M., 1982. 'Philippine internal conditions: issues for U.S. policy'. Washington, Library of Congress, Congressional Research Service, Issue Brief IB 82102.

Niksch, L.A., 1982. 'Internal conditions in the Philippines: deterioration and its causes'. Pacific Basic Economic Review, (Wharton Economic Forecasting Associates) V(2).

Niksch, L.A. and Niehaus, M., 1981. 'The internal situation in the Philippines: current trends and future prospects'. Washington: Library of Congress, Congressional Research Service.

Noble, L.G., 1976. 'The Moro National Liberation Front in the Philippines', Pacific Affairs, 49(3):405-424.

Ofreneo, R.P., 1970. 'The Philippine press: 1945-1972, problems and trends', unpublished Master of Arts dissertation, University of the Philippines.

Onate, B.T., 1982. 'High wheat imports induced "surplus" rice for exports: policy or strategy'. Paper presented during the Philippine Agricultural Economics and Development Association pre-Convention, Los Banos, 12 February 1982.

Ongkingco, P.S., Galvez, J.A. and Rosgrant, M.W., 1982. 'Irrigation and rice production in the Philippines status and projections', Los Banos, International Food Policy Research Institute, International Fertilizer Development Centre and the International Rice Research Institute, rice policies in Southeast Asia project, working paper No. 3.

Organization for Economic Co-operation and Development (OECD) (annual). <u>Geographic Distribution of Financial Flows to Developing Countries</u>, Paris.

Pauker, G.J., 1983. 'Security and economics: the military expenditures of the ASEAN countries'. Paper presented to second US-ASEAN conference on economic development and political stability: alternative scenarios for the 1980s. Berkeley.

People's Liberation Movement, 1980. 'Program-Manifesto'. Typescript.

Pomeroy, W.J., 1974. <u>An American Made Tragedy: Neo-colonialism and Dictatorship in the Philippines</u>. New York: International Publishers.

Population, Resources, Environment and the Philippine Future (PREPF), 1980. <u>Probing Our Future: The Philippines 2000 A.D.</u>. Manila.

Power, J.H. and Sicat, G.P., 1971. <u>The Philippines: Industrialisation and Trade Policies</u>. London: Oxford University Press.

Pringle, R., 1980. <u>Indonesia and the Philippines: American Interests in Island Southeast Asia</u>. New York: Columbia University Press.

Psinakis, S., 1981. <u>Two 'Terrorists' Meet</u>. San Francisco: Alchemy Books.

Ramos, F.V., 1982-83. 'People's power and peacekeeping', <u>Fookien Times Yearbook</u>, 1982-83.

Ravenal, E.C., 1978. 'The new strategic balance in Asia', <u>Asian Pacific Community</u>, 5:92-116.

Rocamora, J., 1979. 'The political uses of PANAMIN', <u>Southeast Asian Chronicle</u>, 67:11-21.

Roekaerts, M., 1981. 'Church and state in the Philippines: an assessment of the domestic impact of the visit of John Paul II to the Philippines', <u>Pro Mundi Vita Dossiers</u>, Brussels.

Rosenberg, D.A., 1979. 'Liberty versus loyalty: the transformation of Philippine news media under martial law', in D.A. Rosenberg, ed., <u>Marcos and Martial Law in the Philippines</u>. Ithaca: Cornell University Press, pp. 145-179.

Scalapino, R.A., 1980. 'Approaches to peace and security in Asia: the uncertainty surrounding American strategic principles', in S. Charwla and D.R. Sardeson, eds., <u>Changing Patterns of Security and Stability in Asia</u>. New York: Praeger.pp. 1-21.

Schlegel, S.A., 1979. <u>Tiruray Subsistence: From Shifting Cultivation to Plow Agriculture</u>. Quezon City: Ateneo de Manila University Press.

Scorpion Equipment Marketing Corporation, 1982. 'List of planters in the Manopla area which can be mechanized under Hodge system'.

Schalom, S.R., 1981. <u>The United States and the Philippines</u>. Philadelphia: Institute for the Study of Human Issues.

Shoesmith, D., 1977. <u>The Politics of Sugar</u>. Melbourne: Asian Bureau Australia.

Shoesmith, D., 1979. 'Church and martial law in the

Philippines: the continuing debate', in Southeast Asian Affairs 1979. Singapore: Heinemann Educational Books for the Institute of Southeast Asian Studies, pp. 246-257.

Shoesmith, D., 1983a. 'After Aquino: what role for the church?', Asian Bureau Australia Newsletter, 71(October):1-2.

Shoesmith, D., 1983b. 'Islam and Revolution in Mindanao-Sulu', Dyason House Papers, 9(4):2-12.

Socialist Republican Union, 1982. 'Unity through rectification'. Typescript.

Solidaridad Dos, 1980. 'Ang ating gawaing pangteoritika'. Typescript.

Stanley, P.W., 1982. 'U.S. should look beyond Marcos', International Herald Tribune, 24 September 1982.

Stewart, J.G., 1972. 'The Cotabato conflict: impressions of an outsider', Solidarity, VII(4):31-42.

Sussman, G., 1981. 'Telecommunication transfers: transnational corporations, the Philippines and structures of domination'. University of the Philippines, Third World Studies Program, Third World Studies Dependency Papers, Series No. 35, June.

Sullivan, W., 1983-84. Foreign Policy no. 53.

Tan, E.A. and Holazo, V. 1979. 'The Philippines', Philippine Economic Journal, 18(4):450-492.

Tan, S.K., 1977. The Filipino Muslim Armed Struggle 1900-1972. Manila: Filipinas Foundation.

Taylor, G.E., 1964. The Philippines and the United States: Problems of Partnership. New York: Praeger for Council on Foreign Relations.

Te, A. and Herdt, R.W., 1982. 'Fertilizer prices, subsidies and rice production'. Paper presented at the annual convention of the Philippine Agriculture Economic and Development Association, Inc., Manila, 4 June 1982.

Tiglao, R., 1980. 'The political economy of the Philippine coconut industry'. Quezon City: University of the Philippines, Diliman, Third World Studies Center.

Tondo Foreshore Development Authority, 1975. 'Tondo Foreshore social survey'.

Torres, R.D., et al., 1977. 'A report on the living and working conditions of sugar plantation workers of Negros and Iloilo'. Manila, Ministry of Labor, Institute of Labor and Manpower Studies. Research Paper No. 1.

Umali, N.T., 1983. 'The losing course of the Armed Forces of the Philippines and the fascist dictatorship'. Typescript.

United States, Department of Commerce, 1981. 'U.S. direct investment abroad, 1977'. Washington, Bureau of Economic Analysis.

Unnevehr, L.J., 1982. 'The impact of Philippine government intervention in rice markets'. Paper presented at the workshop of the rice policies in Southeast Asia project held in Jakarta, August 17-20 1982.

Villacorta, W.A., 1983. 'Contending political forces in the Philippines today: the political elite and the legal opposition', Contemporary Southeast Asia, :185-204.

Villanueva, H.S., et al., n.d. 'Preliminary observations on mechanical cane harvesting using Massy Ferguson 105', La Granja, La Carlota, Negros Occidental: Philippine Sugar Commision.

Weatherbee, D.E., 1980. 'The United States and Indonesia: new realities in Southeast Asia', Strategic Review, 8(4):56-63.

Weinstein, F.B., 1982. 'The U.S. role in east and southeast Asia', in R.H. Myers, ed., A U.S. Foreign Policy for Asia: the 1980s and Beyond. Stanford: Hoover Institute Press, pp. 114-139.

World Bank, 1980. Aspects of Poverty in the Philippines, Washington.

World Bank, 1983. World Development Report 1983. New York: Oxford University Press.

Wurfel, D., n.d. 'Philippine foreign policy: strategies for regime survival'. University of Toronto, York University, Canada and the Pacific: Agenda for the Eighties, Working Paper No. 15.

Youngblood, R.L., 1981a. 'Ideology and Christian liberation in the New Society'. Paper presented to second annual Philippine Studies Conference, Honolulu, 27-30 June 1981.

Youngblood, R.L., 1981b. 'Church-military relations in the Philippines', Australian Outlook, 35(3):250-361.

Youngblood, R.L., 1982. 'Structural imperialism: an analysis of the Catholic Bishops' Conference of the Philippines'. Comparative Political Studies, XV(1):29-56.

Yu, R. and Bolasco, M., 1981. Church-State Relations. Manila: St. Scholastica's College.

Zasloff, J.J. and Brown, M. 1978. Communist Indochina and U.S. Foreign Policy: Post-war Realities. Boulder: Westview Special e Studies in International Relations.

Presidential Task Force for the Reconstruction and Development of the Southern Philippines (PTF-RAD) 114
Press Foundation of Asia 199
Private Association for National Minorities/ Presidential Assistant on National Minorities (PANAMIN) 126-9
Pundato, Dimasankay 120

Qaddafi, Mummar 115, 119, 122
Queensland 175, 185
Quezon, Manuel 9, 11, 15, 197

Radio Mindanao Network 198
Radio Philippines Network (R.P.N.) 200
Radio Veritas 62
Ramos, Fidel 2, 41, 57, 64, 107
Reagan, Ronald 1, 5, 24-5, 36, 51, 64, 105, 216-7, 221, 223
Reserve Officers Training Course (ROTC) 48, 68, 104
Ricarte, Artemio 9, 11, 15, 174
Rizal, Jose 8, 10-2, 14-6, 27, 174
Roces family 197-8, 200
Romualdez family 22, 200, 204
Rural Credit Programmes 180

Salamat, Hashim 116, 120-2
Salas, Rafael 63
Salonga, Jovito 30
San Miguel Corporation 29, 64
Sandigan 54
SEATO 212-3
Self-Reliance Defense Posture Program (SRDPP) 109
Seventh Fleet 211, 214
Shari'a law 118
Sin, Jaime 11, 14, 15, 30, 31, 35, 72-4, 77-80, 121, 203
Singapore 95, 147-8, 210, 218, 219-20
Solarz-Kennedy resolution 35
Soriano, Emanuel 27
Soriano family 198, 200
Southern Philippines Development Authority (SPDA) 114, 118, 126
Subic Bay Naval Complex 105-6, 109, 164, 209, 211, 213-4, 217-8
Sullivan, William 41, 215-6

Tadhana 8-9
Tamano, Mamintal 121
Tanada, Lorenzo 33-4
T'boli 125-6, 128
technocrats 3, 5-6, 22, 38-9, 42, 43, 44, 48-9, 59-61, 63, 66-7, 106, 123
Ten Point Programme (of the NDF) 122
Thailand 57, 95, 143, 147-9, 208, 213, 215, 219-20
Times Journal 200
Tingguian 127
Tiruray 125